WORDSWORTH SCHOLARSHIP AND CRITICISM, 1973–1984

GARLAND REFERENCE LIBRARY
OF THE HUMANITIES
VOL. 536

WORDSWORTH SCHOLARSHIP AND CRITICISM, 1973–1984

An Annotated Bibliography, with Selected Criticism, 1809–1972

Mark Jones and Karl Kroeber

GARLAND PUBLISHING INC. • NEW YORK & LONDON
1985

Library of Congress Cataloging-in-Publication Data

Jones, Mark, 1957–
Wordsworth scholarship and criticism, 1973–1984.

(Garland reference library of the humanities ; v. 536)
Includes index.
1. Wordsworth, William, 1770–1850—Bibliography.
I. Kroeber, Karl, 1926– . II. Stam, David H.
Wordsworthian criticism, 1964–1973. III. Title.
IV. Series.
Z8985.J66 1985 [PR5888] 016.821′7 84-45384
ISBN 0-8240-8840-9

Printed on acid-free, 250-year-life paper
Manufactured in the United States of America

CONTENTS

II. Chronological Listings of the Scholarship and Criticism

INTRODUCTION

Purpose and Organization

Our aim here is to provide a bibliography of practical use to students of Wordsworth. To that end we have given our principal attention to year-by-year annotated listings for 1973-1983 (with a partial listing for 1984) that strive to give notice of all work of importance, though there was nearly as much scholarship published during that period as in the preceding 150 years. Our first four sections, listing texts and standard reference works, as well as historically important criticism for the whole preceding period, are radically selective (we have, for example, made no effort to list the many biographies) because these materials have been thoroughly described elsewhere, especially in those works listed in Section 2.2. The criterion for our intense selectivity in these sections was that of general significance. In Section 5 we attempt a comprehensive listing for 1973-83, except that no notice is given of dissertations (available in *Dissertation Abstracts*), nor of scholarship in foreign languages, nor of the spate of reprintings of early books on Wordsworth recorded in the *Cumulative Book Index*, and we have neglected the "Romantic Reassessment" publications from Salzburg (which are, for the most part, dissertations). Here, as in Section 4, the listing is arranged alphabetically by year; in the first three sections, which include fewer items, we have used other arrangements we hope are more convenient for users.

The last bibliography of this sort, David Stam's *Wordsworthian Criticism, 1964-1973* (64), appeared in 1974 and provided only a partial listing for 1973 (as we have done for 1984); for the sake of convenience, we have begun our comprehensive listing with 1973, even though this means repeating his few listings for that year. In addition, without duplicating items appearing in Section 4, we have included in an appendix items missing from Stam's bibliography for the years 1971-72.

Bibliographical Format

We have attempted to give the fullest practical bibliographical information for all entries. Especially for items in the select listing of historically important works (Section 4), we generally indicate more recent editions, listing both the most reliable scholarly editions and more readily available popular editions. Full publishing information is given for all such entries, though in the case that a book is reprinted by its initial publisher, for the reprint or second edition we give the date only. For example, in the annotation to entry 53, an edition of Dorothy's Journals is listed with the publishing information, "London: Macmillan, 1941; Rpt. 1959"--meaning that the book was published by Macmillan both times. The reprints we list are the most recent we have come across, not necessarily the most recent to have appeared. When page numbers are given in the annotations or in our topical index, these always refer to the pagination of the last edition we cite (which is usually the most available). But if the entry is for a modern-journal article listed as having subsequently appeared in a book, the page numbers refer to the journal pagination.

In the belief that this information may be of value in assessing usefulness or importance, we have indicated the length of books, whether they contain indexes, and whether they are available in paperback. If an index would not be appropriate (for instance in the case of the Cornell editions), there is no indication; otherwise all books are listed as "indexed" or "not indexed." Because it is impossible to keep track of all such publishing information, the abbreviation "pbk" means no more than that an edition has been available in paperback. This information is given only as a convenience, and where this abbreviation is missing we do not mean to state that there has not been a paperback edition of the work.

Annotations

The annotations attempt to indicate the central contribution of each work and, where appropriate, such things as its critical school or critical debts and the works of the poet with which it is concerned. Since it is a primary objective of our listing to help the user find the most helpful scholarship on a topic, annotations are not free of our value judgments, though we have attempted to be fair.

Book-Review Listings

We list book reviews throughout, but these listings are not comprehensive, and we have concentrated on those books which have produced significant intellectual discussion. In these listings it has been necessary to abbreviate the titles of journals (see "Abbreviations" and "Journals Cited," below). Most review citations give the inclusive page numbers and full name of the reviewer, but occasionally, where we have relied on the Index of Book Reviews in the Humanities or on the Citations Index, we give only the beginning page number and an initialized reviewer's name. For anyone seeking further reviews, both these indexes are highly recommended.

Cross-referencing and Indexes

We have tried to increase the utility of this volume by cross-referencing and by providing two indexes. In the author index reviewers and editors are indicated by the letters "R" and "E" before the reference number. Of the topical index we observe that besides critical subject headings (such as autobiography, the child figure, and memory) it includes (1) names of people, such as the poet's relatives, precursors, and critics; (2) titles of poems, prose works, and collections by Wordsworth, such as Poems in Two Volumes (the user should remember that titles are not always used consistently, "The Ruined Cottage," for example, being used by some critics to refer to Book I of The Excursion, and by others to refer to considerably different early versions); and (3) critical "schools" such as structuralism, deconstructionism, and Marxism, even though many such descriptions are necessarily arbitrary. Each entry in the topical index consists of the reference number of the work cited, and sometimes includes a brief explanation along with the page or chapter reference (which always pertains to the work cited, not to this bibliography). Thus Coleridge's comments on the Ode in chapter 22 of his Biographia (86) are indexed:

86, ch. 22 ("bombast" in)

Page numbers are generally given only when the relevant passage is in a long essay or (if it is in a book) when it is not accessible through the book's index; but in many cases we give the page numbers simply to indicate the scope of the discussion. (On the pagination of these references, see above, "Bibliographical Format.")

Abbreviations Used

We have used abbreviations sparingly. Only in the annotations themselves and in the reviews listings are the titles of journals abbreviated, except that we always use the acronyms for ELH and PMLA, which are best known by these forms. In most cases the subtitles of journals are not given. The user should note that, for the sake of simplicity and consistency, in listing book reviews we have used "RM" to refer to The Romantic Movement: A Selective and Critical Bibliography, since it has been published by several different journals (see Section 2.2.A), and that "RM, 1972" refers to the volume covering 1972, not the volume published in 1972.

In the annotations the only abbreviations are "C" for Samuel Taylor Coleridge, and "W" for William Wordsworth. In addition, we have used the common shortened forms for works with long titles, such as the Intimations Ode, which is referred to simply as the Ode, and "Lines Composed a Few Miles above Tintern Abbey...," which appears as "Tintern Abbey."

In the index, titles of poems and collections are systematically abbreviated; a full list of these will be found on pages 279-80.

Acknowledgments

We wish to express our gratitude to the Columbia University Libraries, above all to the reference librarians and the interlibrary-loan personnel, without whose cordial assistance this bibliography could not have been compiled. And we wish to thank G. T. Tanselle and Carl Woodring for invaluable counsel on several important matters. Finally, for their innumerable if not "unremembered" acts of kindness and of love, which have been both the greatest and the least direct help, and for their extraordinary patience, we are deeply thankful to Irene Jones, Don Jones, Greg Jones, and Bob Ellinwood.

In a work of this kind errors of omission and commission are inevitable. We apologize to victims of our lapses and will be grateful to anyone noting mistakes who reports them to the publisher so that any subsequent edition can be improved.

JOURNALS CITED

Only in the annotations and in the book-review listings have we used abbreviations for journals; those we have used will be found below. The very few abbreviations not currently used by the MLA have been starred.

	Aberdeen University Review
	Agenda
	Aligarh Journal of English Studies (India)
	American Imago: A Psychoanalytic Journal for Culture, Science, and the Arts
AL	American Literature: A Journal of Literary History, Criticism, and Bibliography
	American Notes and Queries
ASch	American Scholar
	Anglia: Zeitschrift für Englische Philologie
	Antigonish Review (New Series)
ArielE	Ariel: A Review of International English Literature (Calgary, Alberta)
ArQ	Arizona Quarterly
	Ball State University Forum (Muncie, IN)
BlakeQ	Blake: An Illustrated Quarterly (Albuquerque, NM)
BlakeN	Blake Newsletter
BlakeS	Blake Studies
	Boundary 2: A Journal of Postmodern Literature
BJA	British Journal of Aesthetics
	British Library Journal
	Bucknell Review: A Scholarly Journal of Letters, Arts, and Science
	Bulletin of Research in the Humanities (New York)
	Bulletin of the American Academy of Arts and Sciences
	Bulletin of the John Rylands Library (Manchester)
	Bulletin of the New York Public Library
	Bulletin of the West Virginia Association of College English Teachers
	Byron Journal
	Cahiers Victoriens et Edouardiens: Revue du Centre d'Etudes ... de l'Université Paul Valery, Montpellier
	Caliban (Toulouse, France)
CQ	Cambridge Quarterly

	CEA Critic: An Official Journal of the College English Association
	Centennial Review (E. Lansing, MI)
	Centrum: Working Papers of the Minnesota Center for Advanced Studies in Language, Style, and Literary Theory
ChLB	Charles Lamb Bulletin
	Choice
	CIEFL Bulletin (Central Institute of English and Foreign Languages, Hyderabad, India)
	Cithara: Essays in the Judaeo-Christian Tradition (St. Bonaventure University, NY)
	Clio: An Inter-disciplinary Journal of Literature, History, and the Philosophy of History
	Colby Library Quarterly (Waterville, ME)
CE	College English
	College Language Association Journal
	Commonweal
	Commonwealth Quarterly
CompD	Comparative Drama
	Comparative Language Association Journal
CL	Comparative Literature (Eugene, OR)
CLS	Comparative Literature Studies
	Concerning Poetry (Bellingham, WA)
	Contemporary Review (London)
CritI	Critical Inquiry (Chicago)
CritQ	Critical Quarterly
	Critical Review (Melbourne, Australia)
	Critical Survey
	Criticism: A Quarterly for Literature and the Arts (Detroit, MI)
DR	Dalhousie Review
	Diacritics: A Review of Contemporary Criticism
DM	Dublin Magazine
DUJ	Durham University Journal
	Dutch Quarterly Review of Anglo-American Letters
	Eighteenth-Century Life
ECS	Eighteenth-Century Studies (Davis, CA)
	ELH [Formerly the Journal of English Literary History]
	Encounter (London)
	Encyclia: Journal of the Utah Academy of Sciences, Arts, and Letters
	English: The Journal of the English Association (London)
ELN	English Language Notes (Boulder, CO)
	English Literature in Transition, 1880-1920

ES	English Studies: A Journal of English Language and Literature
	English Studies in Africa
ESC	English Studies in Canada
	Esquire: A Journal of the American Renaissance
EIC	Essays in Criticism (Oxford, England)
	Essays in Literature (Macomb, IL)
EA	Etudes Anglaises: Grande-Bretagne, Etats-Unis
Expl	Explicator
	Folklore (London)
	Forum for Modern Language Studies (St. Andrews, Scotland)
	Furman Studies (Greenville, SC)
	Genre
GaR	Georgia Review
GR	Germanic Review (Washington, DC)
	Glyph: Textual Studies
	Greyfriar: Siena Studies in Literature
	Hopkins Quarterly
HudR	Hudson Review
	Huntington Library Quarterly: A Journal for the History and Interpretation of American Civilization
	Indian Journal of American Studies
	Innisfree (Hammond, LA)
	Interpretations: Studies in Language and Literature (Memphis, TN)
	Iowa English Yearbook
	Iowa Review
JAAC	Journal of Aesthetics and Art Criticism
	Journal of American Culture
JEGP	Journal of English and Germanic Philology
	Journal of Narrative Technique
	Journal of the American Academy of Religion
AUMLA	Journal of the Australasian Universities Language and Literature Association: A Journal of Literary Criticism, Philology, and Linguistics
KSJ	Keats-Shelley Journal: Keats, Shelley, Byron, Hunt, and their Circles
	Kentucky Review
KR	Kenyon Review
	Language and Style: An International Journal
	The Library: A Quarterly Journal of Bibliography
	Library Journal
*Li	Listener
	Literary Criterion (Mysore, India)
	Literature and Belief (Center for the Study of Christian Values in Literature, Provo, UT)

L&H	Literature and History: A New Journal for the Humanities
	Literature and Psychology (Teaneck, NJ)
	Literature/Film Quarterly
	Literatur in Wissenschaft und Unterricht (Kiel, W. Germany)
*LM	London Magazine
TLS	London Times Literary Supplement
	Manchester Guardian
MR	Massachusetts Review
	Massachusetts Studies in English
MQR	Michigan Quarterly Review
	Milton and the Romantics (Statesboro, GA)
	Milton Quarterly
	Milton Studies
	Modern Drama
MLJ	Modern Language Journal
MLN	Modern Language Notes
MLQ	Modern Language Quarterly
MLR	Modern Language Review
MP	Modern Philology: A Journal Devoted to Research in Medieval and Modern Literature
	Mosaic: A Journal for the Comparative Study of Literature and Ideas
	Nathaniel Hawthorne Journal
	New England Review
	New Letters
	New Literary History (Charlottesville, VA)
*NS	New Statesman
NYHT	New York Herald Tribune Book Review
NYRB	New York Review of Books
NYT	New York Times Review of Books
	North Dakota Quarterly
N&Q	Notes and Queries (New Series when applicable)
	Oral English
OLR	Oxford Literary Review
	Papers of the Bibliographical Society of America
PLL	Papers on Language and Literature: A Journal for Scholars and Critics of Language and Literature
PR	Partisan Review
	Paunch (Buffalo, NY)
PQ	Philological Quarterly (Iowa City, IA)
	Philosophy and Literature
	Philosophy and Rhetoric
	PN Review
	Poetics: International Review for the Theory of Literature
	Polit 1

	Pre-Raphaelite Review
	Princeton University Library Chronicle
	Proceedings of the British Academy
	Prose
	Psycho-Cultural Review
	Publications of the Arkansas Philological Association
	Publications of the Missouri Philological Association
PMLA	Publications of the Modern Language Association
	Punjab University Research Bulletin, Arts
	Quadrant (Sydney, Australia)
QR	Quarterly Review
QQ	Queen's Quarterly (Kingston, Ontario)
	Rackham Literary Studies (Ann Arbor, MI)
	Renaissance and Modern Studies
	Renascence: A Critical Journal of Letters (Catholic Renascence Society, Milwaukee, WI)
	Research Studies (Pullman, WA)
	Review (Blacksburg, VA)
RES	Review of English Studies: A Quarterly Journal of English Literature and the English Language (New Series when applicable)
	Revue des Langues Vivantes
RP&P	Romanticism Past & Present
*RM	The Romantic Movement: A Selective and Critical Bibliography (see Section 2.2.A)
	Salmagundi
	Saturday Review
SR	Sewanee Review
	Soundings: An Interdisciplinary Journal (Santa Barbara, CA)
SAQ	South Atlantic Quarterly
SCR	South Carolina Review
SHR	Southern Humanities Review
SoRA	Southern Review: Literary and Interdisciplinary Essays (Adelaide, Australia)
	Spectator
	Studia Mystica (Sacramento, CA)
	Structuralist Review
	Studies (Dublin)
SiB	Studies in Bibliography: Papers of the Bibliographical Society of the University of Virginia
	Studies in Canadian Literature
	Studies in English Literature (Tokyo)
SEL	Studies in English Literature, 1500-1900
	Studies in Medieval Culture (Kalamazoo, MI)
	Studies in Philology (Chapel Hill, NC)
SIR	Studies in Romanticism (Boston, MA)

SRL	Studies in Romance Languages
	Studies in the Humanities (Indiana, PA)
SVEC	Studies on Voltaire and the Eighteenth Century
	Style (Fayetteville, AR)
	Tennessee Studies in Literature
	Texas Studies in Literature and Language
	Theoria: A Journal of Studies in the Arts, Humanities and Social Sciences (Natal, S. Africa)
	Theoria to Theory: An International Journal of Science, Philosophy, and Contemplative Religion
	Thomas Hardy Yearbook
	Thoreau Journal Quarterly
	Transactions of the Cumberland and Westmoreland Antiquarian and Archaeological Society
	Triveni: Journal of Indian Renaissance
UES	Unisa English Studies (South Africa)
	University of Mississippi Studies in English
UTQ	University of Toronto Quarterly: A Canadian Journal of the Humanities
	University of Windsor Review (Ontario)
	Victorian Periodicals Newsletter
VP	Victorian Poetry (Morgantown, WV)
VS	Victorian Studies (Bloomington, IN)
VQR	Virginia Quarterly Review: A National Journal of Literature and Discussion
	Walt Whitman Review
WHR	Western Humanities Review
WC	The Wordsworth Circle (Philadelphia, PA)
YR	Yale Review: A National Quarterly
YULG	Yale University Library Gazette
YCGL	Yearbook of Comparative and General Literature
YES	Yearbook of English Studies
YWES	Year's Work in English Studies
	Yeats-Eliot Review

PART I
Standard Research Materials

SECTION 1. TEXTS

1.1. COMPLETE EDITIONS OF THE POETRY

1. The Poetical Works of William Wordsworth, Edited from the Manuscripts, with Textual and Critical Notes. Ed. Ernest de Selincourt and Helen Darbishire. 5 Vols. Oxford: Clarendon, 1941-49. Revised ed. 1952-59. indexed.

The standard edition, following the poet's organization of his poems, based on the six-volume edition of 1849-50, the last revised by the poet. (For a list of errors in this edition, see 253.)

2. William Wordsworth: The Poems. Ed. John O. Hayden. 2 Vols. Harmondsworth: Penguin, 1977. Rpt. New Haven, CT: Yale, 1981. 1066+1104 pp. indexed. pbk.

Like Knight's edition of 1882-86, this follows the latest authorial texts while arranging them chronologically, which gives it great advantages in terms of format and accessibility, but also contravenes the poet's intention and creates problems of chronology and consistency (see 949). While truer than de Selincourt and Darbishire (1), particularly to W's punctuation, Hayden still makes some silent emendations and modernizations.

Reviews: M. Dodsworth, English 26(1977), 90; Anthea Morrison, DUJ 40(1979), 289-91; QQ 89(1982), 690.

3. Wordsworth: Poetical Works, with Introductions and Notes. Ed. Thomas Hutchinson. London: Oxford, 1904. Rev. Ed., by Ernest de Selincourt, 1936. xxx+779 pp. indexed. pbk.

The only one-volume paperback edition which can pretend completeness and preserves W's arrangement, this volume (based on the authoritative 1849-50 edition) includes the 1850 Prelude and the prefaces in tiny print, but excludes several fragments, drafts, and works, such as "Home at Grasmere," included in the Oxford five-volume (1) and more recent editions.

4. *The Poetical Works of Wordsworth*. Revised and with a New Introduction by Paul D. Sheats. Boston: Houghton Mifflin, 1982. xlviii+939 pp. indexed.

Reprint of A.J. George's 1904 edition, including a new biographical introduction. Follows the 1849-50 texts, with a chronological arrangement.

1.2 EDITIONS OF INDIVIDUAL POEMS AND COLLECTIONS

Cornell Wordsworth Editions, under the general editorship of Stephen Parrish and Mark L. Reed, have supplemented and superseded parts of the five-volume Oxford Edition (1) (though not entirely--see, for example, Hunt's review of Butler's "The Ruined Cottage," item 20). The rationale of this series is set out succinctly in the preface to Jonathan Wordsworth's *The Music of Humanity* (155) and in two essays by Stephen Parrish, "The Worst of Wordsworth" (408), and "The Editor as Archaeologist" (979), as well as in the individual prefaces and in the statement prefixed to each volume. The Cornell editors propose, in light of Wordsworth's "obsessive" revision, "to bring the earlier Wordsworth into view" by providing reading texts of the earliest versions of his poetry and photographic reproductions of the manuscripts with meticulous transcriptions on facing pages. These volumes not only provide a sounder basis (in the manuscripts and the transcriptions, if not always in the reading texts) for literary criticism, but also make it possible as never before to examine the growth of the poet and his art. They have also sparked some debate regarding the propriety of the "editorial creation" of poems (see Stephen Gill, 949), and the prefaces and reviews, of which we have attempted to provide a thorough listing to date, form a considerable literature of textual editing. Volumes in the Cornell Series are unnumbered, but it is currently projecting its twentieth volume. Still under preparation are:

The Excursion, ed. Michael Jaye
Juvenilia, 1785-1797, ed. Robert Woof, Carol Landon, and Jared Curtis
Last Poems, 1820-1850, ed. Jeffrey Robinson
Late Poems for the Recluse, ed. Joseph Kishel
Lyrical Ballads, 1797-1800, ed. James Butler and Karen Green

Peter Bell, ed. John Jordan
Poems, 1807-1820, ed. Carl Ketcham
The Fourteen-Book Prelude, ed. W.J.B. Owen
The Thirteen-Book Prelude, ed. Mark L. Reed
Sonnet Sequences and Itinerary Poems, ed. Geoffrey Jackson
The White Doe of Rylestone, ed. Kristine Dugas

Among these, *Peter Bell*, *The Fourteen-Book Prelude*, and *Late Poems for the Recluse* will appear very shortly. Those that have appeared so far are interspersed in the following entries, which are arranged alphabetically by the title of the poem or collection edited. (Under each title, editions are listed in order of importance.) See also 160 and 162 for earlier manuscript versions of several shorter poems.

THE BORDERERS

5. *The Borderers, by William Wordsworth*. Ed. Robert Osborn. Ithaca, NY: Cornell, 1982. xv+815 pp.

Includes a textual and historical introduction (pp. 3-40); reading texts of prose and verse fragments from MS. 1 (The Rough Draft Notebook, 1796-97) of the preface on the character of Rivers (1797); parallel reading texts of the early (1797-99) and late (1842) versions; and transcriptions, some with facing photographs, of the manuscripts. Appendices include a reading text and photographs with facing transcriptions of the related manuscript fragment, "Gothic Tale" (1796); a transcription of the "Argument for Suicide" manuscript (1797); and W's notes to *The Borderers*.

Reviews: David Bromwich, *TLS*, 9 Sept. 1983, pp. 963-64; L. Goldstein, *MQR* 23(1984), 455; J. Robinson, *WC* 13(1982), 128.

DESCRIPTIVE SKETCHES

6. *Descriptive Sketches, by William Wordsworth*. Ed. Eric Birdsall, with the assistance of Paul M. Zall. Ithaca, NY: Cornell, 1984. xiv+301 pp.

Includes an introduction on the poem's composition and revisions (pp. 3-23); facing reading texts of the 1793 and

1836 editions, with footnotes including variants and annotations; and photos with facing transcriptions of the various manuscripts (especially of 1793, 1832, and 1836 editions which W revised for subsequent editions). Appendices include an essay presenting manuscript evidence that C's "The Old Man of the Alps" derived from W's early revisions to Descriptive Sketches, and selections from contemporary reviews.

ECCLESIASTICAL SONNETS

7. The Ecclesiastical Sonnets of William Wordsworth: A Critical Edition. Ed. Abbie Findlay Potts. New Haven, CT: Yale, 1922. x+316 pp. indexed.

The best available edition; prints the 1850 texts with a table of variants, and transcriptions of the earlier MS. F, which includes versions of thirty-three of the sonnets. Includes a general introductory essay and copious explanatory notes which are helpful in tracing W's sources.

AN EVENING WALK

8. An Evening Walk, by William Wordsworth. Ed. James Averill. Ithaca, NY: Cornell, 1984. xii+306 pp.

Includes an introduction on the poem's composition, sources, reception, and revisions (pp. 3-19); facing reading texts of the 1793 and 1836 editions, with footnotes including variants and annotations; photos with facing transcriptions of the early manuscripts (DC MSS. 2, 5, and 7, 1787-1792); a complete reading text of a "very nearly finished" 1794 revision, followed by photos with facing transcriptions of the manuscripts (DC MSS. 9 and 10); and photos with facing transcriptions of miscellaneous other manuscripts and editions which W marked up for revisions. Appendices include the Fenwick note and passages from reviews. Averill does not print the final, 1845 version, which is commonly available elsewhere (e.g., 1); its presentation of the 1794 version, which is twice the length of the original and has never been printed entire, is "probably this volume's major contribution."

HOME AT GRASMERE

9. Home at Grasmere: Part First, Book First, of The Recluse by William Wordsworth. Ed. Beth Darlington. Ithaca, NY: Cornell, 1977. xiv+464 pp.

Includes an introduction on the composition of the poem (pp. 3-32); facing reading texts of MS. B (ca. 1800-ca. 1806) and MS. D (ca. 1812-ca. 1832); photographic reproductions with facing transcriptions of these manuscripts, as well as of MS. A (1806), of MS. R (1800-ca. 1806), and of two manuscripts of The Prospectus to The Recluse. Appendices describe the "Publication and Reception of Home at Grasmere" (in 1888), and provide a reading text of the prose portion of the Preface to The Excursion (1814).

Reviews: John Beer, TLS, 1 Sept. 1978, p. 966; Laurence Goldstein, Criticism 20(1978), 429-31; Bishop C. Hunt, RM, 1977, pp. 75-76; M. Isnard, EA 32(1979), 341; Kenneth R. Johnston, WC 9(1978), 214-21; Robert Langbaum, MP 78 (1980), 93-99; Herbert Lindenberger, SIR 18(1979), 303-11; W.J.B. Owen, RES 30(1979), 96-98; R. Sharrock, MLR 76 (1981), 167; VQR 55(1979), 149.

LYRICAL BALLADS

10. Lyrical Ballads: The Text of the 1798 Edition with the Additional 1800 Poems and the Prefaces. Ed. R.L. Brett and A.R. Jones. London: Methuen, 1963. Rev. Ed., 1965. xlix+345 pp. indexed. pbk.

The best scholarly edition of this important collection now in print, unmodernized (but still not entirely faithful to the originals), with variants through 1805 in footnotes. Includes a long historical introduction, text of the 1800 Preface with 1802 variants in footnotes, notes on the poems by both W and the editors, and a short selection of criticism by W's contemporaries.

Review: F.H. Langman, AUMLA 22(1964), 309.

11. Wordsworth and Coleridge: Lyrical Ballads, 1798. Ed. W.J.B. Owen. Oxford: Oxford, 1967. xl+180 pp. pbk.

Includes introduction, commentary, and a text of the 1800

preface collated with the 1802 text. Text of the poems has been extensively modernized, which greatly limits its usefulness as an historical edition.

Reviews: TLS, 21 Sept. 1967, p. 841, and 23 Nov. 1967, p. 1118; George Whalley, QQ 76(1969), 118; R.S. Woof, N&Q 15(1968), 349.

12. Wordsworth and Coleridge: Lyrical Ballads 1805. Ed. Derek Roper. London: Collins, 1968. 2nd Ed. London: MacDonald and Evans, 1976. 432 pp. indexed. pbk.

Extensively modernized text of the last edition of this collection, with copious interpretive notes.

POEMS IN TWO VOLUMES

13. Poems in Two Volumes, and Other Poems, 1800-1807, by William Wordsworth. Ed. Jared Curtis. Ithaca, NY: Cornell, 1983. xxxvii+731 pp.

Includes an introduction on "The Making of Poems, in Two Volumes, 1800-1807" (pp. 3-39); reading texts of the poems edited from the manuscripts, with notes and thorough records of variants (substantives in footnotes); and selected photographic reproductions, with facing transcriptions, of the manuscripts. Also includes reading texts with variants and selective manuscript photos and transcriptions for 42 more poems composed but not published by 1807. Appendices: "Wordsworth's Sonnets and their Arrangement in 1804"; bibliographical description of Poems in Two Volumes and of the Longman Manuscript; and an essay on a recently discovered transcription by Walter Scott of W's "Glen-Almain," with an exact transcription.

Review: Kenneth Johnston, WC 14(1983), 115-16.

14. Poems in Two Volumes 1807. Ed. Helen Darbishire. Oxford: Clarendon, 1914. 2nd Ed. 1952. lii+482 pp. indexed on pp. 346-52.

A type-facsimile edition with a biographical and critical introduction, still valuable for its notes on the poems and its appendix analyzing and tracing the sources of W's metrical forms and rhyme schemes.

THE PRELUDE, 1798-1799

15. *The Prelude, 1798-99, by William Wordsworth*. Ed. Stephen Parrish. Ithaca, NY: Cornell, 1977. ix+313 pp.

Includes an introduction on "The Growth of the Two-Part *Prelude*" (pp. 3-36); a reading text; and photographic reproductions, with facing transcriptions, of the many contributing manuscripts.

Reviews: David Ellis, *CQ* 8(1978), 65-71; Bishop C. Hunt, *WC* 8(1977), 217-19; Robert Langbaum, *MP* 78(1980), 93-99; Jonathan Wordsworth, *TLS*, 11 Nov. 1977, p. 1330.

16. *The Norton Anthology of English Literature*. 3rd Ed. Ed. M.H. Abrams et al. New York: W.W. Norton, 1974. Vol. 2. xlii+2516 pp. indexed. pbk.

Important in the history of W's texts, since it constitutes both the first publication of the two-part *Prelude* of 1798-99, and the first wide publication of the *reading* text of "The Ruined Cottage," MS. D, first published by Jonathan Wordsworth in 1969 (155).

THE PRELUDE, 1805 and 1850

17. *The Prelude 1799, 1805, 1850: Authoritative Texts, Context and Reception, Recent Critical Essays*. Ed. Jonathan Wordsworth, M.H. Abrams, and Stephen Gill. New York: W.W. Norton, 1979. xix+684 pp. pbk.

Prints the 1805 and 1850 texts on facing pages, with the latter in particular edited against manuscripts and corrected texts that make it superior to de Selincourt's edition (below). Includes discussion of stages of composition, many notes, and selections from critical essays on the poems.

Reviews: Bishop C. Hunt, *RM*, 1979, p. 135; Donald H. Reiman, *SIR* 21(1982), 502-509; W.W. Robson, *TLS*, 1 Aug. 1980, pp. 863-64. See also 872.

18. *The Prelude, or Growth of a Poet's Mind, Edited from the Manuscripts with Introduction, Textual and Critical Notes*. Ed. Ernest de Selincourt. Oxford: Clarendon,

1926. Rev. Ed., by Helen Darbishire, 1959. lxxiv+650 pp. indexed.

First publication of the 1805 version of *The Prelude*, printed with the version first published in 1850 on facing pages. This volume had a shaping influence on Wordsworthian criticism for forty years, but is now in large measure superseded by the Norton edition (17).

19. *William Wordsworth: The Prelude, a Parallel Text*. Ed. J.C. Maxwell. Harmondsworth: Penguin, 1971. Rpt. New Haven, CT: Yale, 1981. 573 pp. pbk.

Presents the 1805 and 1850 texts on facing pages, with a modest introduction and endnotes. Maxwell is truer to the 1850 edition than is de Selincourt, and records all deviations from its wording and punctuation, but makes some silent modernizations in spelling, capitalization, and hyphenation, and silently alters much of the punctuation of 1805 to conform with that of 1850.

Reviews: Bishop C. Hunt, *RM*, 1971, 66; *TLS*, 3 Dec. 1971, p. 1526.

THE RUINED COTTAGE

20. *The Ruined Cottage and The Pedlar by William Wordsworth*. Ed. James Butler. Ithaca, NY: Cornell, 1979. xvi+480 pp.

Includes an introduction on the manuscripts and the chronology of composition (pp. 3-35); parallel reading texts of MSS. B (1798) and D (1799) of "The Ruined Cottage"; photographic reproductions with facing transcriptions of the contributing manuscripts; a reading text of MS. E (1803-4) of "The Pedlar," with variants, facing a transcription of MS. M (fair copy for Coleridge in Malta, 1804); and transcriptions of additions to MSS. E and M. Appendices contain reading texts, followed by photographic reproductions with facing transcriptions, of "The Baker's Cart" and "Incipient Madness" (related fragments); and a reading text of W's relevant notes to *The Excursion*. See also 155.

Reviews: Bishop C. Hunt, *RM*, 1981, pp. 126-28; Jonathan Wordsworth, *WC* 10(1979), 244-45 (reply by Butler, 246).

THE "SALISBURY PLAIN" POEMS

21. *The Salisbury Plain Poems of William Wordsworth*: Salisbury Plain, *or* A Night on Salisbury Plain; Adventures on Salisbury Plain *(including* The Female Vagrant); Guilt and Sorrow; *or*, Incidents upon Salisbury Plain. Ed. Stephen Gill. Ithaca, NY: Cornell, 1975. xviii+310 pp.

The first Cornell edition to appear, bearing a foreword by Stephen Parrish explaining the aims of the series. Includes an introduction on the composition, revision, and reception of the various texts (pp. 3-16); reading texts of the first two versions (MSS. 1 and 2, 1793-94 and 1795-*ca.* 1799), each followed by photographs and transcriptions of the manuscripts on facing pages; and a reading text of "Guilt and Sorrow" (1842), with transcriptions of "Incidents upon Salisbury Plain" (1841) MSS. 3 and 4 on facing pages. Three appendices give similar treatment to related fragments and consider "A Possible Source for the Sailor's Story" in contemporary journalism.

Reviews: Paul Betz (with list of corrigenda), *WC* 7 (1976), 181-85; Jared Curtis, *JEGP* 75(1976), 605-609; Bishop C. Hunt, *RM*, 1975, p. 56; W.J.B. Owen, *RES* 28 (1977), 355-58; Jonathan Wordsworth, *TLS*, 3 Dec. 1976, p. 1524.

THE WAGGONER

22. *Benjamin the Waggoner by William Wordsworth*. Ed. Paul F. Betz. Ithaca, NY: Cornell, 1981. xii+356 pp.

Includes an introduction on the poem's composition and revision (pp. 3-30); parallel reading texts of *Benjamin the Waggoner* MS. 1 (1806) and *The Waggoner*, First Edition (1819) with variants from manuscripts and editions through 1849; photos with facing transcriptions of the various manuscripts, including *Benjamin the Waggoner* MS. 2 (1806) with variants from MS. 1; and a transcription with selected photos of *Benjamin the Waggoner* MS. 3 (1812). Appendices offer photos with facing transcriptions of C's proposed revisions to MS. 1, and a note suggesting that T.J. Wise rather than W dated MS. 2 "1806."

Reviews: R. Ashton, _TLS_, 15 Jan. 1982, p. 57; Laurence Goldstein, _MQR_ 21(1982), 527; Bishop C. Hunt, _RM_, 1981, pp. 145-57; Paul Magnuson, _WC_ 13(1982), 130; Donald H. Reiman, _SIR_ 21(1982), 502-509.

THE WHITE DOE OF RYLSTONE

23. _The White Doe of Rylstone, by William Wordsworth_. Ed. Alice Comparetti. Ithaca, NY: Cornell, 1940. 311 pp.

The best available edition, this volume simply reproduces Hutchinson's text (3), but also lists variants in footnotes and provides in its introduction and notes a wealth of information on the poem's composition and publication, sources, literary form, and reception.

1.3. STANDARD AND RECENT SELECTIONS OF POETRY AND PROSE (listed chronologically)

24. _William Wordsworth: Selected Poems and Prefaces_. Ed. Jack Stillinger. Boston: Houghton Mifflin, 1965. xix+582 pp. pbk.

A generous selection, including all of the 1850 _Prelude_ and 80 pages of notes, both W's and the editor's.

25. _William Wordsworth: Selected Poetry and Prose_. Ed. Geoffrey H. Hartman. New York: New American Library, 1970. xl+448 pp. pbk.

Includes a preface first printed in _Yale Review_ and revised as "Nature and the Humanization of the Self in Wordsworth" (316) and 45 pages of selected prose.

26. _Wordsworth: Selected by Lawrence Durrell_. Harmondsworth: Penguin, 1973. 168 pp. pbk.

Not seen.

27. William Wordsworth: A Selection. Ed. Monica Davies. London: University Tutorial, 1974. viii+205 pp.

Includes a long introduction, a modest sampling of lyrics, and copious interpretive notes.

28. William Wordsworth: Selected Poems. Ed. Walford Davies. London: Dent, 1975. xxv+227 pp.

Includes a brief introductory essay and notes.
Review: Anthea Morrison, DUJ 69(1976), 164-66.

29. William Wordsworth. Ed. Stephen Gill. London: Oxford, 1984. xxxii+752 pp. indexed.

A chronologically ordered selection giving texts from the first editions or, for poems W withheld for long periods or never published, from the manuscripts. On the rationale for this edition, see the note on the Cornell Series (sec. 1.2, above), Gill's introduction, and his essay, 949. Includes brief notes and 85 pages of selected prose.

1.4. STANDARD AND RECENT EDITIONS OF THE PROSE WORKS

A. COMPLETE PROSE

30. The Prose Works of William Wordsworth. Ed. W.J.B. Owen and Jane Worthington Smyser. 3 Vols. Oxford: Clarendon, 1974. xxiv+1355 pp. indexed.

A superb edition superseding all earlier works, fully and usefully annotated, including careful comparative presentation of different Prefaces to Lyrical Ballads, and publishing some things such as W's essay on "The Sublime and the Beautiful" for the first time. But this edition does not include comments on the poems by the poet, either from his letters or those dictated to Isabella Fenwick, which may be found, for example, in Volume 3 of Alexander Grosart's edition of the prose (London: Moxon, 1876).
Reviews: Brian Cosgrove, Studies 64(1975), 49-58; Frances Ferguson, MLN 89(1974), 1057; Stephen Gill, N&Q 221

(1976): 123-25; Andor Gomme, TLS, 17 Jan. 1975, pp. 61-63 (reply by Owen, 4 March, p. 279, and response by Gomme, 28 March, pp. 339-40); Geoffrey Hartman, YR 64(1975), 418-22; James A.W. Heffernan, ES 56(1975), 558; Alan G. Hill, RES 26(1975), 479-82; Karl Kroeber, MP 75(1978), 315-18; J.C. Maxwell, MLR 69(1974), 846; John R. Nabholtz, JEGP 74(1975): 249; E. Pereira, UES 14,i(1976), 50-52; Carl Woodring, WC 5(1974), 139-40.

B. WORDSWORTH'S LITERARY THEORY

31. Literary Criticism of William Wordsworth. Ed. Paul M. Zall. Lincoln: University of Nebraska, 1966. xvii+212 pp. indexed.

32. Wordsworth's Literary Criticism. Ed. W.J.B. Owen. London: Routledge & Kegan Paul, 1974. xi+236 pp.

Zall and Owen provide almost the same important critical texts.

Reviews: Howard Mills, EIC 25(1975), 232-44; Dennis Taylor, WC 6(1975), 193-94.

33. The Critical Opinions of William Wordsworth. Compiled by Markham L. Peacock, Jr. Baltimore: Johns Hopkins, 1950. Rpt. New York: Octagon, 1969. xxvi+469 pp. indexed.

A useful, encyclopedically arranged compilation of the poet's observations on a range of literary topics, helpfully cross-referenced.

C. OTHER PROSE

34. The Illustrated Wordsworth's Guide to the Lakes. Ed. Peter Bicknell. Exeter: Webb and Bower, 1984. 208 pp. indexed.

Text of the authoritative 1835 edition, copiously illustrated with contemporary drawings, engravings, and paintings (many in color) as well as modern color photos. Includes a succinct historical introduction and an appendix containing W's protests against the incursion of the

railroads.
Review: Jonathan Keates, TLS, 22 June 1984, p. 690.

35. William Wordsworth's Convention of Cintra: A Facsimile of the 1809 Tract. Intro. by Gordon Kent Thomas. Provo, UT: Brigham Young, 1983. xiii+216 pp. pbk.

Composite facsimile with brief introduction on the historical context.

1.5. LETTERS AND DOROTHY'S JOURNALS

A. WORDSWORTH'S AND DOROTHY'S LETTERS

The standard edition of The Letters of William and Dorothy Wordsworth, 6 vols., ed. Ernest de Selincourt (Oxford: Clarendon, 1935-39), is being thoroughly re-edited with the inclusion of much new material, under the general editorship of Alan G. Hill. These second-edition volumes, listed separately, are supplemented by a number of volumes which follow.

36. Volume 1: The Early Years, 1787-1805. Revised by Chester L. Shaver, 1967. xvii+729 pp. indexed.

Reviews: Patrick Anderson, Spectator, 28 July 1967, pp. 104-105; William W. Heath, MLR 10(1969), 187; Karl Kroeber, RM, 1967, pp. 44-45; J.R. MacGillivray, UTQ 37 (1968), 309-20; C.L. Morrison, RES 20(1969), 510; Hans Schnyder, ES 51(1970), 263-65; Jack Stillinger, JEGP 67 (1968), 316; TLS, 6 July 1967, p. 596; Enid Welsford, N&Q 15(1968), 350; Jonathan Wordsworth, Anglia 88(1970), 401-404.

37. Volume 2: The Middle Years, Part 1, 1806-1811. Revised by Mary Moorman, 1969. xxvi+546 pp. indexed.

Reviews: William W. Heath, MLR 10(1969), 187-91; John Holloway, Spectator, 11 April 1970, pp. 481-82; J.C. Maxwell, N&Q 17(1970), 189-90; C.L. Morrison, RES 20 (1969), 510-11; Hans Schnyder, ES 53(1972), 568; TLS, 27 Nov. 1969, p. 1367.

38. _Volume 3: The Middle Years, Part 2, 1812-1820_. Revised by Mary Moorman and Alan G. Hill, 1970. xx+691 pp. indexed.

Reviews: David V. Erdman, _RM_, 1970, 49; John Holloway, _Spectator_, 11 Apr. 1970, p. 481; J.C. Maxwell, _N&Q_ 20 (1973), 72-73; W.J.B. Owen, _MLR_ 66(1971), 397-99; Hans Schnyder, _ES_ 53(1972), 568.

39. _Volume 4: The Later Years, Part I, 1821-1828_. Revised by Alan G. Hill, 1978. xxxii+730 pp. indexed.

Erroneously labelled "Volume 3" on the spine.
Reviews: James H. Averill, _SIR_ 18(1979), 299-304; John Beer, _TLS_, 1 Sept. 1978, p. 966; Peter Conrad, _NS_, 23 June 1978, pp. 848-49; M. Dodsworth, _English_ 27(1978), 296; J. Dunn, _Li_, 17 Aug. 1978, p. 221; Stephen Gill, _N&Q_ 26(1979), 595-96; William Heath, _WC_ 10(1979), 247-48; Bishop C. Hunt, _RM_, 1979, pp. 130-31; M. Isnard, _EA_ 33 (1980), 82.

40. _Volume 5: The Later Years, Part 2, 1829-1834_. Revised by Alan G. Hill, 1979. xxii+789 pp. indexed.

Reviews: James H. Averill, _SIR_ 21(1982), 496-501; Beth Darlington, _WC_ 12(1981), 146-48; Bishop C. Hunt, _RM_, 1980, p. 137-38; Stephen Logan, _N&Q_ 23(1981), 344-48 (with list of errata); W.J.B. Owen, _RES_ 34(1983), 227-28.

41. _Volume 6: The Later Years, Part 3, 1835-1839_. Revised by Alan G. Hill, 1982. xxv+794 pp. indexed.

Review: Beth Darlington, _WC_ 14(1983), 117-19.

42. _Letters of William Wordsworth: A New Selection_. Ed. Alan G. Hill. Oxford: Oxford, 1984. xxx+330 pp. indexed. pbk.

A judicious selection of 162 whole letters (rather than extracts), including eight never printed before, with a brief general introduction.

43. _The Love Letters of William and Mary Wordsworth_. Ed. Beth Darlington. Ithaca, NY: Cornell, 1981. 265 pp. indexed.

A recently discovered collection of letters of 1810 and 1812 between W and his wife, which throws much light on their domestic concerns and provides evidence of their intense fondness for each other. Stephen Parrish describes the discovery of these letters in 979.

Reviews: John Bayley, NYRB, 18 Feb. 1982, p. 13; David Bromwich, TLS, 3 Dec. 1982, p. 1340; Margaret Drabble, Li, 29 Apr. 1982, p. 20; Bishop C. Hunt, RM, 1981, pp. 147-48; John T. Ogden, DR 61(1981-2), 750; P.M. Spacks, SIR 21(1982), 661; Claire Tomalin, TLS, 30 Oct. 1981, p. 1255; VQR 58(1982), 88.

44. My Dearest Love: Letters of William and Mary Wordsworth, 1810. Ed. Beth Darlington. Printed at the Scolar Press for Trustees of Dove Cottage, 1981. 81 pp.

A beautiful--and expensive--six-color facsimile edition, presenting the earliest seven of the love letters (22 July-25 Aug. 1810) found in 1977 (see 43), with facing transcriptions.

Review: Jonathan Wordsworth, WC 12(1981), 210.

B. LETTERS OF WORDSWORTH'S CORRESPONDENTS AND FAMILY

Listed below (alphabetically by writer) are only those volumes which focus on W as recipient or derive their primary interest from connection with him. Many others could be added: the newly edited letters of Lamb contain much of interest to Wordsworthians, as do those of Coleridge and Keats. For editions of these and of other Romantic poets' letters, see the MLA volume cited under Kroeber (67).

45. De Quincey to Wordsworth: A Biography of a Relationship, with the Letters of Thomas De Quincey to the Wordsworth Family. Ed. John E. Jordan. Berkeley and Los Angeles: University of California, 1962. xi+391 pp. indexed.

Interperses sixty letters dating from 1803 to 1848 with the fullest account available of the long and varied relationship.

46. The Letters of Sara Hutchinson from 1800 to 1835. Ed. Kathleen Coburn. Toronto: University of Toronto, 1954. xxxvii+474 pp. indexed.

169 letters of W's wife's sister, a member of the Wordsworth household (and amanuensis) for nearly thirty years.

47. Owen, W.J.B. "Letters of Longman & Co. to Wordsworth, 1814-36." _The Library_ 9(1954): 25-34.

Texts of the letters, with notes referring to W's own letters.

48. _Wordsworth and Reed: The Poet's Correspondence with His American Editor, 1836-1850, and Henry Reed's Account of His Reception at Rydal Mount, London, and Elsewhere in 1854_. Ed. Leslie N. Broughton. Ithaca, NY: Cornell, 1933. xviii+288 pp. indexed.

Contains W's letters to and from the editor of the first complete American edition of W's poems (1837), on matters of business, literature, and friendship.

49. _The Correspondence of Henry Crabb Robinson with the Wordsworth Circle, 1808-1866_. Ed. Edith J. Morley. 2 Vols. Oxford: Clarendon, 1927. xii+904 pp. indexed.

Valuable for study of the later W; includes not only the correspondence on both sides between W and his long-time friend and advocate, but also that pertaining to W between Robinson and others.

50. _Letters of Dora Wordsworth_. Ed. Howard P. Vincent. Chicago: Packard, 1944. ix+98 pp. not indexed.

Thirty letters (1825-32) from W's daughter to Maria Jane Jewsbury, a friend and an admirer of W, with six by William and Dorothy.

51. _The Letters of John Wordsworth_. Ed. Carl H. Ketcham. Ithaca, NY: Cornell, 1969.

Includes the letters of W's favorite brother, most of them published for the first time, introduced by a long biographical essay including a detailed account of the shipwreck in which John died.

52. The Letters of Mary Wordsworth, 1800-1855. Ed. Mary E. Burton. Oxford: Clarendon, 1958. xxix+363 pp. indexed.

Until the publication of the love letters (43 and 44) the only edition of W's wife's correspondence. Mark Reed (82, appendix 10) prints an additional letter to Mrs. Thomas Cookson, 3 Nov. 1806.

C. DOROTHY'S JOURNALS

53. Journals of Dorothy Wordsworth: The Alfoxden Journal 1798; The Grasmere Journals 1800-1803. Ed. Helen Darbishire, 1958; 2nd ed. by Mary Moorman. London: Oxford, 1971. xx+232 pp. indexed. pbk.

Dorothy's journals provide a valuable account of the Wordsworths' daily life and occasional sources for W's poetry (poems and sources are acutely compared by Pottle, 122, and Brownstein, 180). But they are also worth reading for their own sake, as Brownstein and Darbishire's preface to this volume argue. Appendices to this edition include short poems by W to which Dorothy refers, and two of Dorothy's own short poems. But this edition does not include Dorothy's detailed accounts of tours to Scotland and the continent, 1803-1828, which are included in de Selincourt's Journals of Dorothy Wordsworth, 2 vols. (London: Macmillan, 1941; Rpt. 1959). See also 365, 559, 565.

SECTION 2. CONCORDANCES AND BIBLIOGRAPHIES

2.1. CONCORDANCES

54. Cooper, Lane. *A Concordance to the Poems of William Wordsworth Edited for the Concordance Society*. London: Smith & Elder, 1911. Rpt. New York: Russell & Russell, 1965. xiii+1136 pp.

Based on Hutchinson's edition of 1904, this volume does not treat later finds, such as the 1805 *Prelude*. See also Cooper's description of the concordance's making, 102.

55. Beckwith, Thomas, and Patricia McEahern. *A Complete Concordance to the* Lyrical Ballads *of Samuel Taylor Coleridge and William Wordsworth: 1798 and 1800*. New York: Garland, forthcoming. *ca.* 900 pp.

Concords not only the poetry of the first two editions, but also selected words of the 1800 Preface.

2.2. BIBLIOGRAPHIES OF WORDSWORTH CRITICISM

A. APPEARING ANNUALLY

The Romantic Movement: A Selective and Critical Bibliography, which appears from 1937-1949 in *ELH*, 1950-1964 in *Philological Quarterly*, 1965-1980 in *English Language Notes*, and since 1981 from Garland Publishing, includes reviews of books and annotations of many articles, and lists reviews of books in other journals. It has been reprinted and usefully cross-indexed through 1970 as *The Romantic Movement Bibliography, 1936-70, A Master Cumulation*, 7 Vols., ed. A.C. Elkins and L.J. Forstner (Ann Arbor, MI: Pierian Press, 1973, 3289 pp.). Since 1970 *The Wordsworth Circle* has provided surveys of Wordsworthian scholarship in essay form, and for the past several years has devoted its summer issue to long reviews of current books. Studies in Romanticism now reviews most major Wordsworthian scholarship. The Wordsworth sections in the PMLA Bibliography (which is now arranged by work, rather than simply by author) and the Modern Humanities Review Association Bibliography (usually a year or two behind the PMLA Bibliography) are comprehensive but unannotated.

B. STANDARD BIBLIOGRAPHIES OF WORDSWORTH CRITICISM (Arranged by period covered)

56. Ward, William S., compiler. Literary Reviews in British Periodicals 1798-1820: A Bibliography, with a Supplementary List of General (Non-Review) Articles on Literary Subjects. 2 Vols. New York: Garland, 1972. xix+633 pp.

Supplemented by two volumes covering the periods 1821-1826 (1977; xiii+301 pp.) and 1789-1797 (1979; xvii+342 pp.), these comprehensive but unannotated volumes devote several pages to W.

Review: Carl Woodring, KSJ 23(1974), 139-42.

57. Bauer, N.S. "Wordsworth's Poems in Contemporary Periodicals." Victorian Periodicals Newsletter 11(1978): 61-76.

A very helpful list of poems quoted in British reviews, magazines, and weekly papers from 1798 to 1836, with an essay generalizing on the use of the quotations and pointing out the importance of the periodicals in establishing W's reputation.

58. Bauer, N. Stephen. "Early Burlesques and Parodies of Wordsworth." Journal of English and Germanic Philology 74(1975): 553-69.

Lists 47 burlesques and parodies dating between 1801 and 1836, and comments perceptively on their significance both as criticism and as an index of W's reputation.

59. Bauer, N. Stephen. "Romantic Poetry and the Unstamped Political Press, 1830-1836." *Studies in Romanticism* 14(1975): 411-24.

Illuminating discussion of the uses political journalists made of the Romantic poets in articles and advertisements; lists the citations from W in "unstamped, pro-reform, and radical journals" in an appendix.

60. Bauer, N[eil] S[tephen]. *William Wordsworth: A Reference Guide to British Criticism, 1793-1899*. Boston: G.K. Hall, 1978. xii+467 pp. indexed.

Excellent annotations and cross-referencing, thoroughly comprehensive, designed to dovetail with Logan's work (61).

Review: Russell Noyes, *WC* 10(1979), 249-50 (with short list of omissions).

61. Logan, James Venable. *Wordsworthian Criticism: A Guide and Bibliography*. Columbus: Ohio State, 1947. Rpt. 1961. xii+304 pp. indexed.

The bibliography (pp. 157-275) is annotated, but not always incisively. Fairly comprehensive for 1900-44, quite selective on earlier years.

62. Henley, Elton F. *A Check List of Masters' Theses in the United States on William Wordsworth*. Charlottesville: Bibliographical Society of the University of Virginia, n.d. [*ca.* 1960]. i+41 pp. indexed.

Through 1959. Neither annotated nor very helpfully indexed.

63. Henley, Elton F., and David H. Stam. *Wordsworthian Criticism, 1945-1964: An Annotated Bibliography*. Rev. Ed. New York: New York Public Library, 1965. 107 pp. indexed.

Continues Logan's work in both matter and format.

64. Stam, David H. *Wordsworthian Criticism, 1964-1973: An Annotated Bibliography Including Additions to Wordsworthian Criticism 1945-1964*. New York: New York Public Library and Readex Books, 1974. 116 pp. indexed.

Same format as the above, to which there are seven pages of additions and corrections. Stam is not comprehensive for the later years, especially 1971-73, for which the user will find additional listings in the present volume.

65. Bernbaum, Ernest, James V. Logan, Jr., and Ford T. Swetnam, Jr. "Wordsworth." In *The English Romantic Poets: A Review of Research and Criticism*, ed. Frank Jordan. 3rd Ed. New York: Modern Language Association, 1972, pp. 69-134.

Swetnam's revision of the bibliographical essay previously published in the 1950 and 1956 editions, listing books and articles through 1970.

66. Maxwell, J.C., and S.C. Gill. "Wordsworth, 1770-1850." In *English Poetry: Select Bibliographical Guides*, ed. A.E. Dyson. London: Oxford, 1971, pp. 167-87.

An excellent, very selective bibliographical essay and list putting the entire period in perspective to 1970.

67. Kroeber, Karl. "Wordsworth." In *The English Romantic Poets: A Review of Research and Criticism*, ed. Frank Jordan. 4th Revised Ed. New York: Modern Language Association, 1985.

Supersedes earlier editions of this essential work of 1972, 1956, and 1950; includes detailed comments on bibliographies, biographies, editions, and criticism through 1984.

68. Bennett, James R. "The Comparative Criticism of Blake and Wordsworth: A Bibliography." *The Wordsworth Circle* 14 (1983): 99-106.

An extremely helpful listing, well annotated and chronologically arranged, covering everything to the present.

2.3. DESCRIPTIVE CATALOGUES AND RELATED ITEMS

While there is no systematic descriptive bibliography of Wordsworth aside from Wise's slight volume (76), the catalogues of special collections, listed below with related items (alphabetically by author), are extremely useful.

69. Bauer, N. Stephen. "Wordsworth and the Early Anthologies." The Library 27(1972): 37-45.

    A valuable account of W's initially reluctant contribution to the lucrative anthologies, with a checklist of 36 English and Scottish volumes printing W's poetry between 1798 and 1836. See also the next item.

70. Bauer, N. Stephen. "Wordsworth and the Early Anthologies: II." The Library 30(1975): 244-45.

    Supplements the above with eighteen entries dating from 1804 to 1836.

71. Butler, James A. "Wordsworth in Philadelphia Area Libraries, 1787-1850." The Wordsworth Circle 4(1973): 41-64.

    Union list of lifetime editions and related items in nineteen Philadelphia area libraries, including Swarthmore's large collection, with brief descriptions.

72. Healey, George Harris. The Cornell Wordsworth Collection: A Catalogue of Books and Manuscripts Presented to the University by Mr. Victor Emanuel. Ithaca, NY: Cornell, 1957. xiii+458 pp. indexed. 24 plates.

    The best catalogue, a valuable resource for studies of W's texts: numbers and thoroughly describes the W manuscripts and editions in Cornell's considerable collection. Also includes a descriptive list of works relating to W and C.

73. Noyes, Russell. The Indiana Wordsworth Collection: A Catalogue. Boston: G.K. Hall, 1978. xvi+288 pp. indexed.

Lists and to some extent describes items in the large W collection of the Lilly Library at Indiana University, including not only W and C editions and manuscripts, but also parodies, pictures, portraits, and criticism of the poets.

74. Patton, Cornelius Howard. The Amherst Wordsworth Collection: A Descriptive Bibliography. Amherst, MA: Trustees of Amherst College, 1936. xi+304 pp. indexed.

Besides the descriptions of W and C editions and manuscripts, this volume includes an annotated bibliography of works belonging to the college relating to W and C.

75. Shaver, Chester L., and Alice C. Shaver. Wordsworth's Library: A Catalogue Including a List of Books Housed by Wordsworth for Coleridge from c. 1810 to c. 1830. New York: Garland, 1979. xliii+363 pp.

Consolidates information from three major sources, the Houghton Library Catalogue (1929), the 1859 catalogue of the sale of W's books, and the "Widener Collection notebook recording loans made from W's library at Rydal Mount between 1824 and 1858." A very useful volume.
Reviews: James A. Butler, ELN 18(1981), 301-304; Bishop C. Hunt, RM, 1979, p. 133.

76. Wise, Thomas J. A Bibliography of the Writings in Prose and Verse of William Wordsworth. Printed for private circulation, 1916. Rpt. London: Dawsons, 1971. xv+268 pp.

Still useful, though Wise's legendary dishonesty can occasionally be misleading.

77. Woof, R.S. "Wordsworth's Poetry and Stuart's Newspapers: 1797-1803." Studies in Bibliography 15(1962): 149-89.

Lists W's poems in the Courier and the Morning Post--some submitted by C. See also Jane Smyser, "Coleridge's Use of Wordsworth's Juvenilia," PMLA 65(1950): 419-26.

SECTION 3. STANDARD BIOGRAPHY AND CHRONOLOGY

The following is an extremely selective listing; there are a great many biographies, which are well covered by Logan (61) and by Kroeber (67).

78. Moorman, Mary. William Wordsworth, a Biography: The Early Years, 1770-1803. Oxford: Clarendon, 1957. xvi+652 pp. indexed. pbk.

Reviews: Helen Darbishire, LM 4(July 1957), 67-70; Malcolm Elwin, QR 295(1957), 334-44; Z.S. Fink, MP 57 (1960), 209-11; Barbara Lupini, English 11(1957), 191-92; George W. Meyer, MLN 73(1958), 444-48; I. Newell, QQ 65(1958), 351-53; W.J.B. Owen, RES 10(1959), 94-97; Hans Schnyder, ES 40(1959), 326-27; Bennett Weaver, RM, 1957, pp. 166-67; George Whalley, NS, 9 March 1957, p. 314; P.M. Zall, CL 10(1958), 271-72.

79. Moorman, Mary. William Wordsworth, A Biography: The Later Years, 1803-1850. Oxford: Clarendon, 1965. xvi+632 pp. indexed. pbk.

The standard biography; reliable and fair. Supersedes George McLean Harper's William Wordsworth: His Life, Works, and Influence, 2 vols., 1916; rev. and enlarged, 1929.

Reviews: F.W. Bateson, NYRB, 29 Dec. 1966, p. 13; John Bayley, Spectator, 26 Nov. 1965, p. 696; Denis Donoghue, NS, 26 Nov. 1965, p. 834; Donald J. Gray, VS 10(1967), 297-99; Geoffrey Hartman, NYHT, 6 March 1966, p. 4; John E. Jordan, CQ 8(1966), 281-82; Patrick Murray, Studies 59 (1970), 215-18; Russell Noyes, ELN 4(1966), 144-48; W.J.B. Owen, RES 17(1966), 334-36; Herbert Peschmann, English 16(1966): 20; Herbert Read, Li, 4 Nov. 1965, p. 721; Mark L. Reed, N&Q 14(1967), 28-30; Hans Schnyder, ES 51(1970), 263-65; H.A. Smith, MLR 63(1968), 208; TLS, 20 Jan. 1966, pp. 33-34; Bennett Weaver, RM, 1965, pp. 43-49.

80. Onorato, Richard J. The Character of the Poet: Wordsworth in The Prelude. Cambridge, MA: Princeton, 1971. x+435 pp. indexed.

The best extended psychoanalytic biography of the poet.
Reviews: Thomas McFarland, YR 61(1972), 279; Jeffrey Mehlman, WC 4(1973), 206-208 (reply by Onorato, 209-10); TLS, 11 Feb. 1972, p. 162; Leon Waldoff, JEGP 72(1973), 144-47; Jonathan Wordsworth, MLQ 33(1972), 460-63.

81. Reed, Mark L. Wordsworth: The Chronology of the Early Years, 1770-1799. Cambridge: Harvard, 1967. xi+369 pp. indexed.

See annotation to the next volume. Contains a "General Chronological List of Wordsworth's Writings with Their First Published Appearances" (pp. 15-36), a biographical "Chronology, 1741-1799" (pp. 37-286), and several valuable essays on the dating of W's early activities, juvenilia, and major works such as The Borderers and "The Ruined Cottage."
Reviews: Kenneth T. Abrams, RM, 1967, pp. 43-44; Edward Bostetter, SEL 7(1967), 741-66; J.R. MacGillivray, UTQ 37 (1968), 309-20; C.L. Morrison, RES 20(1969), 510; Jack Stillinger, JEGP 66(1967), 463-65; TLS, 7 Sept. 1967, p. 801; George Whalley, QQ 76(1969), 118.

82. Reed, Mark L. Wordsworth: The Chronology of the Middle Years, 1800-1815. Cambridge: Harvard, 1975. xiii+782 pp. indexed.

Indispensable books. Marvellously detailed and lucid accounts of seemingly all known facts about the poet and his circle with exact, helpful analyses of how major poems were composed and revised. This volume contains a "General Chronological List of Wordsworth's Writings with Their First Published Appearances" (pp. 11-54), and a more general biographical "Chronology, 1800-1815" (pp. 55-609). Appendices include addenda and corrigenda for The Chronology of the Early Years (above), a table for the renumbering of the Dove Cottage Papers, 1785-1814, and several valuable essays on the composition and dating of W's major poems, including The Prelude and The Excursion.
Reviews: Beth Darlington, RES 28(1977), 370; Bishop C. Hunt, RM, 1975, pp. 58-59; Carl H. Ketcham, WC 6(1975),

191-92; Jonathan Wordsworth, *TLS*, 26 March 1976, pp. 354-55 (see also F.W. Bateson, *TLS*, 9 April, p. 430; J. Wordsworth, *TLS*, 30 April, p. 520; F.W. Bateson, *TLS*, 7 May, p. 553; J. Wordsworth, *TLS*, 21 May, p. 614; Robert Woof, *TLS*, 28 May, pp. 646-47).

PART II
Chronological Listings of the Scholarship and Criticism

SECTION 4. SELECTED CRITICISM, 1809-1972

Reviews of the period have been selected and reprinted in 83 and 84; following these is a chronological selection of the most important criticism by the poet's more illustrious contemporaries, by the Victorians, and by twentieth-century critics. For fuller treatments of this material, see works listed in Section 3.

83. Hayden, John O., ed. _Romantic Bards and British Reviewers: A Selected Edition of the Contemporary Reviews of the Works of Wordsworth, Coleridge, Byron, Keats and Shelley_. Lincoln: University of Nebraska, 1971. xix+427 pp.

Handy selection of the most important reviews from W's own day, lightly annotated, with an introductory survey (pp. ix-xix) and a helpful selective bibliography (pp. 429-33). Arranged by poem reviewed.
Reviews: Donald H. Reiman, _KSJ_ 21/22(1972/73), 264-6; Duane Schneider, _ChLB_ 1(1973), 19-27.

84. Reiman, Donald H., compiler. _The Romantics Reviewed: Contemporary Reviews of British Romantic Writings. Part A: The Lake Poets_. 2 vols. New York: Garland, 1972. xxxi+892 pp.

Photographic reproduction, quite complete through 1824, arranged by journal. Includes good brief annotations by the compiler, but does not include newspaper notices.
Review: Carl Woodring, _KSJ_ 23(1974), 139-42.

ROMANTIC VIEWS

85. Byron, George Gordon, Lord. _English Bards and Scotch Reviewers: A Satire_. London: J. Cawthorn, 1809 (anonymously).

Satirical and condescending; witty.

86. Coleridge, Samuel Taylor. Biographia Literaria; or Biographical Sketches of My Literary Life and Opinions. London: Fenner, 1817. Rpt. Ed. John Shawcross. 2 Vols. London: Oxford, 1907. Rpt. Ed. G. Watson. London: Dent, 1956. pbk. Rpt. Ed. James Engell and W. Jackson Bate. Princeton, NJ: Princeton, 1983. cxxxvi+409 pp. indexed. pbk.

The source of much later criticism of W; of special importance are chapters 17-22, with their detailed analyses of several poems. For C's response to The Prelude, see his poem "To William Wordsworth" (1806; first published 1817).

87. Hazlitt, William. "On the Living Poets." In Lectures on the English Poets. London: Taylor & Hessey, 1818. Rpt. in The Complete Works of William Hazlitt, ed. P.P. Howe. London: Dent, 1930-34. Vol. 5, pp. 143-68. Rpt. in Selected Writings, ed. Ronald Blythe. Harmondsworth: Penguin, 1970, pp. 219-31.

Offers a perceptive contemporary appreciation of the originality of the "Lake Poets," especially W, "the most original poet now living."

88. Shelley, Percy Bysshe. Peter Bell the Third. London: C.&J. Ollier, 1819 (anonymously). Rpt. in Poetical Works, 1839.

Shrewd satire by a poet much influenced by W. Of related interest are Shelley's sonnet, "To Wordsworth" (1816), and John Hamilton Reynolds' parody, Peter Bell: A Lyrical Ballad (1818).

89. Hazlitt, William. "My First Acquaintance with Poets." The Liberal 3(April, 1823). Rpt. in The Complete Works (see 87), Vol. 17, pp. 106-22, and in Selected Writings (see 87), pp. 43-65.

Far more on C than on W, but contains valuable descriptions of W, particularly of his method of recitation.

90. Hazlitt, William. The Spirit of the Age: Or, Contemporary Portraits. London: H. Colburn, 1825. Rpt. in The Complete Works (see 87), Vol. 11.

Pursuing his earlier observations (87) on the humility of W's subject matter and the simplicity of his verse, Hazlitt draws parallels between the revolutionary import of W's poetic and the age's political revolutions, in the chapter "Mr. Wordsworth" (pp. 86-95). All of Hazlitt's works listed here contain trenchant opinions by a keen observer of the poet's character, his art, and its place in the age.

91. De Quincey, Thomas. "Lake Reminiscences." Tait's Edinburgh Magazine n.s. 6(Jan., Feb., Apr., 1839): 1-12, 90-102, 246-54. Rpt. as "The Lake Poets: William Wordsworth" in The Collected Writings of Thomas De Quincey, ed. David Masson. Edinburgh: Adam and Charles Black, 1889-90. Vol. 2, pp. 229-302. Rpt. in Recollections of the Lakes and the Lake Poets, ed. David Wright. Baltimore: Penguin, 1970, pp. 119-206.

Valuable personal reminiscences, including frank verbal portraits and characters of W, Mary, and Dorothy, and some shrewd comments.

92. De Quincey, Thomas. "On Wordsworth's Poetry," Tait's Edinburgh Magazine n.s. 12(Sept., 1845): 545-54. Rpt. in The Collected Writings (see 91), Vol. 11, pp. 294-325.

An excellent essay blaming W's slow rise to fame on his "injudicious" 1800 Preface and on his "too original" perception of natural phenomena; contains some severe criticism of The Excursion, especially books 1 and 4, to which De Quincey prefers the shorter and earlier poems.

VICTORIAN VIEWS

93. Bagehot, Walter. "Wordsworth, Tennyson, and Browning; or Pure, Ornate, and Grotesque Art in English Poetry." National Review 19(1864): 27-67. Rpt. in Literary Studies. London: Longman, 1879. Vol. 2, pp. 326-81. Rpt. in

The Collected Works of Walter Bagehot, ed. Norman St. John-Stevas. Cambridge, MA: Harvard, 1965-78. Vol. 2, pp. 321-66.

Vivid contrasts emphasizing W's intensity, economy, and lucidity of style.

94. Shairp, J[ohn] C. "Wordsworth, the Man and the Poet." North British Review 41(1864): 1-54. Enlarged and revised in Studies in Poetry and Philosophy. Edinburgh: Edmonston & Douglas, 1868, pp. 1-103.

The first essay usefully to distinguish epochs in the poet's career. The second half (from p. 54) is of most interest, the first half being chiefly biographical.

95. Brooke, Stopford A. Theology in the English Poets. Cowper, Coleridge, Wordsworth, and Burns. London: Henry S. King, 1874. Rpt. London: Dent & Sons, 1910. xii+275 pp. not indexed.

Excellent on the spiritual dimensions of W's poetry; first careful criticism of The Prelude.

96. Pater, Walter. "Wordsworth." Fortnightly Review 21(1874): 455-65. Rpt. in Appreciations, With an Essay on Style (London: Macmillan, 1889; rpt. Oxford: Blackwell, 1967), pp. 39-64.

Sensitive and penetrating evaluation praising the depth and authenticity of the poet's emotions.

97. Stephen, Sir Leslie. "Wordsworth's Ethics." Cornhill Magazine 34(1876): 206-26. Rpt. in Hours in a Library, 3rd Series. London: Smith, Elder & Co., 1879. Rpt. in Leslie Stephen: Selected Writings in British Intellectual History, ed. Noël Annan. Chicago: University of Chicago, 1979, pp. 197-227.

Effectively argues that the poet's ideas are important. Sees W reconciling idealist and empirical traditions, but tasks W with an insufficient view of evil in nature.

98. Arnold, Matthew, ed. *The Poems of Wordsworth*. London: Macmillan, 1879. Rpt. London: Macmillan, 1961. xxxi+331 pp.

The introduction to this volume of selections largely determined the nature of W's reputation until the publication of A.C. Bradley's work (see 99, 100), and it remains influential. Dismissing W's "philosophy," Arnold praises his poetry as vitally inspiriting. The introduction, titled "Wordsworth," is reprinted in Arnold's *Essays in Criticism*, 2nd Series (London: Macmillan, 1888), and is more readily available in Trilling's collection, *The Portable Matthew Arnold* (New York: Viking, 1949). See also Arnold's "Memorial Verses" (1850).

TWENTIETH-CENTURY VIEWS

99. Bradley, A[ndrew] C. *English Poetry and German Philosophy in The Age of Wordsworth*. Manchester: The University Press, 1909. 29 pp.

Contains a careful treatment of Wordsworth in relation to Hegel.

100. Bradley, A[ndrew] C. *Oxford Lectures on Poetry*. London: Macmillan, 1909. Rpt. Bloomington: Indiana University, 1961. 395 pp. not indexed.

Includes two seminal essays: "Wordsworth" (pp. 99-148), stressing the ambiguities and complexities that enrich the poet's openness and simplicity; and "The Long Poem in Wordsworth's Age" (pp. 177-205), which attributes to the Romantics' genius for subjectivity and lyric the mediocrity of their long poems. The former is reprinted in part in 165.

101. Greenbie, Marjory Latta Barstow. *Wordsworth's Theory of Poetic Diction*. New Haven, CT: Yale, 1917. Rpt. New York: AMS, 1977. xv+187 pp. indexed.

Includes careful analysis of the diction of *Lyrical Ballads* in the light of the theories found in W's prefaces.

102. Cooper, Lane. "The Making and the Use of a Verbal Concordance." Sewanee Review 27(1919), 188-206.

Interesting description of the procedures used in compiling the Concordance to the Poems of Wordsworth (54), with a study of the poet's vocabulary.

103. Beatty, Arthur. William Wordsworth: His Doctrine and Art in Their Historical Relations. Madison: University of Wisconsin, 1922. 3rd ed., 1960. 310 pp. indexed.

Historically important work describing W's debt to David Hartley and associational psychology, and finding W's transcendentalism founded upon his knowledge of sensationalist philosophy.

104. Whitehead, A[lfred] N. Science and the Modern World. New York: Macmillan, 1925. Rpt. New York: New American Library, 1960. xii+304 pp. indexed.

Chapter Five, "The Romantic Reaction," argues for the continuing significance of W's resistance to the abstractions of Newtonian science in the light of twentieth-century physics' conceptions of natural process. Reprinted in part in 161.

105. Huxley, Aldous. "Wordsworth in the Tropics." Yale Review 18(1929): 672-83. Rpt. in Do What You Will, Essays by Aldous Huxley. London: Chatto & Windus, 1929, pp. 123-39.

Claims that travel in equatorial regions would have taught W that nature is not kindly but alien to man. Witty and stimulating, if unfair to the poet.

106. Rader, Melvin M. Presiding Ideas in Wordsworth's Poetry. Seattle: University of Washington, 1931. Rpt. New York: Gordian, 1968. 95 pp. indexed.

The first book to take serious account of the 1805 Prelude published in 1926 (18), reacting against Beatty (103) by stressing idealist sources for Wordsworthian psychology. Somewhat updated in Rader's Wordsworth: A Philosophical Approach (Oxford: Clarendon, 1967).

107. Eliot, T[homas] S[tearns]. The Use of Poetry and The Use of Criticism: Studies in the Relation of Criticism to Poetry in England. London: Faber & Faber, 1933. 2nd Ed. 1964. 156 pp.

The chapter on "Wordsworth and Coleridge" (pp. 67-85) is original in its insights; Eliot sees W as possessed of the more significant critical mind.

108. Willey, Basil. The Seventeenth-Century Background: Studies in the Thought of the Age in Relation to Poetry and Religion. London: Chatto & Windus, 1934. Rpt. Garden City, NY: Doubleday, 1953. 316 pp. indexed. pbk.

An excellent chapter "On Wordsworth and the Locke Tradition" surveys the poet's debt to empirical thought. Reprinted in 142, 161.

109. Sperry, Willard L. Wordsworth's Anti-Climax. Cambridge, MA: Harvard, 1935. Rpt. New York: Russell & Russell, 1966. vii+228 pp. not indexed.

Locates the cause of W's decline in his aesthetics, which are analyzed in terms of the poet's views on philosophy, politics, and religion.

110. Beach, Joseph Warren. The Concept of Nature in Nineteenth-Century English Poetry. New York: Macmillan, 1936. Rpt. New York: Russell & Russell, 1966. 618 pp. indexed.

The examination of W's concept of nature in chapters 3-6 is thorough and well-balanced, taking full account of Beatty's arguments (103) but pointing up some of Beatty's oversights, notably the poet's debt to the Cambridge Platonists.

Reviews: E.K. Brown, UTQ 6(1937), 141-47; C.F. Harrold, VQR 13(1937), 303-306; Emile Legouis, EA 1(1937), 73-74; Warner G. Rice, JEGP 36(1937), 599-602.

111. Leavis, F[rank] R[aymond]. Revaluation: Tradition and Development in English Poetry. London: Chatto & Windus, 1936. Rpt. New York: Norton, 1963. viii+275 pp. not indexed. pbk.

Chapter 5, a general essay on W (pp. 154-202), has been influential especially in its high estimate of The Excursion, book 1. Leavis helpfully comments on what Arnold calls the "illusion" of philosophy in W's verse, qualifies Shelley's portrait of the "unsexual" W, and relates his poetic decline to maturation and the demands his "generously active sympathies" made on him.

112. Bush, Douglas. Mythology and the Romantic Tradition in English Poetry. Cambridge, MA: Harvard, 1937. Rpt. New York: Norton, 1969. xxvi+647 pp. indexed. pbk.

A conscientious searching out of sources, useful as a reference work.

Reviews: AL 9(1937), 277-78; Leonard Bacon, SRL, 10 July 1937, p. 7; Stanton A. Coblentz, NYT, 1 Aug. 1937, p. 2; William Clyde De Vane, MP 35(1937), 211-213; A. Koszul, JEGP 38(1937), pp. 7-8; Gilbert Norwood, UTQ 6 (1937), 593-97; C.G. Osgood, MLN 53(1938), 439-41; C.D. Thorpe, RM, 1937, pp. 7-8; TLS, 19 June 1937, p. 461; Edna Lou Walton, NYHT, 19 Sept. 1937, p. 23.

113. James, D[avid] G. Scepticism and Poetry: An Essay on the Poetic Imagination. London: G. Allen & Unwin, 1937. Rpt. New York: Barnes & Noble, 1960. 274 pp.

Though dense and contorted, the chapter on W, "Visionary Dreariness" (pp. 141-69), was one starting point for David Ferry's important study (131). Reprinted in 154.

Reviews: Spectator, 9 April 1937, p. 678; TLS, 20 March 1937, p. 200.

114. Willey, Basil. The Eighteenth-Century Background: Studies on the Idea of Nature in the Thought of the Period. London: Chatto & Windus, 1940. Rpt. New York: Columbia, 1962. 301 pp. indexed. pbk.

The final chapter, "Nature in Wordsworth," is a judicious analysis, pointing out the importance to W of

eighteenth-century attitudes toward nature, and stressing against the position of Beatty (103) the idealistic and transcendentalizing tendencies in W's philosophy.
Reviews: Walter Grahan, JEGP 41(1942), 246-48; A.O. Lovejoy, MLN 58(1953), 485-87; D.M. Low, RES 18(1942), 118-21; Melvin Rader, MLQ 4(1943), 116-17.

115. Havens, R[aymond] D. The Mind of a Poet: Volume One, A Study of Wordsworth's Thought, and Volume Two, The Prelude, A Commentary. Baltimore, MD: Johns Hopkins, 1941. Rpt. 1962. xviii+670 pp. indexed.

An extensive work emphasizing transcendental aspects of W's thought; the commentary on the 1850 Prelude in Volume 2 is highly detailed and still useful.
Reviews: Joseph Warren Beach, MLN 57(1942), 473-76; Ernest Bernbaum, JEGP 42(1943), 133-37; Helen Darbishire, RES,19(1943), 97-100; Waldo H. Dunn, NYT, 8 March 1942, p. 34; J.R. MacGillivray, UTQ 12(1943), 233-34; George McLean Harper, SRL, 21 Feb. 1942, p. 21; George Wilbur Meyer, MLQ 4(1943), 120-22 (with exchange, pp. 515-18); Bennett Weaver, RM, 1942, pp. 13-15; John Edwin Wells, PQ 22(1943), 88-89.

116. Knight, G[eorge] Wilson. The Starlit Dome: Studies in the Poetry of Vision. London: Oxford, 1941. Rpt. 1971. xiv+330 pp. indexed.

The opening eighty-page chapter on W is a valuable exploration of fundamental symbols and significantly recurrent imagery.
Review: Kathleen Tillotson, RES 19(1943), 323-24.

117. Miles, Josephine. Wordsworth and the Vocabulary of Emotion. Berkeley: University of California, 1942. Rpt. New York: Octagon, 1965. xi+181 pp. not indexed.

Although based on word-counts, this book is more than a mere compilation of statistics, and poses important questions about the relation of language to feeling.
Reviews: Joseph E. Baker, PQ 23(1944), 94-95; Bennett Weaver, RM, 1943, pp. 20-22; Rene Wellek, MLN 58(1943), 644-45.

118. Trilling, Lionel. "Wordsworth's 'Ode: Intimations of Immortality.'" English Institute Annual 1941, ed. Rudolf Kirk. New York: Columbia, 1942, pp. 1-28. Rpt. in The Liberal Imagination. New York: Viking, 1950, pp. 125-54.

An important essay arguing that the poem is not a lament for failed poetic powers. Reprinted in 142 and 165. See also Vendler's revisionary essay (612).

119. Stallknecht, Newton P. Strange Seas of Thought: Studies in William Wordsworth's Philosophy of Man and Nature. Durham, NC: Duke, 1945. 2nd Ed. Bloomington: Indiana University, 1958. Rpt. 1966. xi+290 pp. indexed.

An opinionated but vigorous work which stresses that W drew not only on idealistic philosophical sources but also on some mystical traditions, notably that embodied in the works of Jacob Boehme.

Reviews: Carlos Baker, MLN 61(1946), 202-203; Edith C. Batho, MLR 40(1945), 318-19; Frederika Beatty, NYT, 23 Sept. 1945, p. 25; Helen Darbishire, RES 22(1946), 69-71.

120. Lyon, Judson Stanley. The Excursion: A Study. New Haven, CT: Yale, 1950. Rpt. Hamden, CT: Archon, 1970. x+154 pp. indexed.

Not a lively work, nor one critically inspired, but it marshalls effectively many of the facts most relevant to the poem's composition and aims.

Reviews: Helen Darbishire, RES 3(1952), 81-82; James V. Logan, MLN 66(1951), 51-53; J. Bard McNulty, MLQ 14 (1953), 122-23; TLS, 16 June 1950, p. 375; Bennett Weaver, JEGP 50(1951), 276-78.

121. MacLean, Kenneth. Agrarian Age: A Background for Wordsworth. New Haven, CT: Yale, 1950. xiii+108 pp. indexed.

Though somewhat superseded by later historical works, this remains a good introduction to the intricate social-political problems of the poet's era.

Reviews: F.W. Bateson, RES 4(1953), 189-90; Edith C. Batho, MLR 47(1952), 273; V.R. Stallbaumer, MLQ 14

(1953), 313-14; TLS, 6 July 1952, p. 415 (see also W.J.B. Owen, TLS, 13 July, p. 437).

122. Dunklin, Gilbert T., ed. Wordsworth: Centenary Studies Presented at Cornell and Princeton Universities. Princeton, NJ: Princeton, 1951. Rpt. Hamden, CT: Archon, 1963. 169 pp. indexed.

An extremely valuable small collection of seven essays, four of which are of particular interest: E.L. Griggs, in "Wordsworth through Coleridge's Eyes," amasses much relevant material to argue that in their collaboration "the gain was Wordsworth's." In "The Eye and the Object," Frederick Pottle examines W's imaginative divergence from Dorothy's Journal, his source for "I Wandered Lonely as a Cloud." Lionel Trilling, in "Wordsworth and the Iron Time," astutely compares W's thought with Judaism, suggesting that W's stress on endurance and common life explains his small appeal to an age seeking violent stimulants. And John Crowe Ransom contributes a masterful essay of general comment, "Wordsworth: Notes toward an Understanding of Poetry."

Reviews: Edith C. Batho, RES 5(1954), 95-96; William A. Borst, NYHT, 11 Nov. 1951, p. 20; S. Mandel, SRL, 29 March 1952, p. 32; George Meyer, JEGP 51(1952), 114-18; Josephine Miles, JAAC 11(1952), 82-83; TLS, 26 Oct. 1951, p. 672; Bennett Weaver, RM, 1951, pp. 129-30.

123. Marsh, Florence. Wordsworth's Imagery: A Study in Poetic Vision. New Haven, CT: Yale, 1952. Rpt. Hamden, CT: Archon, 1963. 146 pp. indexed.

Lists and discusses important recurrent images.

Reviews: J. Remenyi, JAAC 13(1954), 117-18; Roger Sharrock, RES 5(1954), 312-14.

124. Abrams, M.H. The Mirror and the Lamp: Romantic Theory and the Critical Tradition. New York: Oxford, 1953. Rpt. 1979. 406 pp. indexed. pbk.

W is central in this famous book, which sees Romanticism as characterized by the emergence of an art centered on expressiveness. But Abrams does full justice to W's links to his eighteenth-century predecessors.

Reviews: G. Boas, KR 16(1954), 124-28; Malcolm Brown,

MLQ 17(1956), 76-77; Geoffrey Bullough, YWES 24(1953), 260-61; M. Herrick, JEGP 53(1954), 252-53; John Holloway, RES 6(1955), 94-96; Arnold Isenberg, JAAC 12(1954), 527; T.M. Raysor, MP 51(1954), 281-83; Rene Wellek, CL 6 (1954), 178-81; A.S.P. Woodhouse, MLN 70(1955), 374-77.

125. Potts, Abbie Findlay. Wordsworth's Prelude: A Study of Its Literary Form. Ithaca, NY: Cornell, 1953. Rpt. New York: Octagon, 1966. xii+392 pp. indexed.

Helpful in citing many of the poem's sources, especially among eighteenth-century poets. Uses the 1805 version.

Reviews: Edith C. Batho, MLR 51(1956), 459-60; Joseph W. Beach, MLN 70(1955), 302-304; Frederick A. Pottle, MP 52(1955), 280-82; B. Redman, SRL, 20 March 1954, p. 20; Newton Stallknecht, KR 16(1954), 482-86; Bennett Weaver, JEGP 53(1954), 253-56; Frederick T. Wood, ES 36 (1955), 177.

126. Bateson, F[rederick] W[ilse]. Wordsworth: A Re-Interpretation. London: Longmans, 1954. 2nd ed. 1956. ix+227 pp. indexed.

An influential study arguing the importance of W's internal biography to an understanding of his poetry, most famous for its emphasis on W's feelings for Dorothy, a position moderated in the second edition.

Reviews: H. Fausset, Manchester Guardian, 22 Oct. 1954, p. 4; R. Halsband, Saturday Review, 2 Apr. 1955, p. 23; TLS, 12 Nov. 1954, p. 722; George Whalley, NS, 1 Jan. 1955, p. 21.

127. Jones, [Henry] John [Franklin]. The Egotistical Sublime: A History of Wordsworth's Imagination. London: Chatto & Windus, 1954. Rpt. 1964. ix+212 pp. indexed.

Much interested in the continuity of W's whole career, Jones argues that W's best poetry is that which successfully expresses a paradoxical quality of "solitude-in-relationship." Original and interesting criticism.

Reviews: DM 30(Oct.-Dec. 1954), 55-56; David Jesson-Dibley, English 10(1954), 107; Li, 18 Feb. 1954, p. 307; Norman Nicholson, LM 1(1954), 97-102; TLS, 5 March 1954, pp. 145-46; Bennett Weaver, RM, 1955, pp. 943-44; George Whalley, NS, 17 April 1954, p. 508.

128. Mayo, Robert. "The Contemporaneity of the _Lyrical Ballads_." _PMLA_ 69(1954): 486-522.

A seminal essay, arguing that the poems are not drastically different in theme or style from much of the popular poetry of the day. Reprinted in part in 300. Mayo's topic is considered further in several studies, e.g., Charles Ryskamp, "Wordsworth's _Lyrical Ballads_ in their Time" (145), pp. 357-72; J.E. Jordan, "The Novelty of the _Lyrical Ballads_" (160), pp. 340-58; and the book-length studies of Mary Jacobus (390) and Heather Glen (950).

129. Unwin, Rayner. _The Rural Muse: Studies in the Peasant Poetry of England_. London: Allen & Unwin, 1954. 202 pp. indexed.

W is differentiated from the eighteenth-century "peasant poets."

Review: Ralph Lawrence, _English_ 10(1954), 108-109.

130. Langbaum, Robert W. _The Poetry of Experience: The Dramatic Monologue in Modern Literary Tradition_. New York: Random House, 1957. Rpt. New York: Norton, 1963. 246 pp. indexed. pbk.

Sees the Romantic poets, especially W, as originating developments in lyric form leading to the dramatic monologue.

Reviews: John Bayley, _Spectator_, 26 July 1957, p. 143; H. Corke, _Encounter_ 9(Oct. 1957), 80-82; B. Fuson, _CE_ 20 (1960), 259-60; T. Gunn, _LM_ 5(Feb. 1958), 62-65; John Jones, _NS_, 3 Aug. 1957, p. 550; W. Rueckert, _JEGP_ 58 (1959), 518-20; _TLS_, 2 Aug. 1957, p. 950; Chad Walsh, _NYHT_, 4 Aug. 1957, p. 6.

131. Ferry, David. _The Limits of Mortality: An Essay on Wordsworth's Major Poems_. Middleton, CT: Wesleyan, 1959. Rpt. 1965. xi+181 pp. indexed.

An important work, the first to develop suggestions appearing in Bradley's commentaries (99, 100) that W's "love of nature" was complicated and even contradictory. Ferry, who reads W's "nature" poems as hostile to nature except as a symbol of eternity, perceives W as resisting the limits imposed by the natural world on man's visionary and sacramental potentialities.

Reviews: Stephen M. Parrish, MP 60(1962), 143-45; P. Ure, N&Q 7(1960), 274-75; Bennett Weaver, RM, 1960, p. 194.

132. Perkins, David. The Quest for Permanence: The Symbolism of Wordsworth, Shelley, and Keats. Cambridge, MA: Harvard, 1959. Rpt. 1969. viii+305 pp. indexed.

Devotes the first three chapters to W, arguing that the poet yearns for a "more stable" reality than he found under the new conditions of life at the end of the eighteenth century, characterized by instability and accelerating change, and is troubled by the "gulf between human nature...and the rest of nature."

Reviews: P. Bartlett, Expl 19(1960), rev. 1; Edward E. Bostetter, RM, 1959, pp. 141-42; J. Gray, QQ 67 (1960), 314-15; H.E. Hugo, JAAC 19(1960), 240-41; John Jones, RES 13(1962), 205-206; Leonidas M. Jones, KSJ 9, pt. 2(1960), 135-37; Lionel Stevenson, SAQ 59(1960), 456-57; J. Stillinger, JEGP 59(1960), 581-84; R.S. Woof, DR 41(1961), 93-95.

133. Danby, John F. The Simple Wordsworth: Studies in the Poems 1797-1807. London: Routledge & Kegan Paul, 1960. Rpt. 1968. viii+152 pp. not indexed.

Emphasizes the importance of W's "simple" lyrics by showing their concealed complexity and rhetorical skill.

Reviews: Patrick Cruttwell, HudR 14(1961-62), 400; John Holloway, Li, 2 Feb. 1961, p. 234; John Jones, NS, 6 Jan. 1961, p. 25; TLS, 23 Dec. 1960, p. 830; Bennett Weaver, RM, 1961, pp. 676-77; Frederick T. Wood, ES 42 (1961), 400.

134. Hirsch, E[ric] D., Jr. Wordsworth and Schelling: A Typological Study of Romanticism. New Haven, CT: Yale, 1960. Rpt. Hamden, CT: Archon, 1971. xiii+214 pp. indexed.

An interesting comparative study of the poet and the German philosopher; several shrewd analyses of major poems.

Reviews: Richard H. Fogle, CL 19(1962), 305; W.J.B.

Owen, RES 12(1961), 430-32; Howard Sergeant, English 13 (1960), 108; H.A. Smith, MLR 56(1961), 412-13; Newton Stallknecht, MLN 76(1961), 58-64; Bennett Weaver, RM, 1960, pp. 195-96.

135. Kroeber, Karl. Romantic Narrative Art. Madison: University of Wisconsin, 1960. Rpt. 1966. xi+225 pp. indexed. pbk.

Treats The Prelude as a "personal epic" and comments on W's role in Romantic literary balladry.

Reviews: Frederick L. Beaty, KSJ 11(1962), 103-105; Peter Butter, MLR 57(1962), 92-93; Geoffrey Carnall, RES 13(1962), 206-208; John D. Jump, MP 59(1961), 138-40; Martin K. Nurmi, RM, 1960, p. 170; C.J. Rawson, N&Q 9 (1962), 429-30; Jack Stillinger, JEGP 61(1962), 187-89.

136. Bloom, Harold. The Visionary Company: A Reading of English Romantic Poetry. Garden City, NY: Doubleday, 1961. Revised and enlarged, Ithaca, NY: Cornell, 1971. xxv+477 pp. pbk.

The chapter on W contains original readings, often with a shrewd eye for overlooked detail, of most of the principal works.

Reviews: Carlos Baker, KSJ 12(1963), 113-15; James Benziger, Criticism 5(1963), 185-88; Paul de Man, MR 3(1962), 618-23; C.S. Lewis, Encounter, June 1963, p. 74; James V. Logan, RM, 1961, p. 655; Robert O. Preyer, YR 51(1962), 316-19; J.W.R. Purser, RES 14(1963), 209-11; TLS, 20 Apr. 1962, p. 266.

137. Peckham, Morse. Beyond the Tragic Vision: The Quest for Identity in the Nineteenth Century. New York: George Braziller, 1962. 380 pp. indexed.

Analyzes W in relation not only to the painter Constable, but also to the German painter Friedrich (ch. 7) and to Goethe (ch. 6). In his later The Triumph of Romanticism (Columbia: University of South Carolina, 1970), Peckham makes an interesting comparison of Wordsworth and Constable.

Reviews: Kenneth Neil Cameron, YCGL, 1963, pp. 93-94; William C. De Vane, YR 52(1962), 112-18; Martin K. Nurmi, RM, 1962, pp. 437-38.

138. Piper, H[erbert] W. The Active Universe: Pantheism and the Concept of Imagination in the English Romantic Poets. London: Athlone, 1962. viii+243 pp. indexed.

Argues with some effectiveness for W's development of a concept of imagination, rooted in the pantheistic imagination of intellectuals such as Priestley and Erasmus Darwin, different from that which C describes in the Biographia Literaria (86) and not unlike Wittgenstein's ideas of "seeing as."

Reviews: K.C. Brown, BJA 4(1964), 82-83; Martin K. Nurmi, RM, 1962, p. 446; Roger Sharrock, RES 16(1965), 84; H.A. Smith, MLR 58(1963), 414; Derek Stanford, English 14(1963), 202; Jack Stillinger, JEGP 62(1963), 690; TLS, 19 Apr. 1963, p. 266.

139. Bostetter, Edward E. The Romantic Ventriloquists: Wordsworth, Coleridge, Keats, Shelley, Byron. Seattle: University of Washington, 1963. Revised, 1975. xiv+357 pp. indexed.

Questions the "triumphant affirmation" of the Romantic poets, devoting a long chapter to W's doubts and difficulties regarding man's relation to nature. Examines the great lyrics from "Tintern Abbey" to "Ode to Duty," the 1805 Prelude, and The Excursion, arguing that the unfinished Recluse is symptomatic of the poet's inability to sustain his youthful optimism.

Reviews: James V. Baker, Criticism 7(1965), 199-200; Richard H. Fogle, JEGP 66(1967), 155-56 John E. Grant, KSJ 14(1965), 93-96; A.J.K., RM, 1963, p. 443; Donald Weeks, JAAC 24(1965), 322-23; H.A. Smith, MLR 59(1964), 465-66; TLS, 2 July 1964, p. 572.

140. Frye, Northrop, ed. Romanticism Reconsidered: Selected Papers from the English Institute. New York: Columbia, 1963. Rpt. 1968. ix+133 pp. pbk.

Four notable essays, including M.H. Abrams' "English Romanticism: The Spirit of the Age," which defines W's centrality to Romantic art.

Reviews: Martin K. Nurmi, RM, 1963, pp. 436-37; Mark Roberts, EIC 15(1965), 118-30; TLS, 27 Aug. 1964, pp. 757-58.

141. Lindenberger, Herbert. On Wordsworth's Prelude. Princeton, NJ: Princeton, 1963. xix+316 pp. indexed.

Perhaps the best book devoted solely to The Prelude (using the 1805 version); treats the poem's structure, language, and reception in a series of chapters that deliberately do not attempt unity. Many of Lindenberger's discussions (especially chs. 2 and 3, on style) are useful also for understanding the wider range of W's philosophical verse.

Reviews: Alan Grob, JEGP 63(1964), 808; E.D. Hirsch, Jr., YR 53(1963), 115; Carl F. Keppler, ArQ 19(1963), 284-85; John R. Nabholtz, MP 62(1965), 361; H.A. Smith, MLR 59(1964), 115; TLS, 13 Sept. 1963, p. 690; R.S. Woof, DR 44(1964), 233-35.

142. Davis, Jack, ed. Discussions of Wordsworth. Boston: D.C. Heath, 1964. xiii+178 pp. not indexed. pbk.

Reprints thirteen important essays and extracts, eight of which are listed elsewhere: by Coleridge (86), Arnold (98), Bradley (100), Willey (108), Leavis (111), Trilling (118), Abrams (124), and Jones (127). Also of interest is Norman MacLean's "An Analysis of a Lyric Poem" (1942), treating "It is a beauteous evening, calm and free."

143. Hartman, Geoffrey H. Wordsworth's Poetry 1787-1814. New Haven, CT: Yale, 1964. 2nd ed. 1971. xxv+418 pp. indexed. pbk.

For two decades the central critical work on W and focus for innumerable debates. Includes many detailed analyses of specific poems; the commentaries on the major works are frequently referred to by subsequent critics. Hartman argues that the poet developed by "converting apocalypse into akedah...as a preparatory humanizing of an otherworldly power of imagination," for which the "everyday world was often so inadequate that imagination preferred withdrawal or ecstasy." (Quotations are from Hartman's "Retrospect" in the second edition.) Especially influential have been Hartman's psychological, as opposed to historical, readings of the verse.

Reviews: Morris Dickstein, PR 33(1966), 139-42; A. Fletcher, YR 54(1965), 595-98; Daniel Hughes, Criticism 7(1965), 389-91; Kenneth Johnston, WC 3(1972), 149-59;

Karl Kroeber, RM, 1964, pp. 44-45; Robert Langbaum, ELH 33(1966), 271-84; Herbert Lindenberger, MLQ 27(1966), 212-20; Manfred McKenzie, SoRA 2(1966), 174-78; W.J.B. Owen, MLR 61(1966), 685-86; Christopher Ricks, NYT, 28 Jan. 1965, p. 10; TLS, 29 April 1965, p. 332; J.R. Watson, RES 17(1966), 94-96; Donald Weeks, JAAC 24 (1965), 321-22.

144. Perkins, David. Wordsworth and the Poetry of Sincerity. Cambridge, MA: Harvard, Belknap Press, 1964. viii+285 pp. indexed.

Considers the poet's response to the developing demand that poetry be written with personal sincerity. Analyzes W's style as fundamentally exemplary, directed to what the poet perceives to be the needs of life rather than merely of art. Thoughtful criticism of a kind not recently fashionable.

Reviews: P. Drew, Li, 15 Oct. 1964, p. 601; B.S. Johnson, Spectator, 28 Aug. 1964, p. 280; R.W. King, MLR 61(1966), 113-14; Karl Kroeber, RM, 1964, p. 46; W.J.B. Owen, RES 16(1965), 440; TLS, 5 Nov. 1964, p. 1000; Jonathan Wordsworth, NS, 30 Oct. 1964, p. 661.

145. Hilles, Frederick W., and Harold Bloom, eds. From Sensibility to Romanticism: Essays Presented to Frederick A. Pottle. New York: Oxford, 1965. viii+585 pp. indexed. pbk.

A valuable collection of essays on Romanticism, including several of importance to Wordsworthians. Cleanth Brooks's "Wordsworth and Human Suffering: Notes on Two Early Poems" ponders W's position, in "The Old Cumberland Beggar" and "The Ruined Cottage," that good may come of loneliness, loss, and death. Charles Ryskamp, in "Wordsworth's Lyrical Ballads in their Time," compares W with Cowper and Gay, finding his originality in his quasi-dramatic psychological exposition, and in honest sentiment (cf. 128). Geoffrey Hartman considers W's role in developing a new Romantic lyric form from neoclassic epigram and the related genre of inscription, and places much emphasis on the influence of the Greek Anthology, in "Wordsworth, Inscriptions, and Romantic Nature Poetry" (reprinted in Beyond Formalism [New Haven, CT: Yale, 1970], which also includes two other essays of interest). M.H. Abrams, in an influential essay commenting on

C and "Tintern Abbey," describes "Structure and Style in the Greater Romantic Lyric."
Reviews: CQ 8,i(1966), 95-96; John D. Jump, RES 5 (1966), 331-33; James Kinsley, MLR 61(1966), 680-83; TLS 23 Dec. 1965, p. 1198.

146. Wilkie, Brian. Romantic Poets and Epic Tradition. Madison: University of Wisconsin, 1965. xi+276 pp. indexed.

Arguing that epic is a tradition, not a genre, Wilkie includes The Prelude especially by elucidating its "epic pattern," or structure of "mission and ordeal." Though he specifically treats the 1805 version, Wilkie holds that W's revisions serve to clarify this pattern.
Reviews: Ernest Bernhardt-Kabisch, ELN 3(1965), 142-47; John Buxton, RES 17(1966), 215-17; Robert Gleckner, Criticism 9(1967), 380-81; Carl F. Keppler, ArQ 21(1965), pp. 286-88; Karl Kroeber, RM, 1967, p. 17; James V. Logan, SAQ 65(1966), 168; M.N. Nagler, CL 19 (1967), 380-81; Stephen M. Parrish, KSJ 15(1966), 126-28; Donald H. Reiman, JEGP 64(1965); James Scoggins, CE 27(1966), 645-46; Stuart M. Sperry, Jr., MP 64(1967), 263-64; William Walling, Commonweal 82(1965), pp. 197-99.

147. Woodring, Carl R. Wordsworth. Boston: Houghton Mifflin, 1965. pbk. Rpt. Cambridge, MA: Harvard, 1968. vii+227 pp. indexed.

The best brief introduction to the poet's art.
Reviews: Roland Bartel, CL 22(1970), 92-93; John Colmer, MLR 66(1971), 399-41; Karl Kroeber, RM, 1965, p. 46; J. Hillis Miller, SEL 9(1969), pp. 737-49; H.A. Smith, MLR 63(1968), 208-10.

148. Groom, Bernard. The Unity of Wordsworth's Poetry. London: Macmillan, 1966. xiii+224 pp. indexed.

Probably the most effective argument for not dismissing W's later poetry and for recognizing the continuity in the poet's development.
Reviews: Edward Bostetter, SEL 7(1967), 741-66; David V. Erdman, RM, 1966, p. 41; M. Thorpe, English 17(1968), 62; TLS, 2 March 1967, p. 168.

149. Murray, Roger N. Wordsworth's Style: Figures and Themes in the Lyrical Ballads of 1800. Lincoln: University of Nebraska, 1967. ix+166 pp. indexed.

Contains some fine analyses of the poet's rhetoric.
Reviews: Karl Kroeber, Style 1(1967), 165-68; J.R. MacGillivray, UTQ 37(1968), 309-20.

150. Gerard, Albert S. English Romantic Poetry: Ethos, Structure, and Symbol in Coleridge, Wordsworth, Shelley, and Keats. Berkeley: University of California, 1968. ix+284 pp.

Includes three sensitive and perceptive readings of W, with helpful surveys of earlier criticism: argues that "The Thorn" is unified, the narrator, thorn, and Martha being equally important; praises the poet's honesty for not pretending to reconcile the concrete and the mystical in "Tintern Abbey"; and examines the structure and biographical context of "Resolution and Independence," finding the poem among W's earliest considerations of a transcendent God.
Reviews: Richard H. Fogle, KSJ 18(1969), 111-12; U. Laredo, UES 1(March 1969), 97-98; TLS, 21 Nov. 1968, p. 1304; W.J.B. Owen, RES 20(1969), 262-64.

151. Noyes, Russell. Wordsworth and the Art of Landscape. Bloomington: Indiana University, 1968. xi+282 pp. indexed. pbk.

Not profound, but accurate and informative survey.
Reviews: D.S. Bland, N&Q 17(1970), 191; James A.W. Heffernan, ES 54(1970), 365-67; John R. Nabholtz, ELN 6 (1969), 296-98; J.R. Watson, RES 20(1969), 357-58.

152. Heffernan, James A.W. Wordsworth's Theory of Poetry: The Transforming Imagination. Ithaca, NY: Cornell, 1969. xii+280 pp. indexed.

A valuable discussion of W's poetic theory, stressing his movement, after 1800, toward a view of poetry as "transformation" rather than as "transcription," and as originating in imagination rather than in feeling. Heffernan finds much to praise in W's later poetry.
Reviews: J.A. Clarke, CritQ 13(1971), 88; Karl Kroe-

ber, RM, 1969, pp. 48-49; Thomas McFarland, YR 59(1970), 439; Richard D. McGhee, SHR 4(1970), 374-75; Mark L. Reed, WHR 24(1970), 410-11; E.J. Schulze, MQR 11(1972), 144; J. Stillinger, JEGP 69(1970), 179.

153. Owen, W[arwick] J.B. Wordsworth as Critic. Toronto: University of Toronto, 1969. xiii+239 pp. indexed.

Complements Heffernan's book (152), with little to say about ideas, mostly dogged explanations of particularities.

Reviews: Stanley Freiberg, DR 50(1970), 419-21; Karl Kroeber, RM, 1969, p. 50; Hermann Peschmann, English 19(1970), 104-105; Brian Wilkie, ELN 8(1970), 58-61.

154. Thomson, A[lastair] W., ed. Wordsworth's Mind and Art. Edinburgh: Oliver & Boyd, 1969. vii+235 pp. indexed.

A good anthology of critical essays old and new, including one by E.A. Horsman, "The Design of Wordsworth's Prelude," challenging the impressive reading by Hartman (143).

Reviews: Stephen Gill, N&Q 17(1970), 188-89; TLS, 25 Sept. 1969, p. 1067.

155. Wordsworth, Jonathan. The Music of Humanity: A Critical Study of Wordsworth's Ruined Cottage Incorporating Texts from a Manuscript of 1799-1800. New York: Harper and Row, 1969. xvi+293 pp. indexed.

An important book that began the disentanglement of "The Ruined Cottage" and "The Pedlar" in their original form from book 1 of The Excursion. Jonathan Wordsworth uses these early versions to argue for the significance of his ancestor's early, humanitarian poetry. Includes slightly editorialized reading texts of MS. D, differing from book 1 most notably in its omission of the Pedlar's biography and in its conclusion; of "The Pedlar"; and of a discarded passage. See also Butler's edition (20) and, on the relation of "The Pedlar" story to the larger poem, 525 and 671.

Reviews: F.W. Bateson, NS, 22 Aug. 1969, pp. 246-47; Karl Kroeber, RM, 1969, p. 51; Mary Moorman, ArielE 1, ii(1970), 39-41; Mark L. Reed, JEGP 69(1970), 528; TLS, 27 Nov. 1969, p. 1367.

156. Heath, William W. Wordsworth and Coleridge: A Study of Their Literary Relations in 1801-1802. Oxford: Clarendon, 1970. xiv+182 pp. indexed.

Through some careful, even intricate comparisons, defines how the imagination works as an agent of discovery.

Reviews: John Colmer, MLR 68(1973), 394; Mary Jacobus, RES 23(1972), 86; Karl Kroeber, RM, 1971, p. 65; Russell Noyes, WC 2(1971), 101-103; H. Peschmann, English 21 (1971), 57; Craig Raine, N&Q 20(1973), 69-71; TLS, 16 April 1971, p. 453 (reply by Mary Moorman, p. 504).

157. Prickett, Stephen. Coleridge and Wordsworth: The Poetry of Growth. Cambridge: Cambridge, 1970. vii+214 pp. indexed.

A careful comparative study emphasizing the religious foundations of both poets' ideas of imagination.

Reviews: Irene H. Chayes, RM, 1970, p. 41; John Colmer, MLR 66(1971), 399-401; Robert D. Hume, JAAC 29 (1971), 428; W.J.B. Owen, Mosaic 4(1971), 111-17; H. Peschmann, English 19(1970), 104-105; Craig Raine, DUJ 32(1970), 75-77; Jack Stillinger, JEGP 70(1971), 166-70; TLS, 2 Oct. 1970, p. 1129; R. Headlam Wells, N&Q 20 (1973), 71-72.

158. Wittreich, Joseph A. The Romantics on Milton: Formal Essays and Critical Asides. Cleveland, OH: Case Western Reserve, 1970. xxiii+594 pp. indexed.

The chapter on W (pp. 102-54) provides many brief quotations demonstrating W's attitudes to Milton.

Reviews: David V. Erdman, RM, 1970, p. 22; Kenneth Muir, N&Q 20(1973), 77-78; TLS, 6 Aug. 1971, p. 953.

159. Woodring, Carl R. Politics in English Romantic Poetry. Cambridge, MA: Harvard, 1970. ix+385 pp. indexed.

The chapter on W (pp. 85-147) is the best and most reliable discussion of the relation of the poetry to political events and contains several excellent commentaries on major works, e.g., The Borderers.

Reviews: Stuart Curran, RM, 1970, pp. 22-23; David V. Erdman, SIR 10(1971), 60-65; J.R. de J. Jackson, ELN 10

(1972), 53-54; John D. Jump, RES 23(1972), 214-16; Jerome J. McGann, MP 70(1973), 243-57; Max F. Schulz, MLQ 33(1972), 83-86; R.F. Storch, WC 2(1971), 32-37; Brian Wilkie, JEGP 70(1971), 559-64.

160. Wordsworth, Jonathan, and Beth Darlington, eds. Bicentenary Wordsworth Studies in Memory of John Alban Finch. Ithaca, NY: Cornell, 1970. xli+490 pp.

Nineteen essays, many of them focused on problems posed by W's manuscripts, make up this important volume. Also contains texts, edited from the manuscripts, of the "Ballad-Michael," "A Night-Piece," the discharged-soldier passage of The Prelude, and "Salisbury Plain." (Though these essays are not listed separately here, the reader is directed to them in the index.)

Reviews: Choice 8(1971), 1171; Bishop C. Hunt, WC 2 (1971), 117-21; J.R. de J. Jackson, UTQ 42(1973), 296; Library Journal, 15 Dec. 1970, p. 4263; J.R. Watson, RES 23(1972), 508-11; George Whalley, QQ 81(1974), 265-77.

161. Abrams, M[eyer] H. Natural Supernaturalism: Tradition and Revolution in Romantic Literature. New York: Norton, 1971. 550 pp. indexed. pbk.

W is central to this impressive scholarly exploration of "the secularization of inherited theological ideas and ways of thinking." Abrams sees the Prospectus to The Recluse as defining the fundamental Romantic commitment to a faith in man's ability to realize on earth hopes rooted in the principal religious traditions of Western culture.

Reviews: Robert Martin Adams, HudR 24(1972), 687-93; P.H. Butter, MLR 68(1973), 157-59; A.R. Chrisolm, AUMLA 38(1972), 279-81; John Clubbe, Mosaic 7,iii(1974), 137-50; Frederick Garber, MLQ 34(1973), 206-13; Spencer Hall, SHR 8(1974), 246-48; E.D. Hirsch, Jr., WC 3(1972), 17-20; J.R. de J. Jackson, UTQ 42(1973), 289-91; U.C. Knoepflmacher, SEL 12(1972), 802-20; Herbert Lindenberger, ELN 10(1972), 151-54; Thomas McFarland, YR 41 (1972), 279-97; Jerome J. McGann, MP 70(1973), 243-57; Graham Martin, Spectator, 4 March 1972, pp. 358-59; Morse Peckham, SIR 13(1974), 359-65; Lawrence Poston, OLR 13(1972), 96-98; Stuart M. Sperry, Jr., YCGL 21 (1972), 86-89.

162. Curtis, Jared R. Wordsworth's Experiments with Tradition: The Lyric Poems of 1802, with Texts of the Poems Based on Early Manuscripts. Ithaca, NY: Cornell, 1971. xii+227 pp. not indexed.

Texts of thirty poems, many of them of major importance, with full commentaries.

Reviews: Paul F. Betz, SIR 12(1973), 580-84; Hermann Fischer, Anglia 98(1980), 248-52; Stephen Gill, RES 24 (1973), 99; Stuart M. Sperry, Jr., JEGP 72(1973), 140-43; TLS, 6 Oct. 1972, p. 1186.

163. Garber, Frederick. Wordsworth and the Poetry of Encounter. Urbana: University of Illinois, 1971. xii+195 pp. indexed.

Exploring "The Solitary Reaper" at length as a sort of paradigm, and commenting on many of W's greater lyrics and on the 1850 Prelude, Garber finds central to W's art instants when the poet encounters a person, scene, or object that in some way baffles him. Though he finds varying degrees of "otherness," Garber believes that for W the self and object are always ultimately discrete, so he finds no "mystic experience" in W's poetry.

Reviews: Beth Darlington, RES 24(1973), 384; B. Lupini, English 21(1972), 111; James Scoggins, MLQ 34(1973), 337; Stuart M. Sperry, Jr., JEGP 72(1973), 140; TLS, 6 Oct. 1972, p. 1186.

164. Thomas, Gordon K. Wordsworth's Dirge and Promise: Napoleon, Wellington, and the Convention of Cintra. Lincoln: University of Nebraska, 1971. viii+182 pp. indexed.

A somewhat plodding study centered on W's important Cintra pamphlet; an earlier study of relevance is A[lbert] V. Dicey's The Statesmanship of Wordsworth, An Essay (Oxford: Clarendon, 1917).

Reviews: Bishop C. Hunt, RM, 1971, p. 69; J.R. de J. Jackson, UTQ 42(1973), 289.

165. Abrams, M.H., ed. Wordsworth: A Collection of Critical Essays. Englewood Cliffs, NJ: Prentice Hall, 1972. 214 pp. indexed.

A good anthology of previously published criticism, offering judicious selections from nine of the most important books on W since 1954, and reprinting seven important essays whole or in part, including those of Bradley (100), Whitehead (104), and Mayo (128), Paul de Man's "Intentional Structure of the Romantic Image" (1960), and Cleanth Brooks's essay on the Ode, "Wordsworth and the Paradox of the Imagination" (1947).

166. Barrell, John. The Idea of Landscape and the Sense of Place, 1730-1840: An Approach to the Poetry of John Clare. Cambridge: Cambridge, 1972. x+244 pp.

Idiosyncratic, but contains an excellent contrast of W and John Clare.

SECTION 5. SCHOLARSHIP AND CRITICISM, 1973-1984

Some works, and all editions, published during this period have been listed separately as Standard Research Materials in Part I. Otherwise the listings below are meant to be comprehensive through 1983.

1973

167. Alpaugh, David. "Embers and the Sea: Beckettian Intimations of Mortality." Modern Drama 16(1973): 317-28.

Reads Beckett's Embers as a response to the Ode, especially to the ideals of "natural piety" and love of nature.

168. Altieri, Charles. "From Symbolist Thought to Immanence: The Ground of Postmodern American Poetics" Boundary 2 1(1973): 605-41.

Sees twentieth-century poetry and poetics as grounded in the "two poles" of Romanticism: while Modernism may be traced to C's symbolist poetic, contemporary poets (and to some extent the imagists) owe more to the more objective "immanentist" poetic of W.

169. Altieri, Charles. "Wordsworth's Wavering Balance: The Thematic Rhythm of The Prelude." The Wordsworth Circle 4(1973): 226-40.

An intelligent challenge to Hartman's view (143) that W's imagination is solipsistic and apocalyptic, arguing that memory and sympathetic imagination enable W to be "enlarged by" his experience of "natural rhythms," the repeated errors and losses described in The Prelude, "and led by them to a confidence in natural process." Since the autobiographical poet "follows natural rhythms," he speaks not solipsistically but for the community.

170. Ansari, Asloob Ahmad, ed. *Essays on Wordsworth: A Bi-Centenary Tribute*. Aligargh, India: Aligarh Muslim University, 1973. 135 pp.

Nine celebratory essays of little value.

171. Avni, Abraham. "Overlooked Biblical Allusions in Wordsworth." *Notes & Queries* 20(1973): 43-44.

Lists several overlooked allusions, noting in particular that the "inner shrine" of "It is a beauteous evening, calm and free" alludes to 1 Kings 6.

172. Bagchi, P. "A Note on Wordsworth's Sonnet, 'I heard (alas! 'twas only in a dream).'" *Notes & Queries* 20 (1973): 44.

Locates a source in Plato's *Phaedo*.

173. Barfoot, C.C. "Key Perspective, the Tonality of Tense in Some Poems of Wordsworth." *English Studies* 54,i(1973): 22-37.

Compares W's modulations of verb tense in "Elegiac Stanzas," "The Solitary Reaper," and "Resolution and Independence" to the "structural and dramatic exploitation of tonality, of key" in classical music.

174. Beer, John. "Blake, Coleridge, and Wordsworth: Some Cross-currents and Parallels, 1789-1805." In *William Blake: Essays in Honour of Sir Geoffrey Keynes*, ed. Morton D. Paley and Michael Phillips. Oxford: Clarendon, 1973, pp. 231-59.

Conjectures on mutual influence of W and Godwin (pp. 239-43), and on Blake's influence on W (pp. 253-59), suggesting that W may have seen *The Book of Thel*.

175. Beyette, Kent. "Wordsworth's Medical Muse: Erasmus Darwin and Psychology in 'Strange Fits of Passion Have I Known.'" *Literature and Psychology* 23(1973): 93-101.

Discusses Darwin's influence, and relies heavily on the cancelled final stanza of "Strange Fits" to suggest that Lucy's death, like Harry's chills in "Goody Blake and Harry Gill," is the effect of a delusion.

176. Borck, Jim Springer. "Wordsworth's The Prelude and the Failure of Language." Studies in English Literature, 1500-1900 13(1973): 605-16.

Discusses W's distrust of language as a belief that in time language "dissolves" something of the original meaning, and compares passages from the 1805 and 1850 Preludes to show, not very convincingly, this "progressive linguistic decay."

177. Boyd, David V. "Wordsworth as Satirist: Book VII of The Prelude." Studies in English Literature, 1500-1900 13 (1973): 617-31.

A good treatment of the book (in the 1850 version) as satire, noting especially its formal satiric structure, "as complex and intricate as that of a fugue."

178. Brewster, Elizabeth. "George Crabbe and William Wordsworth." University of Toronto Quarterly 42(1973): 142-56.

Compares and contrasts the poets' styles and concerns, noting a greater similarity in later years, cautiously suggesting mutual influence, and attributing the tepidity of their relationship to Jeffrey's having pitted them against one another in 1807.

179. Brisman, Leslie. Milton's Poetry of Choice and Its Romantic Heirs. Ithaca, NY: Cornell, 1973. xii+335 pp. indexed.

Details W's anxiety of influence, with particular attention to W's relation to Milton in "A little further onward" (pp. 213-18), in "Ode to Duty" (pp. 234-46), and in W's revisions of several poems (pp. 262-96).
Reviews: Leslie Tannenbaum, BlakeS 6(1973), 94-95; David Wagenknecht, SIR 14(1975), 85-91.

180. Brownstein, Rachel Mayer. "The Private Life: Dorothy Wordsworth's Journals." Modern Language Quarterly 34 (1973): 48-63.

Sensitive criticism of Dorothy's journals on their own merits, also including an apt contrast of Dorothy's account of the leech-gatherer with W's "Resolution and Independence."

181. Bugliari, Jeanne. "Whitman and Wordsworth: The Janus of Nineteenth Century Idealism." Walt Whitman Review 19 (1973): 63-67.

Frequently oversimplified comparison and contrast, arguing that W melancholically contemplated the past, while Whitman more sanguinely watched the future.

182. Caviglia, Anne Marie. "A Very Rare Wordsworthian Pun." The Wordsworth Circle 4(1973): 158-59.

Reads "Composed upon Westminster Bridge," line 14, as a sexual pun. See also 272.

183. Cottle, Basil. "Wordsworth and His Portraits: Two Unpublished Letters." Notes & Queries 20(1973): 285-86.

Prints two letters from a private collection, one to Samuel Rogers, 19 April 1831, and one to C. Marks, 29 Nov. 1846, with some remarks on W's portraits and friendships with painters.

184. Cowell, Raymond, ed. Critics on Wordsworth. London: Allen & Unwin, 1973. xi+114 pp. not indexed.

Brief excerpts from previously published criticism, ranging from 1798 to 1970.

185. Das, S.K. Wordsworth on Imagination: An Approach to His Poetry. Calcutta: Pioneer Publications, n.d. [ca. 1973] 228 pp.

Not seen.

186. Dyson, A.E. "Symbiosis in Wordsworth." Critical Survey 6 (1973): 41-43.

In an argument closely following that of E.D. Hirsch, Jr., in Validity and Interpretation (New Haven, CT: Yale, 1967), Dyson presents two possible readings of "A slumber did my spirit seal" and weakly suggests that they are "symbiotic."

187. Eakin, Sybil S. "The Spots of Time in Early Versions of The Prelude." Studies in Romanticism 12(1973): 389-405.

An oft-cited essay showing how W's revisions reveal changing conceptions of mind and nature--the spots of time argue nature's tutelage in early versions, and the mind's predominance by 1805.

188. Eason, Ros. "Wordsworth and Ordinary Sorrow: 'The Ruined Cottage.'" Critical Review 16(1973): 39-55.

Finds W's general belief in the value of solitude and of inanimate nature complicated and qualified by the tale of Margaret (uses Excursion, book 1, as text).

189. Fergenson, Laraine. "Was Thoreau Re-reading Wordsworth in 1851?" Thoreau Journal Quarterly 5,iii(1973): 20-23.

Comments on W's influence generally and notes echoes in the Journal entries of 1851.

190. Ferguson, Frances C. "The Lucy Poems: Wordsworth's Quest for a Poetic Object." ELH 40(1973): 532-48. Rpt. in Wordsworth: Language as Counter-Spirit (447), pp. 173-94.

An ingenious essay noting that from poem to poem Lucy is "ever more decisively traced out of existence," and ascribing her absence to W's increasing diffidence in the capacity of memory and language to represent reality. The various stances W adopts toward Lucy's death, it is argued, show a similar doubt about expressionist poetics, so that the poems are ultimately renunciatory or ascetic. Very helpful on the poems' relation to audience.

191. Goldstein, Laurence. "The Auburn Syndrome: Change and Loss in 'The Deserted Village' and Wordsworth's Grasmere." ELH 40(1973): 352-71. Rpt. in Ruins and Empire (456), pp. 163-83.

An interesting argument that the center of W's spiritual strength was not so much the spots of time, which he could revisit in memory, as the physical spot of Grasmere. Therefore, as "The Tuft of Primroses" attests, W's spiritual and poetic decline may be attributed to the spoliation of Grasmere after 1805. See also 307.

192. Gomme, A.H. "Some Wordsworthian Transparencies." Modern Language Review 68(1973): 507-20.

Explores W's use of third-person characters to portray aspects of himself in the "boy" of "Home at Grasmere," in "There was a Boy" and in the Wanderer of The Excursion (especially book 1).

193. Grob, Alan. The Philosophic Mind: A Study of Wordsworth's Poetry and Thought, 1797-1805. Columbus: Ohio State University, 1973. xii+279 pp. indexed.

Traces changes in Wordsworth's philosophic position from that of philosophic naturalism in the early poetry to a metaphysic stressing transcendence in the later work.

Reviews: Daniel P. Deneau, ArQ 31(1975), 91-93; James A. W. Heffernan, SIR 13(1974), 255-67; Bishop C. Hunt, RM, 1973, p. 67; John E. Jordan, WC 5(1974), 180-82; Susan Morgan, MP 72(1975), 431-32; TLS, 24 May 1974, p. 560.

194. Hamlin, Cyrus. "The Poetics of Self-Consciousness in European Romanticism: Hölderlin's Hyperion and Wordsworth's Prelude." Genre 6(1973): 142-77.

Compares Hyperion (in the German) and the 1850 Prelude as "reflective autobiographical narratives" concerned with what Bloom calls "the dialectic of consciousness and imagination." Both poets, Hamlin argues, were influenced by Fichte's theory of self-consciousness, and strove to reconcile imaginative experience and reflective narration to achieve true self-consciousness, or "intellectual intuition."

195. Hayden, Donald E. "William Wordsworth: Early Ecologist." In _Studies in Relevance: Romantic and Victorian Writers in 1972_, ed. Thomas Meade Harwell. Salzburg, Austria: Universität Salzburg, 1973, pp. 36-52.

Cites W's writings, activities, and his influence in preserving the Lake District.

196. Heath, William W. "Wordsworth's Experiments with Truth." _The Wordsworth Circle_ 4(1973): 87-98.

Considers "Nutting" and the drafts for it to show how the autobiographer experiments with his childhood to make it yield "truth" not just for the writer but also for the reader.

197. Hubert, Thomas. "Simms's Use of Milton and Wordsworth in _The Yemassee_: An Aspect of Symbolism in the Novel." _South Carolina Review_ 6,i(1973): 58-65.

Notes Simms's enthusiasm for W's poetry, and finds W's influence in Simms's use of the sublime.

198. Hugo, F.J. "The Wordsworthian Sense of the Relation Between Mind and the External World." _Theoria_ 40 (1973): 33-39.

Argues that for W the relation is one of "fundamental unity," not of discrete subject and object, and cites "I Wandered Lonely as a Cloud" and "There was a Boy."

199. Johnson, Lee M. _Wordsworth and the Sonnet_. Copenhagen: Rosenkilde & Bagger, 1973. 183 pp. indexed.

The only book entirely given over to W's many sonnets; not fully satisfactory as a history of W's composition of sonnets, but makes useful suggestions about the arrangements of the main sequences.

Reviews: Beth Darlington, RES 26(1975), 225-26; A.H. Elliott, N&Q 22(1975), 425-26; N.F. Ford, Style 9(1975), 134; A.J. Hartley, DR 54 (1974), 396; James A.W. Heffernan, ES 56(1975), 458; Warren U. Ober, MLR 70(1975), 396-401; Paul D. Sheats, WC 5(1974), 145-48.

200. Jordan, Frank. "Scott and Wordsworth; or, Reading Scott Well." The Wordsworth Circle 4(1973): 112-23.

An astute and well written comparison of Scott and W, their language, characters, and especially their quasi-dramatic narrative art of eliciting the reader's "imaginative participation."

201. Kestner, Joseph A., III. "Rousseau and Wordsworth: La Nouvelle Heloise and Two Lyrical Ballads." Iowa English Yearbook 23(1973): 56-59.

Finds possible echoes of Rousseau's novel in "We are Seven" and "The Tables Turned."

202. Kinnaird, John. "Hazlitt as Poet: The Probable Authorship of Some Anonymous Verses on Wordsworth's Appointment as Stamp-Distributor." Studies in Romanticism 12 (1973): 426-35.

Reprints a satire from the Morning Chronicle, 1813, and attributes it to Hazlitt (an attribution challenged in 555), commenting usefully on Hazlitt's attitude to W and on the sense in which contemporaries thought of the Lake Poets' "apostacy."

203. Land, Stephen K. "The Silent Poet: An Aspect of Wordsworth's Semantic Theory." University of Toronto Quarterly 42(1973): 157-69.

A clear, succinct analysis of W's theory of language in relation to eighteenth-century theories (Locke's being found most similar), explaining the figure of the "silent poet" and the frequent ineloquence and coyness of W's narrators by noting W's distrust of language and his belief that thought (and poetry) is pre-verbal.

204. McFarland, G.F. "Wordsworth and Julius Hare." Bulletin of the John Rylands Library 55(1973): 403-33.

Biographical essay, with far less on W than on Hare, cleric, co-author of Guesses at Truth (which he dedicated to W), and personal friend from 1824 until W's death in 1850.

205. Mellown, Muriel J. "Changing Patterns of Communication in Wordsworth's Lyrical Ballads and 1807 Poems." Yearbook of English Studies 3(1973): 161-69.

Argues that the Lyrical Ballads almost all depict failures in human communication, while the 1807 Poems treat communication more optimistically, so that the two collections mark a shift in W's interest from nature to society.

206. Minot, Walter S. "Wordsworth's Use of diurnal in 'A Slumber Did My Spirit Seal.'" Papers on Language and Literature 9(1973): 319-22.

Suggests puns on "urn" and, more tentatively, on "die."

207. Montgomery, Marion. The Reflective Journey Toward Order: Essays on Dante, Wordsworth, Eliot, and Others. Athens: University of Georgia, 1973. xv+312 pp. indexed.

W is the central figure in this collection of loosely related essays attempting to trace his lyricism and his concern with the self to that of Eliot and the twentieth-century novel, though Montgomery's style is diffuse and not critically incisive.

Reviews: R.W. Hill, SCR 9(1977), 61; JML 4(1974), 239; A.C. Labriola, GaR 27(1973), 445.

208. Moore, Maxine. "Melville's Pierre and Wordsworth: Intimations of Immorality." New Letters 39,iv(1973): 89-107.

An astounding exposition of parallels and verbal echoes revealing that Pierre is a "parody on the life and work of Wordsworth"--on his esteem for nature, duty, and resolution; on his style; and on his relationships with women, including Annette and Caroline. As Moore points out, this may help define "the extent and nature of the general rumor" regarding W's French connection at the time of his death.

209. Noyes, Russell. "Why Read The Excursion?" The Wordsworth Circle 4(1973): 139-51.

Gives as the chief reason the poem's embodiment of "W's doctrine of philosophical optimism." Not luminous criticism, but includes a ten-page paraphrase which may help those who still wish not to read the poem.

210. Ober, Warren U. "Nature, the Imagination, and the Conversion of Peter Bell." Yearbook of English Studies 3 (1973): 170-80.

Examines Peter Bell, the "most nearly perfect" embodiment of the theories of W's 1802 Preface, arguing that "revisionary critics" such as Hartman (143) and Ferry (131), who stress W's alienation from man and nature, have neglected this crucial poem precisely because it reaffirms W's belief in the sanative powers of nature and of the imagination.

211. Ogden, John T. "The Power of Distance in Wordsworth's Prelude." PMLA 88(1973): 246-259.

Compares W's sensitive use of spatial perspective to his use of temporal perspective, especially in orienting himself, distancing events, and "allowing room for... imagination." Uses the 1850 Prelude, examining the descriptions of London and of the fair at the foot of Helvellyn (books 7 and 8) in particular.

212. Owen, W.J.B. "The Sublime and the Beautiful in The Prelude." The Wordsworth Circle 4(1973): 67-86.

Sketches the similarities between Burke's Philosophical Inquiry and W's "The Sublime and the Beautiful," and, without asserting that W had read Burke, argues from the 1805 Prelude that W "habitually sees the environment in terms of" the Burkean categories, which W considers immutable psychic laws. See also 407 and 1060.

213. Parrish, Stephen Maxfield. The Art of the Lyrical Ballads. Cambridge: Harvard, 1973. xvii+250 pp. indexed.

A recasting of earlier essays emphasizing W's rhetorical purposes. In "The Poet's Art" Parrish argues that W placed great importance on meter, and did not believe that poetry was "the spontaneous overflow of powerful feeling." In "Partnership," he writes off "statements of accord" between W and C as publicity, and stresses the poets' personal, religious, and artistic differences to argue that the collaboration was more blighting than fruitful for both. Of two essays entitled "The Ballad as Drama," the first calls "The Thorn" to witness that, contrary to Mayo's influential argument (128), W's ballads are innovative, especially in their movement toward dramatic monologue; the second argues that Lyrical Ballads is "centered on the pastoral mode," and sees W as backed by a modern pastoral tradition, including Burns in particular, which aimed not at idealizing country life, but at portraying its "psychological truth."

Reviews: Richard H. Fogle, SHR 9(1975), 217; Stephen Gill, RES 26(1975), 221-25; James A.W. Heffernan, SIR 13 (1974), 255-67; Warren U. Ober, MLR 70(1975), 396-401; Stuart M. Sperry, Jr., JEGP 73(1974), 445; Jack Stillinger, WC 4(1973), 201-203; TLS, 1 March 1974, p. 206.

214. Partridge, Monica. "Romanticism and the Concept of Communication in a Slavonic and a Non-Slavonic Literature." Renaissance and Modern Studies 17(1973): 62-82.

Draws parallels between the first-generation English Romantics and the Russian Romantic poets, especially between W's Lyrical Ballads and Pushkin's Ruslan and Lyudmila (1820), both of which emphasize the common man and "the inadequacy of human communication."

215. Pollin, Burton R. "Permutations of Names in The Borderers, or Hints of Godwin, Charles Lloyd, and a Real Renegade." The Wordsworth Circle 4(1973): 31-35.

Conjectures on W's sources for names and reasons for changing them in early drafts of the play.

216. Pottle, Frederick A. "Wordsworth in the Present Day." *Romanticism: Vistas, Instances, Continuities* (231), pp. 115-33. First published in *Proceedings* of the American Philosophical Society 116(21 Dec. 1972): 443-49.

A sensitive essay of appreciation suggesting that the "respect" presently paid W is due to his "power of *earning* direct statement," his psychologizing, and his "ecological sentiment," among other things.

217. Riffaterre, Michael. "Interpretation and Descriptive Poetry: A Reading of Wordsworth's 'Yew-Trees.'" *New Literary History* 4(1973): 229-56.

A brilliant structuralist reading which attempts to show that even in descriptive poetry the words refer not to things but to other words. See also 317 and 629.

218. Roazen, Deborah H. "George Eliot and Wordsworth: 'The Natural History of German Life' and Peasant Psychology." *Research Studies* 41(1973): 166-78.

Finds Eliot's view of rural life similar to W's but closer, more detailed, and less idealized, chiefly citing *Adam Bede* and an 1856 essay by Eliot.

219. Roberts, Mark. *The Tradition of Romantic Morality*. London: Macmillan, 1973. xv+398 pp. indexed.

In Chapter 4, "Wordsworth and the Apotheosis of Rationalism," Roberts astonishingly remarks that W's influence on poetry has been negligible, and simplistically examines the Preface to *Lyrical Ballads* to argue that W's chief importance is as a conduit for eighteenth-century rationalist morality.

220. Rose, Stanley C. *The Boy Wordsworth*. Dubuque, IA: Kendall/Hunt, 1973. xiv+90 pp. not indexed.

A brief account of W's boyhood derived from the accounts in Moorman (78), earlier biographers, and *The Prelude*.

221. Ruoff, Gene W. "Religious Implications of Wordsworth's Imagination." Studies in Romanticism 12(1973): 670-92.

Argues that for W, imagination functions "within the world of phenomenal reality rather than serving as a means of transcending it," and has a fallible, circumscribed authority much as mysticism has in orthodox Christianity.

222. Ruoff, Gene W. "Wordsworth's 'Yew-Trees' and Romantic Perception." Modern Language Quarterly 34(1973): 146-60.

A fine discussion of the poem arguing that in juxtaposing the trees W contrasts but mediates between what Eliade calls sacred and profane vision.

223. Schier, R.D. "Experience of the Noumenal in Goethe and Wordsworth." Comparative Literature 25(1973): 37-59.

Compares the first monologue in Faust II with the crossing-of-the-Alps passage in the 1850 Prelude, book 6, to argue that, while mutual influence and even sympathy is out of the question, the poets' works show a "profound identity of imagery, thought, vision, and subject."

224. Sewall, Bronwen D. "The Similarity Between Rousseau's Emile and the Early Poetry of Wordsworth." Studies in Voltaire and the Eighteenth Century 106(1973): 157-74.

A rudimentary sketch of the similarities between the writers' treatments of childhood and maturation, nature, and religion.

225. Shattuck, Roger. "This Must Be the Place: Wordsworth to Proust." Romanticism: Vistas, Instances, Continuities (231), pp. 177-97.

Contrasts the sense of place in W and Proust, but has nothing new to offer on W; along the way we are told that Milton echoes "his contemporaries, including Voltaire and Rousseau, Hume, and Kant."

226. Sheats, Paul. The Making of Wordsworth's Poetry, 1785-1798. Cambridge, MA: Harvard, 1973. xvii+301 pp. indexed.

One of the most judicious studies of the early works, being especially good in discussions of the juvenilia. Traces the development of W's art and emphasizes the poet's concern with political issues posed by the French Revolution.

Reviews: Daniel P. Deneau, SHR 10(1976), 182; Stephen Gill, RES 26(1975), 221-25; George H. Gilpin, MP 73 (1976), 313-16; K. Grose, English 23(1974), 75; James A.W. Heffernan, SIR 13(1974), 255-67; Bishop C. Hunt, RM, 1974, pp. 63-64; Warren U. Ober, MLR 70(1975), 396-401; David Perkins, WC 4(1973), 197-200; Stuart M. Sperry, Jr., JEGP 73(1974), 445; TLS, 1 March 1974, p. 206.

227. Sherbo, Arthur. "A Note on The Prelude." The Wordsworth Circle 4(1973): 11-12.

Notes an echo of Shakespeare's Sonnet 66 in the 1850 Prelude, 3:594-611.

228. Strand, Mark. "Landscape and the Poetry of Self." Prose 6(1973): 169-83.

Contrasts The Prelude with "confessional" poetry by Berryman and Lowell, and relates W's greater generality to the demands of landscape art.

229. Teich, Nathaniel. "On the Manuscript Source for the Publication of the Fenwick Notes." The Wordsworth Circle 4(1973): 110-11.

Demonstrates that Knight's 1896 Poetical Works did not use the (now missing) original copy of the Fenwick notes, and so has no independent authority regarding them.

230. Thorburn, David. "Conrad's Romanticism: Self-Consciousness and Community." Romanticism: Vistas, Instances, Continuities (231), pp. 221-54.

A good sketch of Conrad's affinities with Romanticism, and with W in particular, noting similarities in their beliefs, characters, and artistic form, and pointing out the influence of W's Preface to the _Lyrical Ballads_ on Conrad's famous Preface to "The Nigger of the _Narcissus_."

231. Thorburn, David, and Geoffrey Hartman, eds. _Romanticism: Vistas, Instances, Continuities_. Ithaca, NY: Cornell, 1973. 284 pp. indexed.

Includes 216, 225, and 230.
Review: Stuart A. Ende, _WC_ 5(1974), 141-44.

232. Timko, Michael. "Wordsworth's 'Ode' and Arnold's 'Dover Beach': Celestial Light and Confused Alarms." _Cithara_ 13,i(1973): 53-63.

Sees "Dover Beach" as a "direct answer" to the Ode's "illusion and self-deception," opposing Arnold's "assertion of man's human-ness" to W's emphasis on man's relation to nature.

233. Wilkie, Brian. "Wordsworth and the Tradition of the Avant-Garde." _Journal of English and Germanic Philology_ 72(1973): 194-222.

Argues that the "packaging" of the _Lyrical Ballads_ was original if the substance was not (cf. 128), and sees W's theoretical statements in the 1800 and 1815 Prefaces and in the "Essay, Supplementary" (1815) as harbingers of modern avant-gardism, as defined by Renato Poggioli's _The Theory of the Avant-Garde_ (1961).

234. Williams, Raymond. _The Country and the City_. New York: Oxford, 1973. 335 pp. indexed. pbk.

An important study of literary representations of the country and the city, stressing their social significance and consisely describing the historical importance of W's practice (pp. 128-33, 149-52).

235. Wlecke, Albert O. _Wordsworth and the Sublime_. Berkeley: University of California, 1973. xii+163 pp. indexed.

Grounding his thesis in close examination of "Tintern Abbey" and C's "random speculations" on the sublime, Wlecke lucidly argues that W's sublime or visionary experiences, especially those which make "the humble seem sublime," are unwitting moments of self-consciousness, the "something far more deeply interfused" of which W has a "sense sublime" being the action of his own mind. See also 257.

Reviews: Richard H. Fogle, _SHR_ 9(1975), 228; Bishop C. Hunt, _RM_, 1974, pp. 69-70; John Ogden, _WC_ 4(1973), 204-205; Gilbert Thomas, _English_ 23(1974), 36.

236. Wordsworth, Jonathan, and Stephen Gill. "The Two-Part _Prelude_ of 1798-99." _Journal of English and Germanic Philology_ 72(1973): 503-25.

Describes the manuscripts and (so far as possible) the process of composition, noting the early version's distinctness from the 1805 _Prelude_--it was expanded, not simply continued. Somewhat uneasily suggests its status as a completed "poem," and relates its expansion to work on "The Pedlar" and the recusancy of _The Recluse_.

1974

237. Baum, Joan. "The Relevance of Wordsworth." CEA Critic 37,i(1974): 18-20.

Finds W relevant indeed for his "love of nature, faith in Man, and political sympathy," but without acknowledging that all of these have been called in question (e.g., by Ferry, 131).

238. Beauchamp, Gorman. "Wordsworth's Archetypal Resolution." Concerning Poetry 7,i(1974): 13-19.

Regarding the conclusion to "Resolution and Independence" as a "particularly false little homily," Beauchamp explains it by arguing that the poem describes an archetypal encounter which W himself did not comprehend.

239. Birdsall, Eric R. "Wordsworth's Revisions to Descriptive Sketches: The Wellesley Copy." The Wordsworth Circle 5 (1974): 9-14.

Lists the revisions made in Wellesley's copy of the 1793 edition, and deduces that they were entered in 1814 for the 1815 edition, and later for the 1820 edition of W's poems. See also Birdsall's edition (6).

240. Brantley, Richard E. "Spiritual Maturity and Wordsworth's 1783 Christmas Vacation." Studies in English Literature, 1500-1900 14(1974): 479-87.

Argues that the passage in the 1805 Prelude, book 11, on the death of W's father describes the chastisement of pride, and shows the influence of Wesley and Evangelicalism. See also Brantley's book (304), in which this is partially reprinted.

241. Braun, Theodore E.D. "Diderot, Wordsworth, and the Creative Process." Comparative Literature Studies 11 (1974): 151-58.

Compares Diderot's explanation of the creative process in Paradoxe sur le Comedien (pub. 1830) with W's in the 1800 and 1815 Prefaces, focusing in particular on W's paradoxical "spontaneous overflow of powerful feelings" passage. Suggests a common source, but finds it more likely the ideas were "in the air."

242. Brier, Peter A. "Reflections on Tintern Abbey." The Wordsworth Circle 5(1974): 5-6.

Reproduces the Gurney painting of the Abbey (ca. 1803) to show how overgrown it was and suggests that the Abbey figures in W's poem as a symbol of natural religion.

243. D'Avanzo, Mario L. "'Ode on a Grecian Urn' and The Excursion." Keats-Shelley Journal 23(1974): 95-105.

Argues that Excursion 4, 724-860, is a major influence on Keats's ode, and contrasts W's "discursive, reflective, sublime" style with that of Keats's "retailoring."

244. Dings, John. "Bostetter on Wordsworth." Paunch 38(1974): 32-39.

Finds a praiseworthy "tension" between historical explanation and ethical judgment in Bostetter's treatment of W (139), and offers an alternative to his reading of "The Old Cumberland Beggar," arriving at a more lenient judgment of the speaker's plea by considering contemporary attitudes to beggary.

245. Doggett, Frank. "Romanticism's Singing Bird." Studies in English Literature, 1500-1900 14(1974): 547-61.

Briefly sketches the origins of bird imagery, and examines it from the Romantic poets to Hardy. Much more on the other poets than on W, whose "birds are natural creatures, and illustrate ideas rather than symbolize them."

246. Franson, J. Karl. "The Irresponsibility of Wordsworth's Michael." Literary Criterion 11,ii(1974): 29-31.

Criticizes Michael for selfishness in his decision to send Luke away.

247. French, A.L. "The 'Fair Seed-Time' in Wordsworth's Prelude." Critical Review 17(1974): 3-20.

Declares that the 1850 Prelude lacks unity and "dissolves" toward the end, and comments impressionistically on its "visionary passages."

248. Gates, Barbara T. "Wordsworth's Use of Oral History." Folklore 85(1974): 254-67.

Discusses oral history both as a source and as a topic of W's poetry, touching on "Hart-Leap Well" and The Excursion, and contrasting the use of oral and written history in "The Brothers" and "Artegal and Elidure."

249. Goslee, Nancy M. "Under a Cloud in Prospect: Keats, Milton, and Stationing." Philological Quarterly 53 (1974): 205-19.

Suggests that Keats's interest in Milton's "stationing" the objects of his descriptions derives in part from W's similar practice in the Guide to the Lakes and The Excursion (pp. 209-12).

250. Gravil, Richard. "Wordsworth's Ontology of Love in The Prelude." Critical Quarterly 16(1974): 231-49.

Compares W's concept of love with other thinkers', especially Spinoza's "amor intellectis Dei," and argues that it is dialectically integral to imagination in The Prelude (1805).

251. Griska, Joseph M., Jr. "Wordsworth's Mood Disturbance: A Psychoanalytic Approach to Three Poems." Literature and Psychology 24(1974): 144-52.

Considers W's tribulations and disappointments, his physical aches and pains, and the importance of his depression in the Ode, "Resolution and Independence," and "Elegiac Stanzas," to argue that W suffered from "neurotic depression."

252. Hassler, Donald M. "Belief and Death in Wordsworth's *Peter Bell*." *Bulletin of the New York Public Library* 77(1974):251-57.

Argues that the narrator's repudiation of poetic flights and his use of strictly associationist terms to explain Peter's conversion result in an unbearably stark conclusion, a "world of death" and sorrow. But W, Hassler cryptically concludes, "is using death to look beyond death."

253. Hayden, John O. "Substantive Errors in the Standard Edition of Wordsworth's Poetry." *The Library* 29(1974): 454-59.

Corrects errors in the five-volume de Selincourt-Darbishire edition (1), and notes that the errors in accidentals are too numerous to be listed.

254. Hayter, Alethea. "Victorian Brothers and Sisters." *Times Literary Supplement*, 9 Aug. 1974, p. 859.

The first round in a mild and inconclusive dispute about whether W and Dorothy were affectionate simply, inordinately, or incestuously, the latter position being taken only by Lefebure, whose remarks in *Samuel Taylor Coleridge: A Bondage of Opium* (New York: Stein and Day, 1974) provoked the exchange. See also William Hayter, *TLS*, 23 Aug., p. 906; Donald H. Reiman, *TLS*, 13 Sept., pp. 979-80; Roger Fulford, *TLS*, 4 Oct., pp. 1078-79; Mary Moorman, *TLS*, 4 Oct., p. 1079; Donald H. Reiman, *TLS*, 1 Nov., p. 1231; Molly Lefebure, *TLS*, 8 Nov., p. 1261; Mary Moorman, *TLS*, 15 Nov., p. 1288; John Wardroper, *TLS*, 15 Nov., p. 1288; Roger Fulford, *TLS*, 15 Nov., p. 1288; Alethea Hayter, *TLS*, 22 Nov., p. 1317.

255. Hill, Alan G. "New Light on *The Excursion*." *Ariel* 5,ii (1974): 37-47.

Argues that W designed The Excursion on the model of the Octavius, a Christian dialogue by Mincius Felix dating from the second or third century, which may also be a source for the "far more deeply interfused" passage in "Tintern Abbey."

256. Hill, James L. "The Frame for the Mind: Landscape in 'Lines Composed a Few Miles Above Tintern Abbey,' 'Dover Beach,' and 'Sunday Morning.'" Centennial Review 18(1974): 29-48.

Analyzes the art of landscape in the three poems, noting the meeting of mind and nature in "Tintern Abbey" and tracing in Arnold and Stevens "the declining power of the word or poem to mediate between mind and thing."

257. Holland, Patrick. "Wordsworth and the Sublime: Some Further Considerations." The Wordsworth Circle 5 (1974): 17-22.

Turning to W's own essay on "The Sublime and the Beautiful" (see 30, vol. 2), Holland takes issue with Wlecke's suggestion (235) that the poet considered the concepts "a useful fiction," arguing that W took the sublime seriously. Attacks Wlecke's reading of "Tintern Abbey," his skirting of the sublime of fear (crucial, Holland argues, to the young W of The Prelude), and his thesis that W repeatedly tries and fails "to marry his mind to nature." See also 212.

258. Holloway, John. "Poetic Analysis and the Idea of the Transformation-Rule: Some Examples from Herbert, Wordsworth, Pope, and Shakespeare." In Miscellanea Anglo-Americana: Festschrift für Helmut Viebrock, ed. Kuno Schuhmann et al. Munich: Pressler, 1974, pp. 279-97.

Correlates inverted word order with expressions of "marked emotion or intellectuality" in "Anecdote for Fathers" (pp. 285-88) to show the usefulness of the transformation-rule as a concept for literary analysis.

259. Jacobus, Mary. "Peter Bell the First." Essays in Criticism 24(1974): 219-42.

An excellent reading stressing the poem's response to C's "Ancient Mariner" and its use of the Methodist conversion narrative, and arguing that, in demonstrating the powers of nature and imagination rather than of supernaturalism, the poem "is one of Wordsworth's more persuasive acts of literary self-definition."

260. Jaye, Michael C. "Wordsworth at Work: MS. RV, Book II of The Prelude." Papers of the Bibliographical Society of America 68(1974): 251-65.

Examines MS. RV (Dove Cottage MS. 21), the earliest extant manuscript of book 2, to generalize about W's habits of composition. Though unwilling to declare what W's intention was, Jaye sees the two-book version as complete and unified.

261. Jones, Howard Mumford. Revolution and Romanticism. Cambridge, MA: Harvard, Belknap Press, 1974. viii+487 pp.

Takes a quick look at the 1850 Prelude which is perhaps most helpful for a few offhand comments, such as the suggestion that W's youthful radicalism never was in character, or the observation that "seldom or never in this huge autobiography does W record any speech or conversation of his own."

262. Kaufman, Paul. "John Peace to William Wordsworth: Four Unpublished Letters." English Language Notes 11(1974): 193-99.

Prints four long and warm letters to W from the Bristol librarian dating from 1839 and 1845, affording a glimpse of W in old age and shedding light on the men's long-standing friendship.

263. King, E.H. "James Beattie's Literary Essay: 1776, 1783." Aberdeen University Review 45(1974): 389-401.

Sketches the "remarkable similarities in attitude, ideas and aims" between Beattie and W (pp. 398-400).

264. Kirkham, Michael. "Innocence and Experience in Wordsworth's 'The Thorn.'" Ariel 5,i(1974): 66-80.

Dwells on emblems in the poem's landscape and interprets the characters' names allegorically to argue that "The Thorn" dramatizes W's relationship to his "lost innocence" and to his source of poetic power.

265. Kroeber, Karl. "'Home at Grasmere': Ecological Holiness." PMLA 89(1974): 132-41. Revised in Romantic Landscape Vision (329), pp. 116-31.

Suggests that "Home at Grasmere" "is The Recluse," and stresses the importance of the vale as a particular and unified place, W's relation to which anticipates modern appreciation of the "ecosystem."

266. McConnell, Frank D. The Confessional Imagination: A Reading of Wordsworth's Prelude. Baltimore, MD: Johns Hopkins, 1974. ix+212 pp.

Reads the poem as a confession in the Augustinian tradition, of which C is not only the addressee but the "intended convert." Includes sensitive readings of several passages.

Reviews: C. Bond, QQ 84(1977), 139-41; Frances Ferguson, SIR 15(1976), 147-50; Richard Gravil, YES 7(1977), 274-75; Bishop C. Hunt, RM, 1974, pp. 61-62; Richard J. Onorato, WC 7(1976), 179-80; Jonathan Wordsworth, TLS, 14 Nov. 1975, p. 1352.

267. Macmillan, Malcolm Kingsley. "Dialogue Between Blake and Wordsworth Written in Rome Before 17 April 1889 and Left Unfinished by Malcolm Kingsley Macmillan." Blake Newsletter 8(1974), 38-41.

Blake berates W for his emphasis on Nature. Chiefly of antiquarian interest, this dialogue appears not to be a hoax (Macmillan really existed, and left a novel and a collection of letters behind him), but we are told nothing of its origin.

268. Madden, Richard. "The Old Familiar Faces: An Essay in the Light of Some Recently Discovered Documents of

Charles Valentine LeGrice Referring to Lamb, Coleridge and Wordsworth." _Charles Lamb Bulletin_ 6(1974): 113-21.

Reprints poems to W and marginalia to _The Prelude_ written by Le Grice, an old friend of C's, who visited W in 1841 (pp. 118-20).

269. Manley, Seon. _Dorothy and William Wordsworth: The Heart of a Circle of Friends._ New York: Vanguard, 1974. ix+241 pp.

A children's biography.

270. Marchant, Robert. _Principles of Wordsworth's Poetry._ Swansea, Wales: Brynmill Pub. Co., 1974. 112 pp. not indexed.

Marchant's prose is not much fun, especially in his polemical introduction. But his argument that the poems are important for their vital language, rather than for their truth to nature or their philosophy, yields perceptive readings of several lyrics and longer poems, and an interesting discussion (pp. 23-30) of W's interpretive or moralizing endings.

271. Mellown, Muriel J. "The Development of Imagery in 'Home at Grasmere.'" _The Wordsworth Circle_ 5(1974): 23-27.

Arguing for the poem's unity, Mellown finds that its imagery illustrates the themes of relationship, voyage, and paradise, which are figuratively expressed in the culminating passage which was published separately as the Prospectus to _The Recluse_.

272. Minot, W.S., John I. Ades, and Gordon K. Thomas. "Notes on Wordsworthian Puns." _The Wordsworth Circle_ 5(1974): 28-32.

Three responses to Caviglia (182): Ades is dismissive, while Minot and Thomas hold that W punned frequently--the former giving examples, the latter proffering a serious reading of "Composed upon Westminster Bridge" based on a pun on "composed."

273. Mitchell, Jerome. "Wordsworth's Tail-Rhyme 'Lucy' Poem." _Studies in Medieval Culture_ 4(1974): 561-68.

Compares "Three years she grew in sun and shower" with medieval tail-rhyme poems, praising W for using the stanza "unwittingly in the way it was originally intended": for lyric, not narrative.

274. Nabholtz, John R. "The Integrity of Wordsworth's 'Tintern Abbey.'" _Journal of English and Germanic Philology_ 73(1974): 227-38.

Discusses the poem in terms of "odic transitions," arguing that the expressions of doubt clarify the speaker's progress toward affirmation rather than undermining the poem's message, and that the poem achieves a true climax rather than anticlimax in the final address to Dorothy.

275. New, Melvyn. "Wordsworth's Shell of Poetry." _Philological Quarterly_ 53(1974): 275-81.

Argues that the shell borne by the Arab in _The Prelude_, book 5, is not a seashell but a tortoise-shell, from which Hermes first fashioned the lyre.

276. Newey, Vincent. "Wordsworth, Bunyan and the Puritan Mind." _ELH_ 41(1974): 212-32.

While noting W's indifference to Puritanism, Newey helpfully assimilates to Puritan modes of thought W's proclivities to solitude, self-reliance, spiritual autobiography, and especially his interest in commonplace events or people, invested "restrospectively with...predestinarian flavor." Compares _The Prelude_ and _The Pilgrim's Progress_, comments perceptively on "Resolution and Independence," and compares W and Cowper. See also 304.

277. Newmeyer, Edna. "The Language of a 'Butchers Stall': Wordsworth on Milton's Description of Abel's Sacrifice." _Milton Quarterly_ 8(1974): 69-72.

Quotes W's anomalous criticism of Milton's "'inelegant' diction" from W's edition of *Paradise Lost*, and defends Milton.

278. Nuttall, A.D. *A Common Sky: Philosophy and the Literary Imagination.* Berkeley: University of California Press, 1974. 298 pp. indexed.

A fascinating history of "solipsistic fear" in philosophy and literature (chiefly English), with an important discussion of W (pp. 113-46). Nuttall finds W's ballads "a mistake," and uses "The Old Cumberland Beggar" and *Prelude* passages to argue that W's best poetry is unique for its "poetic of percept rather than of literary construct" (in C's terms, of primary rather than secondary imagination; in Auerbach's terms, it is, like Dante's, figural poetry). W's fear of solipsism results in "nostalgia for the object," a longing "to *be* a pure object"--in short, a death-wish which Nuttall sees as typically Romantic.

Reviews: Peter A. Brier, *WC* 5(1974), 211-12; R.L. Lewis, *JAAC* 36(1977), 373-74; David Wykes, *N&Q* 23(1976), 473-74.

279. Olivier, T. "'The Lyrical Ballads' and the 'Preface.'" *Theoria* 43(1974): 63-72.

An uninformed and overly general essay discussing the relation of Preface and poems as their common "concern with what really matters to men."

280. Pearsall, Robert B. "Wordsworth, Housman, and the Metaphor of Hand upon Heart." *American Notes & Queries* 12 (1974): 155.

Traces a line in Housman to W's "'Tis said that some have died for love."

281. Price, John. "Wordsworth's *Lucy*." *American Imago* 31 (1974): 360-77.

A psychoanalytic argument that the speaker of "Strange fits of passion have I known" wishes for Lucy's death. Thus Price assimilates the poem to Bateson's view (126) of the other "Lucy Poems" as W's killing off the object of his incestuous passion.

282. Priestman, Donald G. "The Borderers: Wordsworth's Addenda to Godwin." University of Toronto Quarterly 44 (1974): 56-65.

Argues that the play substitutes love of nature for Godwinian reason as the "handmaiden of benevolence" on the grounds that man's imperfect knowledge of circumstances renders reason fallible.

283. Pulos, C.E. "The Unity of Wordsworth's Immortality Ode." Studies in Romanticism 13(1974): 179-88.

Finds unity by distinguishing between "light," which remains, and the "visionary gleam," a mere manifestation of the light, which is lost; and thereby finds the poem a successful struggle with Romantic melancholy. But the distinctions and identifications made between various terms for light in the poem seem too willful to be convincing.

284. Rader, Melvin. "The Imaginative Mode of Awareness." Journal of Aesthetics and Art Criticism 33(1974), 131-37.

Uses Prelude passages briefly to illustrate Wittgenstein's description of aesthetic vision as "seeing as."

285. Robinson, Jeffrey. "The Prelude, Book XIV, and the Problem of Concluding." Criticism 16(1974): 301-10.

Discusses W's uncertainties about the purpose and success of The Prelude in book 14, and the roles of Dorothy and C in helping the poet overcome his doubts.

286. Robinson, Jeffrey. "Unpublished Letter of William Wordsworth to Henry Robinson of York." The Wordsworth Circle 5(1974): 15-16.

Prints a business letter dated 19 May 1829 (now in collected letters).

287. Schulz, Max F. "The Perseverance of Romanticism: From Organism to Artifact." Clio 3(1974): 165-86.

Uses W and C to define ideals of Romantic art--especially organicism and "the analogy of art to nature"--which modern artists have so modified that they are hardly recognizable as the same ideals.

288. Smyser, Jane Worthington. "The Trial and Imprisonment of Joseph Johnson, Bookseller." Bulletin of the New York Public Library 77(1974): 418-35.

Though it contains almost nothing on W, this well researched account corrects many errors about the trial and prison term of W's first publisher for publishing Wakefield's Reply to the Bishop of Llandaff's Address to the People of Great Britain, and may shed a reflected light on W's own Reply. Refers to W on pp. 418, 434-35.

289. Spiegelman, Willard. "Wordsworth's Aeneid." Comparative Literature 26(1974): 97-109.

Carefully compares W's translation of The Aeneid, books 1-3, with Dryden's and Pitt's, finding W's truer in certain respects, but deficient in its treatment of sensuality, especially in connection with Dido.

290. Spivak, Gayatri Chakravorty. "Decadent Style." Language and Style 7(1974): 227-34.

Considers the shift in verb tense in the opening of The Prelude (1850) in an attempt to redefine decadent style as that which is "self-conscious of the ruptures and discontinuities of literary language."

291. Squires, Michael. The Pastoral Novel: Studies in George Eliot, Thomas Hardy, and D.H. Lawrence. Charlottesville: University Press of Virginia, 1974. vii+228 pp. indexed.

Includes a brief discussion of W's influence on pastoral (pp. 41-51), considering "Michael" and the 1805 Prelude, book 8, to show his movement toward greater realism and the georgic.

292. Stone, Charles F., III. "Narrative Variation in Wordsworth's Versions of 'The Discharged Soldier.'" Journal of Narrative Technique 4(1974): 32-44.

Examines W's special adaptation of narrative for the purposes of autobiography by comparing pre-Prelude and various Prelude versions of the discharged-soldier passage.

293. Stuart, Alice V. "Scott and Wordsworth: A Comparison." Contemporary Review 224(1974): 251-54.

A not very incisive comparison of W's "Fidelity" with Scott's "Helvellyn" (which is based on the same incident). Cf. Priestman's discussion (411, pp. 684-5).

294. Sucksmith, Harvey P. "Orchestra and the Golden Flower: A Critical Interpretation of the Two Versions of Wordsworth's 'I Wandered Lonely as a Cloud.'" Yearbook of English Studies 4(1974): 149-58.

Views the poem as a vindication of W's critical statements in the 1802 and 1815 Prefaces, the revisions being "in accord with W's concept of the imagination."

295. Swearingen, James E. "Wordsworth on Gray." Studies in English Literature, 1500-1900 14(1974): 489-509.

Argues that the poets' views are comparable on many points but differ profoundly on the relation of man to nature, and that this difference lies behind W's criticism of Gray's sonnet in the 1800 Preface. See also 906.

296. Tucker, E.H. "Wordsworth: Poet and Revolutionary." Unisa English Studies 12,i(1974): 19-21.

A simplistic and cliched account of W's decline, with a number of factual errors.

297. Ward, J.P. "Wordsworth and the Sociological Idea." Critical Quarterly 16(1974): 331-55.

Examines topics such as the poet's stress on relationship in "The Old Cumberland Beggar," his use of the family as a "constraining culture" in the Ode, his treatment of the solitary as a "marginal man," and his attitude toward the city to argue that W anticipates developments in nineteenth and early twentieth century sociology, though attributing this chiefly to the climate of ideas; W repeatedly "stumbles upon (though he cannot realize it) the sociological idea."

298. Wilson, James D. "Tennyson's Emendations to Wordsworth's 'Tintern Abbey.'" _The Wordsworth Circle_ 5(1974): 7-8.

Describes the emendations in an 1849 copy belonging to Tennyson, who found the poem a bit repetitive and wordy.

1975

299. Anonymous. "Notes and News." Bulletin of the John Rylands Library 57(1975): 247-58.

Page 251 notes the existence of the manuscript of a W letter (28 Nov. 1808) which de Selincourt and Moorman (37) date 26 Nov. 1808 and list as "untraced."

300. Abrams, M[eyer] H., ed. English Romantic Poets: Modern Essays in Criticism. 2nd Ed. New York: Oxford, 1975. viii+485 pp. not indexed. pbk.

Besides essays of more general interest, reprints several specifically on W: four listed elsewhere, by Willey (108), Trilling (118), Hartman (316), and Sheats ("The 'Lyrical Ballads,'" from his book, 226), as well as a 1969 essay by Jonathan Wordsworth on "Wordsworth's 'Borderers'"--discussing, not W's play, but his interest in "border-figures" (cf. 929).

301. Bassett, Sharon. "Wordsworth, Pater and the 'Anima Mundi': Towards a Critique of Romanticism." Criticism 17 (1975): 262-75.

Explains Pater's enthusiasm for W's vision of nature (96) by sketching its affinities with Pater's aestheticism. Dwelling on W's receptivity, his maternal metaphors for the creative self, and Dorothy's role as "double," Basset praises Pater's "rare accuracy" in using the feminine anima mundi to describe the poet's "central myth of coherence." See also 308.

302. Beyette, Kent. "A Source for the Folklore of the Ass in Wordsworth's Peter Bell." Notes & Queries 22(1975): 405-406.

Suggests John Brand's Observations on Popular Antiquities (1813) as the source for the cross on the ass's shoulders, and comments on the mark's appropriateness for Peter's conversion.

303. Bober, Natalie. William Wordsworth: The Wandering Poet. Nashville and New York: Thomas Nelson, 1975. 191 pp. indexed.

An informal biography to 1802, with nine pages on the rest of W's life.

304. Brantley, Richard E. Wordsworth's 'Natural Methodism.' New Haven, CT: Yale, 1975. xvi+205 pp. indexed.

Argues--not always convincingly--that W is primarily a religious poet whose "practice can best be understood in terms of his pervasive Evangelical idiom." After stressing the influence of Wesley and the Evangelical movement in the Lake District of W's childhood and at Cambridge, Brantley reads The Prelude (chiefly in the 1805 version) as "spiritual autobiography" in the Methodist tradition, and argues that W's view of Nature, even in poems as early as "The Brothers," is informed by Christian typology. See also 259, 276.

Reviews: Michael Baron, English 25(1976), 48-51; C. Bond, QQ 84(1977), 139-41; Wolfgang Franke, Anglia 98 (1980), 252-56; Alan Grob, WC 7(1976), 173-78; Bishop C. Hunt, RM, 1975, p. 55; M. Isnard, EA 31(1978), 392; Vincent Newey, MLR 72(1977), 916-18; W.J.B. Owen, RES 28 (1977), 355-58; Mark L. Reed, MP 75(1977), 97-101; Gene Ruoff, WHR 29(1975), 379-81; Robert Lance Snyder, Criticism 19(1977), 370-72.

305. Butler, James A. "Two New Wordsworth Letters." Notes & Queries 22(1975): 61-63.

Prints two thank-you notes for presentation copies, one to M.P. Kavanagh, 8 July 1839, and one to an unknown addressee, 21 Feb. 1848, the latter for a copy of Bryant's poems. Remarks on Bryant and W.

306. Butler, James A. "Wordsworth's Funeral: A Contemporary Report." English Language Notes 13(1975): 27-29.

Reprints and comments on a letter by Mary Howitt, a popular poet and an acquaintance of W's. Not very enlightening.

307. Butler, James A. "Wordsworth's _Tuft of Primroses_: 'An Unrelenting Doom.'" _Studies in Romanticism_ 14(1975): 237-48.

Argues that the decay of Grasmere recorded in "The Tuft of Primroses" represents the loss of the symbol of "the poet's mental repose," and, since this repose was needed for the philosophic voice of _The Recluse_, helps to explain the poem's incompletion. See also 191.

308. Cahill, Patricia. "Women and Children in _The Prelude_." _Massachussetts Studies in English_ 5,iii(1975-78): 39-47.

Argues that W's explicit treatment of women is sexist, but that far more sensitive is his use of the "anima" and of the child to portray feminine aspects of himself, his imagination, and his relation to nature. See also 301.

309. Cohen, Ralph. "Literary Theory as a Genre." _Centrum_ 3,i(1975): 45-64.

Argues that literary theory is a literary genre, contrasting W's theory of aesthetic pleasure along the way (pp. 49-53) with those of Aristotle and Hume to show the theory's historicity.

310. de Montluzin, Emily Lorraine. "The 'Dedication Scene' in _The Prelude_ and the _Book of Common Prayer_." _Notes & Queries_ 22(1975): 59-60.

Compares the 1850 _Prelude_ 4:334-38 with the "Ministration of Holy Baptism, the Catechism, and the Order of Confirmation" as probable sources.

311. Finch, Geoffrey J. "Wordsworth's Solitary Song: The Substance of 'true art' in 'The Solitary Reaper.'" _Ariel_ 6,iii(1975): 91-100.

A sensitive reading of the poem focusing on W's use of paradoxes to describe true aesthetic experience.

312. Gates, Barbara T. "Wordsworth's Symbolic White Doe: 'The Power of History in the Mind.'" Criticism 17(1975): 234-45.

Argues that the doe is a symbol of the family's history, not just of Emily's, reflecting the degree of power various characters have to draw strength from the past.

313. Harson, Robert R. "Wordsworth's Narrator in 'The Childless Father.'" American Notes & Queries 13(1975): 138-40.

Argues that the narrator is the subject of the poem.

314. Hartman, Geoffrey H. "Evening Star and Evening Land." The Fate of Reading (315), pp. 147-78.

Pages 154-63 deal with W's star imagery, especially in the "Lucy Poems," arguing that his removal of the star from heaven to earth, culminating in his entire transcendence of the conventional star-symbol in "A slumber did my spirit seal," is a surer index of W's originality than his attacks on diction, etc. Previously published in New Perspectives on Coleridge and Wordsworth, ed. Geoffrey Hartman (New York: Columbia, 1972).

315. Hartman, Geoffrey H. The Fate of Reading, and Other Essays. Chicago: University of Chicago, 1975. xvi+352 pp. indexed.

Includes two essays listed separately, 314 and 318.

316. Hartman, Geoffrey H. "Nature and the Humanization of the Self in Wordsworth." English Romantic Poets: Modern Essays in Criticism (300), pp. 123-32.

An excellent brief introductory essay (revising the introduction to 25) with perceptive comments on the Wordsworthian topoi of nature, memory, imagination, and man's humanization.

317. Hartman, Geoffrey H. "The Use and Abuse of Structural Analysis: Riffaterre's Interpretation of Wordsworth's 'Yew-Trees.'" New Literary History 7(1975): 165-89.

Though praising Riffaterre's essay (217) highly, Hartman objects that its structuralist method misrepresents the poem by ignoring its "elision of the human intermediary or observer." Hartman focuses on problems of speaker and "voice" to argue that the poem's theme is fear for the future.

318. Hartman, Geoffrey H. "Wordsworth and Goethe in Literary History." New Literary History 7(1975): 393-413. Rpt. in The Fate of Reading and Other Essays. Chicago: University of Chicago, 1975, 179-200.

Contrasts W's "The Danish Boy" with Goethe's "Der Erlkönig" in order to contrast the effect of the historicist "Northern Enchantment," i.e., the growing interest in ancient Nordic culture, on W (as a poet in a continuous ballad tradition) with its effect on Goethe (as one unencumbered with a continuous tradition).

319. Harvey, Geoffrey M. "The Design of Wordsworth's Sonnets." Ariel 6,iii(1975): 78-90.

Examines W's "Composed Upon Westminster Bridge," "I watch and long have watched with calm regret," and "The world is too much with us," arguing that in each W's skillful use of irony integrates sympathetic perception with intellectual detachment.

320. Herman, Judith B. "The Roman Matron with the Bird-cage: A Note on 'The Sailor's Mother.'" The Wordsworth Circle 6(1975): 302.

Locates a likely source in Plutarch, where a matron and a bird-cage appear together.

321. Hill, Alan G. "Wordsworth, Comenius, and the Meaning of Education." Review of English Studies 26(1975): 301-312.

Discusses W's lifelong ideals of liberal education, tracing them to seventeenth-century thinkers, especially Comenius, whose Orbis Pictus W owned.

322. Holkeboer, Robert, and Nadean Bishop. "Wordsworth on Words." The Wordsworth Circle 6(1975): 307-13.

Helpfully bringing together several of W's statements on language (excluding the prose of Lyrical Ballads), stresses W's concern with expressing the ineffable, and views some of his revisions as motivated by something like the modern distrust of signifiers.

323. Hunt, Bishop C., Jr. "Wordsworth, Haydon, and the 'Wellington' Sonnet." Princeton University Library Chronicle 36(1975): 111-32.

Texts of and commentary on eight letters (now at Princeton) from W to Haydon, 1839-40, including the first manuscript version of "On a Portrait of the Duke of Wellington upon the Field of Waterloo, by Haydon" and several revisions. An excellent demonstration of W's practice, at least in late life, in revision.

324. Jackson, Wallace. "Wordsworth and His Predecessors: Private Sensations and Public Tones." Criticism 17 (1975): 41-58. Rpt. in The Probable and the Marvellous (551), pp. 123-44.

Examines W's use of humble, everyday topics and objects to evoke emotional response, and contrasts the quality and value of his emotion with that in earlier eighteenth-century verse.

325. Jaye, Michael C. "The Prelude, The Excursion, and The Recluse: An Unpublished Prelude Variant." Philological Quarterly 54(1975): 484-93.

Publishes and discusses two unused drafts for a revision of the 1805 Prelude 1:228-38, probably dating from 1813, and pertaining to W's struggles with The Recluse.

326. Johnston, Kenneth R. "'Home at Grasmere': Reclusive Song." Studies in Romanticism 14(1975): 1-28.

A brilliant essay in two parts: superb analysis of tautology, circular structure, and circular imagery, showing how the poem centers in the ineffable and unanswerable and stressing intrinsic factors for its incompletion; and an intriguing contrast between the would-be Recluse and The Prelude. See Johnston's book (1020).

327. Jones, Stanley. "B.R. Haydon on Some Contemporaries: A New Letter." Review of English Studies 26(1975): 183-89.

Sketches Haydon's relations with W, and prints a long, bitter letter written in 1824 on W's failure to lend him money.

328. King, E.H. "James Beattie, William Wordsworth, and the Evolution of Romanticism." In A Festschrift for Edgar Ronald Seary: Essays in English Language and Literature Presented by Colleagues and Former Students, ed. A.A. Macdonald et al. St. Johns: Memorial University of Newfoundland, 1975, pp. 116-29.

Draws attention to similarities between the writers' interests and ideas, arguing that Beattie prepared the way for W and the Romantic movement on the whole. King says much the same thing in his many discussions of the topic, e.g., in his more readily available volume, James Beattie (Boston: Twayne, 1977).

329. Kroeber, Karl. Romantic Landscape Vision: Constable and Wordsworth. Madison: University of Wisconsin, 1975. xi+142 pp. indexed.

Compares paintings and poems to distinguish Romantic from both earlier and later landscape vision, stressing both artists' exploitation of specifics to evoke a diversity of responses. Comments at length on the complications in W's claim for continuity in the spots-of-time passage (1805 Prelude, book 11); on the poet's penchant for the ordinary and unclimactic, and on his unself-deluded love of nature, in "Tintern Abbey"; on "Elegiac Stanzas" as developing rather than altering W's characteristic vision; and on the importance of a localized and unified place as ecosystem in "Home at Grasmere." See also 963.

Reviews: Michael Baron, English 24(1975), 92-94; Kenneth Garlick, N&Q 23(1976), 469-70; Bishop C. Hunt, RM, 1975, p. 57; E.D.H. Johnson, VS 19(1976), 432-33; Kenneth Johnston, WC 7(1976), 165-72; Roderick McGillis, ArielE 6,iv(1975), 109-12; Raimonda Modiano, MLQ 37 (1976), 198-202; Russell Noyes, JEGP 75(1976), 291-93; Stephen Parrish, Criticism 18(1976), 204; A.J. Sambrook, MLR 71(1976), 893-95; Sheila M. Smith, BJA 16(1976), 177-79; J.R. Watson, RES 28(1977), 100-102.

330. La Borsiere, C.R. "Wordsworth's 'Go Back to Antique Ages, If Thine Eyes,' and 'Paradise Lost,' XII, 23-47." Notes & Queries 22(1975): 63.

A note on W's source.

331. Lerner, Laurence. "What Did Wordsworth Mean by 'Nature'?" Critical Quarterly 17(1975): 291-308.

A lucid essay on W's use of "nature," suggesting that he is divided between the viewpoints of Polixenes and Perdita (Winter's Tale, 4.2), seeing nature sometimes as all-encompassing, sometimes as opposed to the merely human and artificial. For Lerner, W's greatest poetry is the amoral "poetry of acceptance" based on the former viewpoint. Sensitive criticism of "The Old Cumberland Beggar."

332. Little, Geoffrey, ed. Barron Field's Memoirs of Wordsworth. Sydney, Australia: Sydney University, 1975. 142 pp. not indexed.

Field's Memoirs, begun in 1837, were read and corrected by W, and left unpublished at his request. Encumbered by long quotations from W, contemporary critics, and others, they are now most valuable for W's corrections (printed in boldface for convenience). This edition (the first publication aside from a few excerpts) is helpfully condensed and edited, including an introductory essay on Field's relations with W and an appendix printing two letters from Field to W. See also 398.

Reviews: Bishop C. Hunt, RM, 1975, pp. 57-58; Lillian

F. Shankman, WC 9(1978), 240-41; V. Smith, ALS 8(1978), 524.

333. Marcus, Leah Sinanoglou. "Vaughan, Wordsworth, Coleridge, and The Encomium Asini." ELH 42(1975): 224-41.

Places "Peter Bell" in the "serio-comic counter tradition of the encomium asini," which reaches back to the Bible and consistently "links the donkey with the lower classes." Comments incisively on W's use of mock-epic technique not to belittle but to elevate, and to attack hierarchical thinking.

334. Martin, B.W. "Wordsworth, Faber, and Keble: Commentary on a Triangular Relationship." Review of English Studies 26(1975): 436-42.

On W's relations with Oxford Movement figures in the early 1840s.

335. Misra, J.B. "Hazlitt and Wordsworth: 'On Going a Journey' in Light of Wordsworth's Poetry." CIEFL Bulletin 11(1975): 83-97.

Does little more than juxtapose passages from Hazlitt's essay and W's poetry to show their "spiritual affinity."

336. Noyes, Russell. "An Unpublished Letter by Wordsworth on Epitaphs." Notes & Queries 22(1975): 60-61.

Prints a letter of 13 Jan. 1844, and notes its faithfulness to the "Essays upon Epitaphs" of 35 years before.

337. Ogden, John T. "The Structure of Imaginative Experience in Wordsworth's Prelude." The Wordsworth Circle 6 (1975): 290-98.

Argues lucidly that W's description of imaginative experience as a sequence of concentration, relaxation, and illumination (exemplified in "There was a Boy"), which fits all the spots of time, also describes the process of recollection and the overarching structure of The Prelude.

338. Owen, W.J.B. "The Borderers and the Aesthetics of Drama." The Wordsworth Circle 6(1975): 227-39.

Seeks to defend the imitation of Shakespeare on the grounds that it was deliberate, and somewhat more helpfully puts the Preface to the play in the tradition of Romantic criticism of Shakespearean characters.

339. Pickering, Sam. "Mrs. Barbauld's Hymns in Prose: An Air-Blown Particle of Romanticism?" Southern Humanities Review 9(1975): 259-68.

Describes the popularity of Mrs. Barbauld's religious children's literature and, without arguing her direct influence, points out the similarity of W's views on childhood, simplicity, and nature.

340. Pradhan, S.V. "Fancy and Imagination: Coleridge Versus Wordsworth." Philological Quarterly 54(1975): 604-23.

Compares and contrasts C's theory with W's, arguing (exclusively from the 1815 Preface) that W's involves an unresolved mix of empirical associationism and transcendentalism. Helpfully details W's debts or similarities to Locke, but is less convincing in showing W's belief in imagination's transcendental power (see 221).

341. Prickett, Stephen. Wordsworth and Coleridge: The Lyrical Ballads. London: Edward Arnold, 1975. 64 pp. indexed. pbk.

A lively little introduction to Lyrical Ballads arguing for the 1798 edition's unity (cf. 517 and 785), with perceptive comments on the nature of the poets' collaboration and on W's genius for flirting with banalities.

Reviews: Michael Baron, English 25(1976), 147; Reeve Parker, WC 9(1978), 221-25.

342. Priestman, Donald G. "Superstition and Imagination: Complementary Faculties of Wordsworth's Narrator in 'The Thorn.'" Journal of Narrative Technique 5(1975): 196-207.

Argues that the superstitious narrator is not gullible but only imaginative, his imagination working unconsciously to assimilate the forms of Martha and the thorn to one another, just as W likens the leech-gatherer and the stone in "Resolution and Independence."

343. Ragussis, Michael. "Language and Metamorphosis in Wordsworth's Arab Dream." Modern Language Quarterly 36(1975): 148-65. Rpt. in The Subterfuge of Art: Language and the Romantic Tradition. Baltimore, MD: Johns Hopkins, 1978, pp. 17-34.

Cites an important source in Ovid, arguing that the dream (in the 1850 Prelude, book 5) is not a restatement but a symbolic resolution of the problems posed by its prologue, which asserts the immortality of the spirit of the word.

344. Ramsey, Jonathan. "Seeing and Perceiving in Wordsworth's An Evening Walk." Modern Language Quarterly 36(1975): 376-89.

A sensitive analysis arguing that in "An Evening Walk" W is already moving from picturesque vision toward the interactive epistemology characteristic of his major poems.

345. Rieger, James. "Wordsworth Unalarm'd." In Milton and the Line of Vision, ed. Joseph Anthony Wittreich, Jr. Madison: University of Wisconsin, 1975, pp. 185-208.

Discusses allusion to Milton in several poems, arguing that W was not anxious about Milton's influence, but used him freely and could even patronize him.

346. San Juan, E., Jr. "The Process of Self-Knowledge in William Wordsworth's 'Ode: Intimations of Immortality.'" Revue des Langues Vivantes 41(1975): 60-67.

Sees the poem as moving through a dialectic of past and present, joy and despair, etc., which is synthesized or transcended through the power of imagination.

347. Schell, Richard. "Wordsworth's Revisions of the Ascent of Snowdon Passage." _Philological Quarterly_ 54(1975): 592-603.

A lucid account of W's revision of the Snowdon passage in MS. W, written in 1804 for the 5-book _Prelude_, to form the conclusion of the 1805 version, showing how the theme of the passage changes from the power of nature to the power of the imagination (cf. 187).

348. Siemon, James. "Poetic Contradiction and 'Resolution and Independence.'" In _Literature and Contradiction_, ed. Brian Caraher and Irving Massey. Buffalo, NY: SUNY Department of English, 1975, pp. 21-34.

Not seen.

349. Stelzig, Eugene L. _All Shades of Consciousness: Wordsworth's Poetry and the Self in Time_. The Hague: Mouton, 1975. 212 pp. indexed.

Sketches the development of self-awareness in philosophy, autobiography, the novel, and meditative poetry which leads to W's retrospective mode, and reads _The Prelude_ and many lyrics of the great decade; Stelzig's readings are chiefly derivative, and his study is pitched toward beginners rather than specialists.
Reviews: Richard Gravil, _MLR_ 73(1978), 413-14; M. Isnard, _EA_ 31(1978), 394; Joseph Kestner, _WC_ 7(1976), 191-94 (with reply by Stelzig).

350. Swingle, L.J. "Romantic Unity and English Romantic Poetry." _Journal of English and Germanic Philology_ 74 (1975): 361-74.

An excellent essay with much on W, arguing against the notion that the English Romantics affirm unity (see also 127). As Swingle argues, W believed in visionary access to unity, but his poetry treats things "as they _appear_" ("Essay, Supplementary," 1815), and is concerned with diversity and opposition, soliciting reconciliation in an active reader.

351. Tave, Stuart M. "Jane Austen and One of Her Contemporaries." In Jane Austen: Bicentenary Studies, ed. John Halperin. New York: Cambridge, 1975, pp. 61-74.

Compares Austen with W on several points--their views on sensationalism and on the city, their preferences for plain language, their interests in low life and garrulous characters, their emphases on "cheerfulness" and duty--ending with a deft comparison of their uses of imagination.

352. Teich, Nathaniel. "Evaluating Wordsworth's Revolution: Romantic Reviewers and Changing Taste." Papers on Language and Literature 11(1975): 206-23.

Examining reviews between 1814 and 1825 to show how W "creates the taste by which he is to be relished," Teich argues that the poet succeeds in substituting imagination for "taste" as the faculty for aesthetic appreciation. Though reviewers describe W's aesthetic "revolution" in political terms, Teich argues that with its emphasis on sympathy, which encompasses "imaginative and moral activities," it is more spiritual than political.

353. Teich, Nathaniel. "Wordsworth's Reception and Coplestone's Advice to Romantic Reviewers." The Wordsworth Circle 6(1975): 280-82.

Comments on contemporary objections to Jeffrey's style of reviewing. Very little on W's reception.

354. Twitchell, James B. "'Hart-Leap Well': Wordsworth's Crucifixion Poem." Tennessee Studies in Literature 20 (1975), 11-16.

Reads the poem as an analogy to the Passion.

355. Twitchell, James B. "The Character of Wordsworth's Leech Gatherer." Research Studies 43(1975): 253-59. Rpt. in The Living Dead: A Study of the Vampire in Romantic Literature. Durham, NC: Duke, 1981, pp. 160-66.

Argues that the speaker of "Resolution and Independence" is not W, and discusses the leech-gatherer as a backward vampire--that is, as a Christ-figure.

356. Vincent, E.R. "Wordsworth, Isola, Lamb." In _Essays in Honour of John Humphreys Whitfield, Presented to Him on His Retirement from the Serena Chair of Italian at the University of Birmingham_, ed. H.C. Davis et al. London: St. George's, 1975, pp. 209-21.

Notes the importance of Italian literature for W (suggesting the influence of Foscolo and Chiabrera on his "Essays upon Epitaphs"), and briefly sketches the lives of Agostino Isola, W's Italian teacher at Cambridge, and of his granddaughter Emma Isola, a friend of the Lambs.

357. Watson, J.R. "Wordsworth's Card Games." _The Wordsworth Circle_ 6(1975): 299-302.

Holds that in his card game (_Prelude_, book 1) W is not emulating Pope but simply depicting humble happiness. Cf. 266, p. 178, and 566.

358. Weiskel, Thomas. "Wordsworth and the Defile of the Word." _Georgia Review_ 29(1975): 154-80. Rpt. in _The Romantic Sublime_ (431), pp. 167-204.

A posthumously published essay discussing imagination in the 1850 _Prelude_ as resistance to the symbolic order or "repression of the signified," examining the beacon and Simplon Pass episodes (books 12 and 6) in particular.

359. Wiener, David. "Wordsworth, Books, and the Growth of a Poet's Mind." _Journal of English and Germanic Philology_ 74(1975): 209-20.

Discusses the various functions of books in the 1805 _Prelude_, especially their role in reconciling the child to reality and leading him to love of nature and of man.

360. Wilhelm, Albert E. "The Dramatized Narrator in Wordsworth's _The Idiot Boy_." _Journal of Narrative Technique_ 5(1975): 16-23.

Contrasts Johnny's synthetic visionary power with the incompetent narrator's dichotomizing mentality.

361. Woodard, Charles R. "Wordsworth and the Romantic Agony." Tennessee Studies in Literature 20(1975): 1-10.

Citing "The Thorn," "Simon Lee," "Alice Fell," and the character of Oswald in The Borderers as examples, Woodard finds W's treatment of suffering morbid, and attributes Mario Praz's exclusion of W from The Romantic Agony (1936) to oversight. Contrast Averill's studies, 364 and 704.

362. Altieri, Charles. "Wordsworth's 'Preface' as Literary Theory." Criticism 18(1976): 122-46.

An impressive essay offering a "naturalist reading" of the Preface and comparing W with Wittgenstein, arguing that--chiefly through his poetics of memory--W integrates idealist themes in an empiricist approach, and thus calls the mind-nature dichotomy in question. With this, Altieri challenges what he sees as false dichotomizing and "neo-idealism" in the views of language and poetry held by Hartman (143), de Man, and Derrida.

363. Averill, James H. "Another Early Coleridge Reference to 'An Evening Walk.'" English Language Notes 13(1976): 270-73.

Cites a line in "Songs of the Pixies" which C stole before he had met W.

364. Averill, James H. "Suffering and Calm in Wordsworth's Early Poetry." PMLA 91(1976): 223-34. Rpt. in Wordsworth and the Poetry of Human Suffering (704), pp. 55-82.

Examines the conclusion to "The Ruined Cottage" in particular, analyzing W's depictions of suffering and calm as dramatizations of catharsis, and relating them to his poetic project of arousing the reader's faculties of sympathy and imagination.

365. Ball, Patricia. The Heart's Events: The Victorian Poetry of Relationships. London: Athlone, 1976. 227 pp. indexed.

Discusses Byron's poems of the separation with W's "Lucy Poems" as two prototypes for Victorian "poetry of relationships." Celebrates the "Lucy Poems" for training narrative away from exterior events toward psychology, or "events of the heart"; they "are W's _In Memoriam_," and are compared with Arnold's Marguerite poems as well. Reviews: M. Allott, _VS_ 20(1977), 431; Alethea Hayter, _TLS_, 15 Oct. 1976, p. 1299; P. Homan, _N&Q_ 25(1978), 270; Jack Kolb, _RES_ 29(1978), 107-8; Andrew Sanders, _DUJ_ 70 (1978), 251-52; S.M. Smith, _BJA_ 17(1977), 285; _VP_ 15 (1977), 189; D. Ward, _English_ 26(1977), 72.

366. Bateson, F.W. "Wordsworth." _Times Literary Supplement_, 9 April 1976, p. 430.

Letter to the editor calling for an edition of Dorothy's journals which reveals the passages blotted out by W's descendants.

367. Bloom, Harold. _Poetry and Repression: Revisionism from Blake to Stevens_. New Haven, CT: Yale, 1976. 293 pp.

In the chapter "Wordsworth and the Scene of Instruction" (pp. 52-82), Bloom finds "Tintern Abbey" dominated by the repressed memory of Milton's invocations in _Paradise Lost_, books 3 and 7; W does not so much strive with Milton as circumvent him, intending a poem of restoration but being forced to find new poetic turf in the subject of memory, which founds an important tradition in modern poetry.

368. Brown, Richard G. "_Peter Bell_: A Key to Its Narrative Structure." _Ball State University Forum_ 17,iv(1976): 12-19.

Does little more than retell the story, pausing occasionally to belabor the obvious, especially "the humanizing effect of the imagination" and W's avoidance of the supernatural.

369. Burke, Richard C. "A Hitherto Unrecorded Wordsworth Holograph." _The Wordsworth Circle_ 7(1976): 83-86.

Describes a holograph of "The Reverie of Poor Susan," signed, dated 1830, and probably presented to Mrs. Hemans, and questions its textual significance.

370. Butler, James A. "Wordsworth, Cottle, and the _Lyrical Ballads_: Five Letters, 1797-1800." _Journal of English and Germanic Philology_ 75(1976): 139-53.

Prints five newly discovered letters from W to Cottle and discusses the men's relations, especially regarding the transfer of the copyright to _Lyrical Ballads_.

371. Celoria, Francis. "Chatterton, Wordsworth and Stonehenge." _Notes & Queries_ 23(1976): 103-104.

Notes W's use of Chatterton's "Battle of Hastings II" in "Salisbury Plain," most of the borrowings being weeded out by the time the poem becomes "Guilt and Sorrow."

372. Chard, Leslie F. "Wordsworth and the Enlightenment: A Reconsideration." _Studies in Voltaire and the Eighteenth Century_ 152(1976): 473-84.

Compares W's dislike of "abstract," as opposed to "true" or "organic," systems--especially as shown in his classification of poems--with the attitude of the encyclopedists.

373. Clausen, Christopher. "Tintern Abbey to Little Gidding: The Past Recaptured." _Sewanee Review_ 84(1976): 405-24.

Rejecting the consolatory element of "Tintern Abbey" and presenting it as a poem of self-division and nostalgia for lost faith and childhood, Clausen argues that W is "the first Victorian poet," whose dilemma is not solved until the "austere self-denial" of Eliot's "Little Gidding."

374. Cohen, Ruth. "The 1800 Ordering of _Lyrical Ballads_: Its Moral Purpose." _Caliban_ 13(1976): 31-44.

Focusing almost entirely on the first volume, Cohen argues that W arranged his poems pedagogically, so that they proceed from moral lesson to lesson, but she concentrates more on the moralism of individual poems than on the logic of W's arrangement.

375. Cooke, Michael G. The Romantic Will. New Haven, CT: Yale, 1976. xviii+279 pp. indexed.

Traces the will "as a prime topos" in Romantic poetry, relating it to the more popular critical topics of imagination and consciousness. Includes illuminating discussions of "The Solitary Reaper," "Tintern Abbey," and "Resolution and Independence," and a chapter examining the "act of will that, though abortive, becomes a...cause of revelation" in the 1850 Prelude, especially in the boat-stealing, Simplon Pass, and Snowdon passages (books 1, 6, and 14). Closes with a look at W's stoicism, which is seen as opposed to poetry, and is fingered as "the enemy of Wordsworth's muse."

Reviews: John Bayley, TLS, 17 June 1977, p. 718; Stuart Curran, JEGP 77(1978), 287-89; David V. Erdman, RM, 1976, p. 39; Dewey R. Faulkner, YR 66(1977), 449-52; Frances Ferguson, MLN 92(1977), 1118-21; Laurence Goldstein, BlakeQ 11(1978), 284-87; Karl Kroeber, KSJ 27 (1978), 135-38; Herbert Lindenberger, MLR 74(1979), 666-67; Morse Peckham, SIR 17(1978), 91-93; John R. Reed, Criticism 19(1977), 193; Mark Roberts, RES 29(1978), 228-30; Peter L. Thorslev, Jr., WC 8(1977), 243-45.

376. Crowe, Stanley J.H. "Rhetoric, 'Reality' and Wordsworth's Excursion." Furman Studies 25,i(1976): 47-58.

Argues that in The Excursion W abandons visionary or prophetic rhetoric in favor of dialectical, "quasi-dramatic form" in an effort to achieve greater objectivity and universality.

377. Dunham, Robert H. "Silas Marner and the Wordsworthian Child." Studies in English Literature, 1500-1900 16 (1976), 645-59.

Examines Marner's regeneration in association with Eppie in terms of W's psychology of childhood and maturation.

378. French, Roberts W. "Wordsworth's Paradise Lost: A Note on 'Nutting.'" Studies in the Humanities 5,i(1976): 42-45.

Agreeing with Ferry (131) that in "Nutting" man is at odds with nature, French sees the boy in the poem as playing the part of Milton's Satan, and as reenacting the destruction of Paradise.

379. Fricke, Donna G., and Douglas C. Fricke, eds. Aeolian Harps: Essays in Literature in Honor of Maurice Browning Cramer. Bowling Green, OH: Bowling Green University, 1976. xvi+293 pp. not indexed.

Includes essays 384 and 420.
Review: VP 15(1977), 382.

380. Gates, Barbara T. "Wordsworth and the Course of History." Research Studies 44(1976): 199-207.

Relates Vico's view of history to W's use of the winding river as a symbol for historical progress, and suggests that W's stress on individualism influenced nineteenth-century historians.

381. Gates, Barbara T. "Wordsworth's Lessons from the Past." The Wordsworth Circle 7(1976): 133-41.

Noting that for W, history is to society as memory is to the individual--a source "for future restoration"--Gates examines the individualism and moralism in W's use of history, especially in "Dion" and The Convention of Cintra.

382. Gattrell, Simon. "Hardy's Under the Greenwood Tree and Wordsworth's 'Phantom of Delight.'" Thomas Hardy Yearbook 6(1976): 26-27.

Notes echoes of W's poem, the plainest of which Hardy removed in revision.

383. Glen, Heather. "The Poet in Society: Blake and Wordsworth on London." Literature and History 3(1976): 2-28.

Compares W's blind-beggar passage (1805 Prelude 7:592 ff.) not only with Blake's "London" but also with Gray and Goldsmith, and argues that in contemplating the beggar W moves from "egocentric meditation upon others" to a truer "affirmation of community." Response by Stan Smith, L&H 4(1976): 94-98.

384. Gould, Keith A. "Panentheism in The Prelude." Aeolian Harps (379), pp. 111-31.

Defining panentheism in the terms of Charles Hartshorne, Gould argues lucidly that The Prelude, especially in the 1850 version, describes the poet's movement toward and discovery of panentheistic faith. Focuses especially on the Gondo Gorge and Snowdon passages (books 6 and 13).

385. Hager, Philip E. "The English Romantics and Education." Antigonish Review 25(1976): 83-92.

A scant discussion of the "monitorial education" system advocated by Andrew Bell (1753-1832) and Joseph Lancaster (1778-1838) with a small compendium of W's and C's reactions.

386. Harvie, J.A. "The Eclipse of the Golden Age." Forum for Modern Language Studies 12(1976): 176-88.

Compares W's opposition to modern science and industry, particularly in the later poems, with that of the Russian poet Baratynsky (d. 1844), and finds W more optimistic.

387. Helmstadter, Thomas H. "Wayward Wisdom: Wordsworth's Humor in the Lyrical Ballads." Mosaic 9,iv(1976): 91-106.

Examines W's satiric but "amiable humor" in a wide range of poems, arguing that it calls on the reader to understand and forgive.

388. Hodgson, John A. "Wordsworth's Dialectical Transcendentalism 1798: 'Tintern Abbey.'" Criticism 18(1976): 367-80.

Argues that the three stages of growth presented in the poem are repeatedly paralleled by three stages of intellectual-spiritual experience, the most important analogy being that both progresses culminate in affection or social sympathy.

389. Holland, Norman N. "Literary Interpretation and Three Phases of Psychoanalysis." Critical Inquiry 3(1976): 221-33.

Surveys readings of "A slumber did my spirit seal," and defends their divergence by analogy to the psychoanalytic concept of identity, defined as "a continuing sameness within change." Though striving for objectivity, Holland argues, our readings must be subjective acts "of personal discovery." Reads "A slumber" according to three phases of psychoanalytic theory: as phallic fantasy, as defense-drama, and as punishment for the reader's dehumanization of others, to demonstrate the difference made by various levels of interpretive sophistication.

390. Jacobus, Mary. Tradition and Experiment in Wordsworth's Lyrical Ballads (1798). Oxford: Clarendon, 1976. x+301 pp. indexed.

Describes W's debts to C, Godwin, Bürger, Cowper, and others, and compares later eighteenth-century verse in an effort to define the poet's own distinctive contribution. See also 128.

Reviews: James H. Averill, SIR 17(1978), 77-83; Michael Baron, English 25(1976), 147-52; David V. Erdman, RM, 1976, p. 78; M. Isnard, EA 31(1978), 395; Jerome J. McGann, MLR 73(1978), 615-16; Norman Nicholson, TLS, 9 July 1976, p. 840; Reeve Parker, WC 9(1978), 221-25; Roger Sharrock, N&Q 26(1979), 350-51; J.R. Watson, RES 28(1977), 358-59.

391. Johnston, Kenneth R. "Wordsworth's Last Beginning: The Recluse in 1808." ELH 43(1976): 316-41.

A close reading of "The Tuft of Primroses" as a unified work, arguing that its unsuccessful attempt to "turn from egocentric to social vision" is important to our understanding both of The Recluse project and of Romanticism. See also Johnston's book (1020).

392. Jordan, John E. Why the Lyrical Ballads? The Background, Writing, and Character of Wordsworth's 1798 Lyrical Ballads. Berkeley: University of California, 1976. xii+212 pp. indexed.

Studies the volume in historical context, comparing less eminent contemporary volumes.

Reviews: James H. Averill, SIR 17(1978), 77-83; Stephen Gill, WC 9(1978), 233-34; A.J. Hartley, DR 57 (1977), 174; John O. Hayden, Criticism 19(1977), 265-67; Roderick Huang, ECS 11(1977), 124-26; Bishop C. Hunt, RM, 1976, p. 79; Lore Metzger, MLQ 39(1978), 200-202.

393. Kerpneck, Harvey. "Arnold, Wordsworth, and 'Memorial Verses.'" English Studies in Canada 2(1976), 163-81.

A close reading of "Memorial Verses" contrasting Arnold's portraits of W, Byron, and Goethe, comparing them with his prose statements, and focusing in particular on his achievement of balance, "tribute this side of idolatry."

394. King, E.H. "Beattie and Coleridge: New Light on the Damaged Archangel." The Wordsworth Circle 7(1976), 142-51.

Contrasts W's with C's use of Beattie to argue W's vast superiority, both moral and intellectual, to C.

395. Kroeber, Karl. "Jane Austen, Romantic." The Wordsworth Circle 7(1976), 291-96.

Comparing Austen, W, Scott, and others to show the Romantic subversion of preconceptions and conventional responses, argues that a concept of Romanticism must consider all the arts.

396. Lim, Paulino M., Jr. "Zen and Wordsworth." The Wordsworth Circle 7(1976): 129-32.

Calling for more study of the relation of W to Zen, describes some similarities, lists works on Zen in English, and proposes directions for research.

397. Little, Geoffrey. [No Title]. _The Wordsworth Circle_ 7 (1976): 16.

Reports an 1837 holograph of "Personal Talk," lines 51-56, and lists variants.

398. Little, Geoffrey. "A Lesson in the Art of Poetry: Barron Field and Wordsworth's Later Revisions." _Journal of the Australasian Universities Language and Literature Association_ 46(1976): 189-205.

Details W's correspondence (beginning in 1828) with Field, whose minute criticisms of W's poetry resulted in revisions, restorations of earlier readings, and explanations. See also Field's _Memoirs_, edited by Little (332), in which Field's letters are published.

399. McAuley, James. "Wordsworth Once More." _Quadrant_ 107 (1976): 40-49.

Attempts to "set in order stages in Wordsworth's development up to 1805," chiefly following the lines of W's own poetic accounts such as "Tintern Abbey." An informative essay, perhaps useful as a general introduction, but it does not contain anything new and is weakened by simplifications (McAuley dismisses the ballads, for example, as "on the whole unsuccessful experiments").

400. McFarland, Thomas. "Creative Fantasy and Matter-of-Fact Reality in Wordsworth's Poetry." _Journal of English and Germanic Philology_ 75(1976): 1-24.

A good essay on W's preference for "reality" arguing that W had a strong predilection for fantasy, which--unhappily repressed in "Peter Bell" and unhappily indulged in "Laodamia"--served him best when reconciled with "reality" in the mixed mode of memory.

401. Manning, Peter J. "Wordsworth, Margaret, and the Pedlar." _Studies in Romanticism_ 15(1976): 195-220.

A rich psychological reading of _The Excursion_, book 1, identifying W with the Pedlar and presenting the poem as W's reworking the loss of his mother and of Annette

Vallon. Argues against dividing the "multi-faceted self-portrait" into "The Pedlar" and "The Ruined Cottage."

402. Metzger, Lore. "Wordsworth's Pastoral Covenant." Modern Language Quarterly 37(1976): 307-23.

A reading of "Michael" which stresses W's ability to recognize adversity without losing his optimistic pastoral vision.

403. Miller, David L. "Dominion of the Eye in Frost." In Frost: Centennial Essays, Vol. 2, ed. Jac Tharpe. Jackson: University of Mississippi, 1976, pp. 141-58.

Lucid comparison of Frost's use "of 'surmise' as a way of accomodating vision to skepticism" with that of W and Keats, finding the emphasis on skepticism much more pronounced in Frost.

404. Newey, Vincent. "The Steadfast Self: An Aspect of Wordsworth." In Literature of the Romantic Period, 1750-1850, ed. R.T. Davies and B.G. Beatty. New York: Barnes & Noble, 1976, pp. 36-55.

Dangerously identifies W with various speakers and characters in "Ode to Duty," "The Ruined Cottage," "Michael," and "Resolution and Independence" to describe his "psychological journey" through the darker side of life, which is compared to Christian's in The Pilgrim's Progress. More helpful is Newey's earlier essay (276).

405. Newmeyer, Edna. "Paradise Preserved or Paradise Regained: Milton and Wordsworth on the Scale of Love." Milton and the Romantics 2(1976): 11-15.

Finds Raphaël's explanations of reason and love to Adam in Paradise Lost central to W's concepts of imagination and love in The Prelude (especially the 1805 version).

406. Osborn, Marijane. "Wordsworth's 'Borderers' and the Landscape of Penrith." Transactions of the Cumberland and Westmoreland Antiquarian and Archaeological Society 76(1976): 144-58.

Sees the literal topography as a kind of bedrock for the poet's dramatization of his social and political ideas, and, presumably, for his psychic problems.

407. Owen, W.J.B. "Wordsworth's Aesthetics of Landscape." _The Wordsworth Circle_ 7(1976): 70-82.

Examining the _Guide to the Lakes_ and the "Unpublished Tour," Owen finds W's aesthetics similar to Burke's, and locates a shift from Gothic to a "modified Burkean aesthetics" in 1790. Cf. 212.

408. Parrish, Steven Maxfield. "The Worst of Wordsworth." _The Wordsworth Circle_ 7(1976): 89-91.

Manifesto for the Cornell project (see Section 1.2). Argues forcefully that because W lived so long, and revised so much as his abilities declined, we need to rescue his "buried masterpieces" and "lost poems" from the later W. For a fuller and more balanced consideration, see Gill's essay (949).

409. Pipkin, James W. "_The Borderers_ and Wordsworth's Emblems of Solitude." _Southern Review (Adelaide)_ 9(1976): 79-92.

Finds the play's significance in its broaching the themes of solitude and man's relation to the external world, and analyzes the major characters as precursors of the Wordsworthian solitary.

410. Prickett, Stephen. _Romanticism and Religion: The Tradition of Coleridge and Wordsworth in the Victorian Church_. Cambridge: Cambridge, 1976. viii+295 pp. indexed.

Full of information and insights on C's and W's impact on Victorian thinkers, both churchmen and laymen. Treatment of W opens with a chapter arguing that his "Language of Nature," with its odd mix of Platonism and Naturalism which so annoyed Blake and C, is (especially for the Victorians) the language not of muddled philosophy but of religious feeling. W's legacy, detailed in chapters on Maurice, Newman, Arnold, and MacDonald, is seen to be not so much ideas as the ability to have and to articulate religious feeling. A ten-page appendix sketches "parallels" between W and Kierkegaard. Pricket is, in addition, often helpful on the poets' relation to eighteenth-century philosophy.

Reviews: Michael Baron, English 25(1976), 147-52; J. Robert Barth, WC 8(1977), 201-204; G. Cullum, SoRA 11 (1978), 205; David V. Erdman, RM, 1976, p. 42; Howard W. Fulweiler, SIR 17(1978), 371-76; J. Gibert, EA 31(1978), 229; E.A. Horsman, AUMLA 47(May, 1977), 67; Trevor Levere, TLS, 22 Oct. 1976, p. 1338; E.D. Mackerness, N&Q 25 (1978), 251; B.W. Martin, RES 38(1977), 479-81; Mary Moorman, DUJ 69(1977), 309-10; Roger Sharrock, English 26(1977), 66-71.

411. Priestman, Donald G. "Wordsworth on the Poetry of Walter Scott." Dalhousie Review 55(1976): 675-88.

Finds W's criticisms of Scott consonant with the principles of the Preface to Lyrical Ballads, and contrasts the moral purpose of W's poetry with the historical purpose of Scott's.

412. Proffitt, Edward. "The Mystery of Voice: The Place of Oral Interpretation in Teaching The Prelude." Oral English 2,ii(1976): 12-13.

Recommends that the poem be read aloud in the classroom; followed by exchange with the editor, pp. 13-15. Neither is of any value.

413. Radner, John B. "The Youthful Harlot's Curse: The Prostitute as Symbol of the City in 18th-Century English Literature." Eighteenth-Century Life 2(1976): 59-64.

Discusses W's Prelude, books 7 and 8 (pp. 61-2), as well as Boswell, Goldsmith, Johnson, Blake, and others, but has nothing new on W.

414. Rai, Alok. "Wordsworth, Coleridge and Poetic Diction." Rajasthan University Studies in English 9(1976): 24-32.

Not seen.

415. Ramsey, Jonathan. "Wordsworth and the Childhood of Language." Criticism 18(1976): 243-55.

Contrasts children's language with the self-conscious and dichotomizing speech of adults in W's poetry, especially "The Idiot Boy" and "Anecdote for Fathers," arguing that in the language of childhood W depicts the childhood of language.

416. Ramsey, Jonathan. "Wordsworth's Silent Poet." Modern Language Quarterly 37(1976): 260-80.

An excellent discussion of W's fondness for "border people," arguing that W saw them, and the "silent poet" pre-eminently, as epitomes of receptivity or "wise passiveness" who "symbolically intercede for us with nature." See also Jonathan Wordsworth's treatments of this topic, 300 and 929.

417. Regueiro, Helen. The Limits of Imagination: Wordsworth, Yeats, and Stevens. Ithaca, NY: Cornell, 1976. 222 pp. indexed.

Dialectical criticism beginning with a defense of the categories of imagination and reality, and finding in the chapter on W that the dialectic takes the form of a relationship between the temporal (i.e., human) and natural worlds. Regueiro argues that W can enter the latter without surrendering imagination only by distancing the poet from the protagonist, most commonly through retrospection.

Reviews: Kenneth John Atchity, WHR 32(1978), 95-96; G.L. Bruns, Criticism 20(1978), 75; Frances Ferguson, GaR 31(1977), 511-16; Bishop C. Hunt, RM, 1976, p. 80.

418. Reid, Ian. "'A Naked Guide-Post's Head': The Wordsworthian Sense of Direction." ELH 43(1976): 538-50.

Notes that W frequently uses imagery of clothing and nakedness in contexts of journeying and direction-finding, and relates this to the Wordsworthian process of restoration, but without finding in it a "codifiable symbolism." Chiefly examines the 1805 Prelude, especially the drowned-man, beacon, and Christmas-vacation passages (books 5 and 11), and "Guilt and Sorrow."

419. Rubenstein, Jill. "Wordsworth and 'Localised Romance': The Scottish Poems of 1831." Studies in English Literature, 1500-1900 16(1976): 579-90.

Argues that in the "localized romance" of Yarrow Revisited, and Other Poems (1831) W combines his own gift for restorative memory with Scott's sense of history and tradition to provide a sense of consolation and continuity in the face of Scott's impending death. See also 993.

420. Rudy, John G. "Structure and Unity in The White Doe of Rylstone." Aeolian Harps (379), pp. 133-48.

Argues that the poem is not fragmented, but structurally opposes the worlds of action and of imagination, Emily's accomplishment being to unify the poem's oppositions.

421. Sabin, Margery. English Romanticism and the French Tradition. Cambridge, MA: Harvard, 1976. xiv+294 pp. indexed.

Central to this book is a brilliant extended contrast between Rousseau and Wordsworth (chs. 1-6), especially distinguishing the autobiography of the Confessions from that of the 1850 Prelude by stressing the writers' differences in purpose and their disagreement on the uses of imagination and memory. Chapter 5 is a fine discussion of W's combination of these two faculties. An important work.

Reviews: E.W. Bruss, CL 30(1978), 371; Michael G. Cooke, SIR 18(1979), 323; P. Henry, MLJ 61(1977), 432.

422. Salvesen, Christopher, and David Palmer. "Wordsworth, Coleridge and Keats." In English Poetry, ed. Alan Sinfield. London: Sussex, 1976, pp. 116-29.

Transcript of a discussion on the general character, and especially on the modernity, of the three poets; chiefly useful, if at all, as an introduction.

423. Simon, Gary. "Craft, Theory & the Artist's Milieu: The Myth-Maker & Wordsworth." Walt Whitman Review 22 (1976): 58-66.

A poorly written, derivative, and overly general essay comparing W with Whitman, arguing that "Tintern Abbey" is "typically expressive" of W's faculties.

424. Smidt, Kristian. "The Beaches of Calais and Dover: Arnold's Counterstatement to Wordsworth's Confession of Faith." _Victorian Poetry_ 14(1976), 256-57.

Compares and contrasts "It is a beauteous evening..." with Arnold's "Dover Beach."

425. Stephenson, William C. "The Mirror and the Lute: Wordsworth's Fine Art of Poetic Auscultation." _Yearbook of English Studies_ 6(1976): 101-12.

Helpful discussion of W's use of sound, echo, and reflection, viewing the more figurative "echoes" between similar experiences as a structuring device in the 1850 _Prelude_, books 1-5.

426. Stevenson, Warren. "Cosmic Irony in Wordsworth's 'A Slumber Did My Spirit Seal.'" _The Wordsworth Circle_ 7 (1976): 92-94.

An excellent accounting for the poem's paradoxes by reading it as "a little dramatic monologue."

427. Sucksmith, Harvey Peter. "Ultimate Affirmation: A Critical Analysis of Wordsworth's Sonnet, 'Composed upon Westminster Bridge,' and the Image of the City in _The Prelude_." _Yearbook of English Studies_ 6(1976): 113-19.

Argues that W's sonnet assimilates the city to his "scheme of things" as the _Prelude_ passages on the city (books 7 and 8) fail to do.

428. Turner, J.F. "'Various Journey, Sad and Slow': Wordsworth's _Descriptive Sketches_ (1791-2) and the Lure of Pastoral." _Durham University Journal_ 69(1976), 38-51.

Rejects biographical explanations of the speaker's melancholy, placing him in the eighteenth-century tradition of the philosophical traveller, but notes W's resistance to conventional "easy escapes" from melancholy, such as pastoral.

429. Warnock, Mary. Imagination. London: Faber & Faber, 1976. 213 pp. indexed. pbk.

Traces the role of imagination in perception from Hume to Wittgenstein, Ryle, and Sartre, and does not claim to break new ground, but the discussion of W's developing conception of the faculty (pp. 102-30), especially in The Prelude, is valuable for its lucidity. Warnock relates W's concept to those of Hume, Kant, and C, and concludes that W's originality lies his belief that images and feelings are formed subconsciously.

Reviews: A. Barnes, JAAC 36(1977), 95; P.N. Furbank, Li, 30 Sept. 1976, p. 406; L.R. Furst, Criticism 19 (1977), 70; S. Gill, RES 28(1977), 509; R. Gleckner, WC 10(1979), 283; D. Pole, BJA 17(1977), 93; R. Scruton, TLS, 15 Oct. 1976, p. 1311.

430. Watson, George. "The Revolutionary Youth of Wordsworth and Coleridge." Critical Quarterly 18,iii(1976): 49-66.

Suggests that both poets' revolutionary sympathies were far more extreme than is often thought, contrasting C's "misleading" accounts of his youth with W's "breathtaking candour" in Prelude 10, and argues that W's disillusionment was philosophical, a "dissatisfaction with doctrines of utopian liberalism rather than with events" in France. See also the responses by Beer (437) and Ellis (445).

431. Weiskel, Thomas. The Romantic Sublime: Studies in the Structure and Psychology of Transcendence. Baltimore, MD: Johns Hopkins, 1976. xi+220 pp. indexed.

An often acute and stimulating, often frustrating and difficult attempt to reassess the Romantic sublime, drawing heavily on Hegelian philosophy, and using both Freudian and structuralist terminology to distinguish between the many species of the sublime (which is seen in general as an inequality between signified and signifier). Weiskel is also largely concerned with the sublime's ethical implications; the treatment of W, who figures prominently throughout, focuses on the poet's efforts to achieve transcendence in the "egotistical" and "liminal" sublime while avoiding the alienation and despair of the Kantian, or "negative" sublime on the one hand, and solipsism or narcissism on the other. Deals with "Resolution and Independence" and the 1850 Prelude in particular.

Reviews: J. Robert Barth, S.J., ELN 15(1978), 219-22; Jerome C. Christensen, Diacritics 8,ii(1978), 10-23; Frances Ferguson, WC 8(1977), 237-42; Michael Fischer, BlakeN 10(1976), 93-95; Thomas R. Frosch, SIR 16(1977), 121-28; Richard Gravil, MLR 74(1979), 664; Joseph M. Griska, Jr. PLL 14(1978), 360-61; Hugh Haughton, TLS, 24 Dec. 1976, p. 1619; Daniel Hughes, Criticism 19(1977), 84-88; E.D. Mackerness, N&Q 25(1978), 251; Melvin Rader, JAAC 35(1976), 253-55; S.M. Smith, BJA 17(1977), 286; Robert Uphaus, SiB 19(1978), 242-44; Carl Woodring, KSJ 27(1978), 133-35; David M. Wyatt, GaR 31(1977), 243-48.

432. Whitney, Ross R. "A New Wordsworth Letter: A Testimonial for Derwent Coleridge." The Wordsworth Circle 7(1976): 87-88.

Describes Derwent's relationship with W, and prints an 1832 letter, since included in the standard edition (40).

433. Wilson, Katherina M. "Imagination and Mysticism." Theoria to Theory, 1976.

Not seen.

434. Ades, John I. "Friendly Persuasion: Lamb as Critic of Wordsworth." The Wordsworth Circle 8(1977): 18-24.

Surveys Lamb's criticism, both epistolary and published, to show its judiciousness.

435. Albrecht, W.P. "Tragedy and Wordsworth's Sublime." The Wordsworth Circle 8(1977): 83-94.

Locates W's idea of the sublime--especially as stated in "The Sublime and the Beautiful" (see 30, vol. 2)--among others' positions. W's sublime is "visionary," depending on the mind, unlike the "visible" sublime of the greater part of eighteenth-century aestheticians; but like his predecessors, and unlike other Romantic thinkers, W appears to find tragedy and the sublime at odds.

436. Beer, John. "Coleridge, the Wordsworths, and the State of Trance." The Wordsworth Circle 8(1977): 121-38.

Traces the word "trance" in W's and C's poetry and argues that for a period, following C's lead, W explored --in "Tintern Abbey," "A slumber did my spirit seal," "Peter Bell," The Prelude, and other poems--the power of trance-like states to foster imaginative sympathy.

437. Beer, John. "The 'Revolutionary Youth' of Wordsworth and Coleridge: Another View." Critical Quarterly 19,ii (1977): 79-87.

Takes issue with Watson (430), arguing that neither poet advocated violent revolution. Watson answers, pp. 86-87.

438. Black, Michael. "On Reading: Some Lines of Wordsworth." Critical Review 19(1977): 71-87.

Analyzes the lines on Newton's statue (1850 Prelude, book 3) at length to indicate the difficulties involved in "explaining" poetry, as well as the necessity of circularly inferring the poet's "intention" from his text. For Black, these lines evince W's modernity: he is the first poet to assimilate Newton's universe.

439. Bornstein, George, ed. Romantic and Modern: Revaluations of Literary Tradition. Pittsburgh: University of Pittsburgh, 1977. xiii+248 pp. indexed.

Includes 460 and 497.

440. Boyd, Julian, and Zelda Boyd. "The Perfect of Experience." Studies in Romanticism 16(1977): 3-13.

Examines W's use of the present perfect in "The Reverie of Poor Susan," "Tintern Abbey," and the Ode (and his avoidance of it in the "Lucy Poems") as a way of spatializing time, and of connecting past experience with the present.

441. Butler, James. "The Chronology of Wordsworth's The Ruined Cottage after 1800." Studies in Philology 74 (1977): 89-112.

Solves several difficulties in dating W's composition and in interpreting Dorothy's references to "The Pedlar" by using watermark evidence to show that MS. E, in which the stories of Margaret and the Pedlar were reunited, was not written until between November 1803 and March 1804 (rather than in 1801-02). Thus Butler is able to hypothesize that W wrote "an independent poem" called "The Pedlar" in 1801-02, and that this poem is what is referred to by "Pedlar" references between 1800 and late 1803. Butler's argument has been taken account of by Reed (82, pp. 665-66). See also Butler's edition of these poems (20).

442. Casagrande, Peter J. "Hardy's Wordsworth: A Record and a Commentary." English Literature in Transition 20 (1977): 210-37.

A thorough influence study citing Hardy's marginalia, compiling his many prose references to W, and focusing mainly on his relation as poet to W's critical theory and consolatory philosophy (especially as this is expressed in the Ode).

443. Cook, Peter A. "Chronology of the 'Lake School' Argument: Some Revisions." Review of English Studies 28 (1977): 175-81.

Corrects the prevalent assumption that Jeffrey's 1802 review of Southey's Thalaba originated the terms "Lakers," "Lake Poets," or "Lake School," showing that the concept had existed since 1797, but that these terms were not used in print until after 1814, and that though Jeffrey popularized them, he did not coin them.

444. Dhavale, V.N. "Frost and Wordsworth." Indian Journal of American Studies 7,ii(1977): 31-44.

Enumerates points--e.g., lack of humor, egocentricity, interest in politics, and a want of "'auditory' imagination" (!)--on which W may be contrasted with Frost, but tends to oversimplify W greatly.

445. Ellis, David. "Wordsworth's Revolutionary Youth: How We Read The Prelude." Critical Quarterly 19,iv(1977): 59-67.

Takes issue with Watson (430), pointing out the difficulties in reading autobiography, and The Prelude in particular, as personal history rather than as "personal myth."

446. Evans, Robley. "The House and the Well in English Romantic Poetry." In Symposium on Romanticism: An Interdisciplinary Meeting, ed. Pierre Deguise and Rita Terras. New London: Connecticut College, 1977, pp. 21-28.

Generalizes from W's use of water imagery to suggest that the early verse is "poetry of movement" while the later is poetry of stasis and enclosure.

447. Ferguson, Frances. Wordsworth: Language as Counter-Spirit. New Haven, CT: Yale, 1977. xvii+263 pp. indexed.

An influential study which, beginning with an examination of W's explicit speculations on language, especially in the Preface to Lyrical Ballads and the "Essays upon Epitaphs," argues that this concern lies behind much of W's poetry, as well as behind his classing of poems.

Reviews: Jonathan Arac, HudR 31(1978), 368; A.J.Hartley, DR 57(1977-78), 783-86; M. Isnard, EA 32(1979), 340; Lawrence Kramer, WC 9(1978), 226-29; Herbert Lindenberger, SIR 17(1978), 236-38; Geoffrey Little, RES 30 (1979), 480-81; Paul Magnuson, YES 10(1980), 294-96; W.J.B. Owen, ELN 16(1979), 339-44.

448. Fox, Arnold B., and Martin Kallich. "Wordsworth's Sentimental Naturalism: Theme and Image in 'The World is Too Much With Us.'" The Wordsworth Circle 8(1977): 327-32.

An unreasonable attack on the sonnet as ununified and sentimental, based on an inadequate reading.

449. Frank, Ellen E. "The Domestication of Nature: Five Houses in the Lake District." Nature and the Victorian Imagination (469), pp. 68-92.

Briefly discusses W's "assimilation of architecture with nature" (pp. 69-74), and Victorian permutations of his attitude.

450. Friedman, Michael. "Wordsworth's Grasmere: A Rentier's Vision." Polit 1, no. 1(1977): 35-60.

Examines W's attitude to the natives of Grasmere, both in the poetry and in biographical documents, arguing that he was unable to overcome a fundamental distance from the common laborer.

451. Garber, Frederick. "Nature and the Romantic Mind: Egotism, Empathy, Irony." Comparative Literature 29 (1977): 193-212.

A wide-ranging essay on the various balances struck by English, German, American, and French Romantics in relating the mind to the outside world, comparing W's "egotism" with Rousseau's, but also noting that W's famous metaphor of the marriage of mind and nature constitutes the "middle way."

452. Gates, Barbara. "The Prelude and the Development of Wordsworth's Historical Imagination." Etudes Anglaises 30(1977): 169-78.

Traces W's development of a vivid historical imagination in the 1805 Prelude, particularly in the passages describing his stay at Cambridge (book 3), his experience of London (book 8), and his reverie on Sarum's Plain (book 12), and suggests that it is a potent "remedy for the poet's ailing spirit."

453. Gatti-Taylor, Marisa. "The Myth of the Child in Wordsworth and Pascoli." Essays in Literature 4(1977): 250-64.

Finds a close correspondence between W's child-figure and the Italian poet's, noting in particular the child's association with nature, its role as fountainhead of poetic power, the "tri-phase" schema of maturation, and the suggestion that there is a sort of salvation in childhood death.

454. Gohn, Jack Benoit. "The Text of Byron's 'Epilogue': A New Line and Some Questions." Notes & Queries 24 (1977): 333-34.

Adds a line to stanza 3 of Byron's parody of the Prologue to "Peter Bell."

455. Gohn, Jack Benoit. "Who Wrote Benjamin the Waggoner? An Inquiry." The Wordsworth Circle 8(1977): 69-74.

A good case for Lockhart's authorship of--or at least for his contribution to--this parody of "Peter Bell."

456. Goldstein, Laurence. Ruins and Empire: The Evolution of a Theme in Augustan and Romantic Literature. Pittsburgh: University of Pittsburgh, 1977. xiv+272 pp. indexed.

Four chapters on W (pp. 114-207) form the heart of this excellent study of ruin, loss, fear, and related themes, which provides an illuminating context for viewing W's turn to conservatism. Goldstein's original readings of several works of the great decade focus on the depth not only of W's anxieties, but also of his strength of affirmation. The final W chapter is a fine discussion of "The Wordsworthian Child."

Reviews: H. Baker, SoR 15(1979), 681; J. Barnard, English 29(1979), 61; W.B. Carnochan, MLQ 39(1978), 193; Robert F. Gleckner, Criticism 20(1978), 336-39; Margery Sabin, SIR 17(1978), 376; Stuart M. Tave, MLR 75(1980), 850; E. Tomarken, GaR 33(1979), 448; Donald Wesling, WC 9(1978), 230-33.

457. Goldstein, Laurence. "Wordsworth and Snyder: the Primitivist and His Problem of Self-Definition." Centennial Review 21(1977): 75-86.

Using W and Snyder as examples, Goldstein argues that the Romantic poet's sense of self and purpose is complicated or threatened by his distrust of language.

458. Griffin, Andrew L. "Wordsworth and the Problem of Imaginative Story: The Case of 'Simon Lee.'" PMLA 92(1977): 392-409.

A sensitive treatment (the fullest to date) of "Simon Lee" as a serious and successful poem, viewing it as elegy and comparing its abandonment of narrative for "silent thought" with the patterns of W's greatest poetry.

459. Hartman, Geoffrey H. "A Touching Compulsion: Wordsworth and the Problem of Literary Representation." Georgia Review 31(1977): 345-61.

A "psychoesthetic" consideration of W's concern with loss and absence (especially of his mother), (1) examining W's touching, seeing, and hearing compulsions as motivated by a wish to reabsorb the mother through nature, and (2) suggesting that the absent person is important (e.g., in the "Lucy Poems") because W distrusts the capacity of writing to "re-present" his losses.

460. Haven, Richard. "Some Perspectives in Three Poems by Gray, Wordsworth, and Duncan." Romantic and Modern (439), pp. 69-88.

Discusses the effect the speaker's relationship to his setting has on the publicity of the poem in Gray's Elegy, W's "Tintern Abbey," and Duncan's "The Fire: Passages 13."

461. Heffernan, Thomas F. "Melville and Wordsworth." American Literature 49(1977), 338-51.

Describes Melville's recently discovered volume of W, recording and commenting on his annotations and markings.

462. Heller, Janet Ruth. "Enjambment as a Metrical Force in Romantic Conversation Poems." Poetics 6(1977): 15-25.

In the context of a more theoretical argument, Heller contrasts W's and C's prosody on the basis of tabular data from three C poems and "Tintern Abbey," lines 1-80.

463. Helms, Randel. "On the Genesis of Wordsworth's Michael." English Language Notes 15(1977): 38-43.

Argues that the Jacob stories in Genesis influenced W's creation of "Michael" from the ballad version.

464. Holland, Patrick. "The Two Contrasts of Wordsworth's 'Westminster Bridge' Sonnet." The Wordsworth Circle 8 (1977): 32-34.

Argues that the city is sublime and beautiful.

465. Holloway, John. The Proud Knowledge: Poetry, Insight, and the Self, 1620-1920. London: Routledge & Kegan Paul, 1977. iv+264 pp. indexed.

Examines various "new ways of constructing a poem" with suggestive brief comment on characterization in "Michael" and The Excursion, book 1 (pp. 82-87); on the 1805 Prelude as quest or Odyssey (pp. 94-102); on ambiv-

alence in the Ode (pp. 182-87); and on "the anti-spectacular" in "The Old Cumberland Beggar" (pp. 213-15).
Review: Brian Martin, N&Q 26(1979), 68-70.

466. Kelley, Erna Emmighausen. "Whitman and Wordsworth: Childhood Experiences and the Future Poet." Walt Whitman Review 23(1977): 59-68.

Compares W's and Whitman's views of the child as having an intuitive sense of "universal unity," especially in The Prelude and "Out of the Cradle Endlessly Rocking."

467. Kelley, Paul. "Rousseau's 'Discourse on the Origins of Inequality' and Wordsworth's 'Salisbury Plain.'" Notes & Queries 24(1977): 323.

Notes verbal echoes in W's opening stanzas.

468. Knoepflmacher, U.C. "Mutations of the Wordsworthian Child of Nature." Nature and the Victorian Imagination (469), pp. 391-425.

An interesting account of how W's child-figure and view of nature were used and abused by the Victorians, especially Arnold, Calverley, Ruskin, Pater, George Eliot, and Dickens. Includes two Victorian illustrations of "We are Seven," also Max Beerbohm's.

469. Knoepflmacher, U.C., and G.B. Tennyson, eds. Nature and the Victorian Imagination. Berkeley: University of California, 1977. xxiii+519 pp. indexed.

Includes 449 and 468, as well as several brief discussions of W's influence and reception among his Victorian successors.

470. Lal, Mohan. "Wordsworth's Concept of Joy." Aligarh Journal of English Studies 2(1977): 11-27.

Notes the religious importance of joy for W, and the relation of W's conception of joy to associationist thinking.

471. Langbaum, Robert. The Mysteries of Identity: A Theme in Modern Literature. New York: Oxford, 1977. x+383 pp. indexed.

The first chapter, part of which appeared in Langbaum's The Modern Spirit (New York: Oxford, 1970), lucidly describes how recognizing unconscious memory and association enabled W to affirm personal identity (a continuous self, or soul) after Locke and Hume; the remainder of the book traces the progress of this solution in Arnold, Eliot, Beckett, Yeats, and Lawrence.

Reviews: Christopher Butler, TLS, 18 Aug. 1978, p. 927; I. Fletcher, VP 17(1979), 278; T. Parkinson, MP 78 (1980), 108; P. Parrinder, JEGP 77(1978), 599; Ronald Schleifer, MLN 93(1978), 1052.

472. Lefebure, Molly. Cumbrian Discovery. London: Victor Gollancz, 1977. 352 pp. indexed.

An unbuttoned walking guide to W's native region with a great deal of information on its history, geological and human, and twenty-one excellent photographs from the late 1800's.

473. Little, Geoffrey. "'Tintern Abbey' and Llyswen Farm." The Wordsworth Circle 8(1977): 80-82.

Suggests that the Wordsworths visited Thelwall on Llyswen farm in May 1798; that, contra Beatty (103) and Reed (81), W's reference to the farm in "Anecdote for Fathers" is real; and (far less convincingly) that the opening lines of "Tintern Abbey" also refer to the farm, which is further up the Wye than is the Abbey.

474. McGavran, James Holt, Jr. "The 'Creative Soul' of The Prelude and the 'Sad Incompetence of Human Speech.'" Studies in Romanticism 16(1977): 35-49.

Raises W's statements on the difficulty of his task (especially in the 1850 Prelude 12:272-86) to special prominence, and argues that the difficulty with human language is itself the poem's "heroic argument."

475. Manning, Peter J. "'Michael,' Luke, and Wordsworth." Criticism 19(1977): 195-211.

A sensitive reading examining W's "self-presentation" in the characters of Michael and especially of Luke.

476. Mazzeno, Laurence W. "Of Fathers, Children, and Poets: Wordsworth's 'Anecdote for Fathers.'" Psycho-Cultural Review 1(1977): 421-33.

A fruitful study of W's revisions, showing how he has improved the poem by making the narrator a more sympathetic father figure. The changes, Mazzeno suggests, reflect an important transformation in W's attitudes toward representatives of paternity. Includes a generous listing of previous criticism (p. 431n).

477. Molesworth, Charles. "Wordsworth's 'Westminster Bridge' Sonnet: The Republican Structure of Time and Perception." Clio 6(1977): 261-73.

Attempts to show the poem's political rhetoric.

478. Morgan, Edwin. "Provenance and Problematics of 'Sublime and Alarming Images' in Poetry." Proceedings of the British Academy 63(1977): 293-313.

Discusses the fate of the sublime in modern poetry, lingering briefly (pp. 295-99) over W's ability to evoke sublimity in confrontations with the forms, not only of nature, but also of human beings.

479. Murthy, S. Laxmana. "Wordsworth's Conception of Poetry." Triveni: Journal of Indian Renaissance 45,iv(1977): 20-28.

A general, unoriginal, and occasionally misleading comment on W's critical statements.

480. Musser, Joseph F., Jr. "William Cowper's Syntax as an Indication of His Relationship to the Augustans and Romantics." Style 11(1977): 284-302.

Contrasts the poets' blank-verse syntax (pp. 294-300), finding Cowper's "modestly subjective," argumentative, and digressive, while W's is "egotistically subjective," meditative, and non-digressive.

481. Nalbantian, Suzanne. _The Symbol of the Soul from Hölderlin to Yeats: A Study in Metonymy_. New York: Columbia, 1977. 151 pp. indexed.

Compares W's poetic use of "soul," especially in the Ode and the Prelude, with that of other poets "to gauge the changing quality of poetic lyricism in the nineteenth century."

Reviews: John Bayley, _TLS_, 17 June 1977, p. 718; W.V. Harris, _GR_ 52(1977), 317; W.K., _RM_, 1977, p. 170; Anthony Thorlby, _N&Q_ 26(1979), 191-92.

482. Owen, W.J.B. "A Shock of Mild Surprise." _The Wordsworth Circle_ 8(1977): 291-305.

Attempts to define a new "poetic mode" of W's by the common effect of several poems--"The Old Cumberland Beggar," "Old Man Travelling," and the discharged-soldier passage of _The Prelude_--on the reader.

483. Owen, W.J.B. "'The Thorn' and the Poet's Intention.'" _The Wordsworth Circle_ 8(1977): 3-17.

A loquacious rehashing of earlier arguments, arguing that the narrator's uncertainty regarding the events of the story is a poeticization of W's uncertainties about why the thorn affected him so strongly, and about how to reproduce its effect. Notes a possible source in ballad (p. 8).

484. Patterson, Charles I., Jr. "The Daemonic in _Peter Bell_." _The Wordsworth Circle_ 8(1977): 139-46.

Finds that W uses classical demons without taking them seriously to create an accurate psychology of Peter's revival, which is effected not by nature but by powers of Peter's own mind.

485. Patterson, Charles I., Jr. "Prophecy and the Prophetic Poet in _The Prelude_." _Southern Humanities Review_ 11(1977): 385-96.

Cites numerous "prophetic" passages to argue (contra Hartman, 143) that _The Prelude_ describes "gradually accruing apocalyptic vision" which the poet does not shy away from as disruptive.

486. Peterfreund, Stuart. "Wordsworth and the Sublime of Duration." _Publications of the Arkansas Philological Association_ 2,ii(1976): 41-46.

Cites the boat-stealing, Simplon Pass, and Snowdon passages of the 1805 _Prelude_ to argue that in the sublime scenes duration grows progressively more important than the suddenness or frightfulness of the sublime object.

487. Peterfreund, Stuart. "Wordsworth, Milton, and the End of Adam's Dream." _Milton and the Romantics_ 3(1977): 14-21.

Studies W's earliest additions to the two-part _Prelude_ to show the development of the _Recluse_ project as emulative of _Paradise Lost_ and _Paradise Regained_, and examines "Home at Grasmere" to argue that W abandoned the project because he was unable to translate Milton's re-achieved paradise into this-worldly terms of process.

488. Pipkin, James W. "The Lucy Poems and Wordsworth's Dream Vision." _Ariel_ 8,iv(1977): 27-41.

Focusing on the speaker's experience rather than Lucy's, interprets his "dream" or "slumber" as a short-lived visionary experience, and sees Lucy's death as a symbol of "the permanence of her imaginative vision" or a sign of grace. Relates this association of death and vision to other poems, especially "Tintern Abbey" and the Ode. Cf. 143, esp. pp. 307-12.

489. Pison, Thomas. "Wordsworth's Autobiography: The Metonymy of Self." _Bucknell Review_ 23,ii(1977): 78-95.

Discusses The Prelude in the light of recent autobiographical theory, and defends the 1850 version as autobiography, arguing that the spots of time in particular make more sense in 1850 than in 1805, having gained in metonymic relationship to their contexts.

490. Pittman, Philip McM. "The Real Language of Men: On Wordsworth and R.S. Thomas." Bulletin of the West Virginia Association of College English Teachers 4,i(1977): 30-42.

Not seen.

491. Pyle, Gerald J., Jr. "J.H. Reynolds's 'Peter Bell.'" Notes & Queries 24(1977): 323-24.

Traces Reynolds's "Here lieth W.W. / Who never more will trouble you, trouble you" to a Literary Gazette letter of 1817.

492. Randel, Fred V. "Wordsworth's Homecoming." Studies in English Literature, 1500-1900 17(1977): 575-91.

Examines patterns of wandering and home-coming in poems written up to 1799, when W settled with Dorothy at Grasmere, seeing "Home at Grasmere" (which was written later, and is not treated at length) as culminating this "spatial configuration of Wordsworth's poetry." Touches on "Descriptive Sketches," the "Salisbury Plain" poems, "Peter Bell," "The Brothers," "Michael," and others.

493. Ray, Laura Krugman. "Kenneth Grahame and the Literature of Childhood." English Language in Transition 20 (1977), 3-12.

Traces the influence of W's and Dickens' child-figures on The Golden Age (1895), by the author of The Wind in the Willows.

494. Roazen, Deborah H. "Middlemarch and the Wordsworthian Imagination." English Studies 58(1977): 411-25.

Notes that Middlemarch, though less pastoral and humble than Eliot's previous novels, still shares W's "concern with basic aesthetic and moral issues" and "ordinary experience"; but suggests that critics think more in terms of affinity, less of influence.

495. Robinson, Jeffrey C. "The Structure of Wordsworth's Memorials of a Tour in Scotland, 1803." Papers on Language and Literature 13(1977): 54-70.

Compares the Memorials to The Prelude as a spiritual journey beginning in doubts about vocation and leading toward imaginative freedom. Discusses all the poems briefly, focusing especially on the frequent female figures, which are seen as forms of Dorothy.

496. Schleifer, Ronald. "Wordsworth's Yarrow and the Poetics of Repetition." Modern Language Quarterly 38(1977): 348-66.

Examines the Yarrow poems in terms of Kierkegaard's concept of repetition, arguing that by repeating himself within the poems and from poem to poem the poet manages, as in The Prelude, "continually to become what he always is." Also treats W's use of Scottish ballads.

497. Schneidau, Herbert N. "Pound and Wordsworth on Poetry and Prose." Romantic and Modern (439), pp. 133-45.

A suggestive essay comparing the poets' views on poetry and prose, relating them to Jakobson's distinction between metaphor and metonymy, and making an interesting though tenuous connection between poetry and aphasia (the "fear that kills" in "Resolution and Independence" being seen as the "fear of losing the power of speech").

498. Sharp, Steven E. "The Unmerited Contempt of Reviewers: Wordsworth's Response to Contemporary Reviews of Descriptive Sketches." The Wordsworth Circle 8(1977): 25-31.

Points out that reviewers misrepresented Descriptive Sketches by neglecting its politics (see also 595), and suggests that W's dislike of reviews may originate here.

499. Smyser, Jane Worthington. "'An eye to perceive and a heart to rejoice': An Essay on Wordsworth." _The Wordsworth Circle_ 8(1977): 35-37. Rpt. as "Wordsworth and Nature: Two Notes," in _Symposium on Romanticism: An Interdisciplinary Meeting_, Ed. Pierre Deguise and Rita Terras. New London: Connecticut College, 1977, pp. 63-68.

Posthumous essay, first read at Connecticut College, pointing out that if W did not teach us to look at mountains, his subjective perception of them was original.

500. Solomon, Gerald. "Wordsworth and 'the Art of Lying.'" _Essays in Criticism_ 27(1977): 141-56.

Traces W's "fantasies" of "Life-in-Death" from the excised passage of the Ode to his own seclusion in Grasmere, and attributes them to the poet's refusal to accept his mother's death. Dwells at length on "It is a beauteous evening..." and more briefly on other poems, often with startling comments (e.g., Solomon sees _W_ as learning "the art of lying" in "We are Seven" and "Anecdote for Fathers"), which are neatly answered by Sturrock (606).

501. Spector, Stephen J. "Wordsworth's Mirror Imagery and the Picturesque Tradition." _ELH_ 44(1977): 85-107.

A good demonstration how W uses and avoids traditional ways of seeing, including not only the picturesque tradition, but also those of Christian iconography and the Narcissus myth. Examines "There was a boy," _The Prelude_, books 1 and 4, _The Excursion_, book 9, "Home at Grasmere," and the _Guide to the Lakes_.

502. Stavros, George. "Oscar Wilde on the Romantics." _English Literature in Transition_ 20(1977): 35-45.

Wilde's coming to terms with W as an ethical poet is central to this discussion.

503. Stevens, Bonnie Klomp. "Biblical Allusion in _Peter Bell_: The Story of Balaam's Ass." _English Language Notes_ 14(1977): 275-78.

Notes the parallel with the story of Balaam in Numbers, of which "'Peter Bell' could almost be interpreted as a parody."

504. Stevenson, John W. "Seeing is Believing: Wordsworth's Modern Vision." Virginia Quarterly Review 53(1977): 86-97.

An overly generalized meditation on W as the precursor of modern "poetry of being" (as opposed to that of non-being).

505. Sturrock, J. "Wordsworth and Vaughan." Notes & Queries 24(1977): 322-23.

Argues that as late as 1814 W did not know Vaughan.

506. Swingle, L.J. "Wordsworth's Contrarieties: A Prelude to Wordsworthian Complexity." ELH 44(1977): 337-54.

Blaming apparent contradictions in W's beliefs for recent critical difficulties, and rejecting the solutions posed by Hartman (143) and Grob (193), argues that the contrarieties, especially within single poems, are elements in dramatic strategies by which W seeks to educate his reader. Comments on "A Night-Piece" and "To My Sister."

507. Tetreault, Ronald. "Wordsworth on Enthusiasm: A New Letter to Thomas Clarkson on the Slavery Question." Modern Philology 75(1977): 53-58.

Prints a letter of 20 March 1824, not in the standard edition (39), including W's "dour and unyielding" response to Clarkson's request for aid in his campaign against slavery, and a post-script from Dorothy to Catherine Clarkson. Explains W's refusal by contrasting Clarkson's "extreme zeal" in the cause with W's ideal of "patient faith."

508. Trotter, David. "Hidden Ground Within: Matthew Arnold's Lyric and Elegiac Poetry." ELH 44(1977): 526-53.

Contains an apt contrast of Arnold and W (pp. 534 ff.), especially in their use of wanderer or beggar figures, finding less risk, and less recognition, in the poetry of Arnold.

509. Watson, J.R. "Lucy and the Earth-Mother." _Essays in Criticism_ 27(1977): 187-202. Rpt. in _Wordsworth's Vital Soul_ (928), ch. 9.

Argues that the "Lucy Poems," like "There was a Boy," derive their power from reference to the "_terra genetrix_" myth, which as described by Eliade involves "the great desire...to be interred in the native soil."

510. Wedd, Mary R. "Dialects of Humour: Lamb and Wordsworth." _Charles Lamb Bulletin_ 19(1977): 46-54.

Examines Lamb's and W's use of humor as "a way of dealing with the unbearable," noting that (as in "Simon Lee") it is not always successful.

511. Weldon, Roberta F. "Hawthorne's Old Apple-Dealer and Wordsworth's Leechgatherer." _Nathaniel Hawthorne Journal_, 1977, pp. 249-59.

A comparison-contrast essay arguing the influence of "Resolution and Independence"--not terribly convincing, and the less fruitful for its simplistic view of W.

512. Wordsworth, Jonathan. "The Five-Book _Prelude_ of Early Spring 1804." _Journal of English and Germanic Philology_ 76(1977): 1-25.

A detailed and complex attempt at reconstructing the version which W decided to expand _ca._ 10 March 1804, including descriptions of the manuscripts. Notes that both W's need to include "external events, social and political," and his wish to put off _The Recluse_, influenced the decision to expand the poem. For a briefer exposition of the structure of the five-book version, see Jonathan Wordsworth's note in the Norton _Prelude_ (17, pp. 516-17). For a different view, see 818.

1978

513. Allaback, Steven, and Alexander Medlicott, Jr. "A Visit with Wordsworth: From the Unpublished Journals of Anna Eliot Ticknor." The Wordsworth Circle 9(1978): 88-91.

From an 1835 visit.

514. Armstrong, Isobel. "'Tintern Abbey': from Augustan to Romantic." In Augustan Worlds, ed. J.C. Hilson et al. Leicester: Leicester University, 1978, pp. 261-79.

Minute, sensitive analysis of the poem's strange use of language, especially prepositions, comparatives, and participles, in the opening lines and the two "supreme moments of mystical experience" (lines 23-49 and 93-102), showing how in each successive passage this "self-transforming" poem enriches the language of the former. For a similar analysis including The Prelude, see 141, ch. 2.

515. Averill, James H. "Wordsworth and 'Natural Science': The Poetry of 1798." Journal of English and Germanic Philology 77(1978): 232-46. Rpt. in Wordsworth and the Poetry of Human Suffering (704), ch. 5.

A fascinating account of W's brief flirtation with science in 1798, largely under C's influence. Argues that W read in Erasmus Darwin's Zoonomia to prepare for The Recluse, but channeled most of his discoveries into Lyrical Ballads, and in poems such as "The Tables Turned" expressed disillusion with Darwin.

516. Baugh, Edward. "The Poem as Autobiographical Novel: Derek Walcott's 'Another Life' in Relation to Wordsworth's 'Prelude' and Joyce's 'Portrait.'" In Awakened Conscience: Studies in Commonwealth Literature, ed. C.D. Narasimhaiah. New Delhi: Sterling, 1978, pp. 226-35.

Compares the West Indian writer's autobiographical poem with W's, speaking more in terms of similarity than of influence. Not helpful on W specifically.

517. Beer, John. Wordsworth and the Human Heart. New York: Columbia, 1978. xx+277 pp. indexed.

Noting eighteenth-century associations with "heart," e.g., Harvey and the cult of sensibility, Beer calls attention to W's precise use of the term in order to define and trace the development of his "humanitarianism," in which C and Dorothy figure largely. Sees the first visit to Tintern Abbey as a major turning point in W's life, and reads the 1798 Lyrical Ballads as a unified work. A fine personality study, helping to explain W's odd position between the various "contrarieties" of passion and sobriety, feeling and thought, society and solitude. Frequently helpful also on his relation to eighteenth-century intellectual currents.

Reviews: James H. Averill, WC 11(1980), 130-32; Michael Baron, English 28(1979), 259-66; G.D. Crossan, AUMLA 53(1980), 79-80; Stephen Gill, TLS, 21 Dec. 1979, p. 166; Bishop C. Hunt, RM, 1979, pp. 125-26; Victoria Longino, N&Q 27(1980), 252; Lucy Newlyn, RES 32(1981), 227-31; D.P., CritQ 21 (1979), 92; Mary Wedd, ChLB 27 (1979), 55-59; Carl Woodring, SAQ 79(1980), 225-26.

518. Bialostosky, Don H. "Coleridge's Interpretation of Wordsworth's Preface to Lyrical Ballads." PMLA 93 (1978): 912-24.

Argues cogently that the Preface has been distorted by our Coleridgean spectacles, clarifying in particular W's comparison of prose and poetry and, with reference to Hartley's distinction between real and nominal language, W's phrase "the language really used by men." See also the exchange with Robert Sternbach, W.J.B. Owen, and Nathaniel Teich in PMLA 94(1979): 326-27, 479-82.

519. Bone, J. Drummond. "Byron's Ravenna Diary Entry: What is Poetry?" Byron Journal 6(1978), 78-89.

Contrasts Byron's poetic with W's and Shelley's, arguing that Byron accepts rather than seeking to transcend temporal process.

520. Borck, Jim Springer. "'The Bitter Language of the Heart' in Wordsworth's The Excursion." The Wordsworth Circle 9 (1978): 182-87.

Argues that the "language of complaint" in The Excursion, especially book 1, focuses on social disconnections and broken links, and that the "language of consolation" (especially the orthodox brand) fails to fix these breaks, or, in short, to console.

521. Brisman, Leslie. Romantic Origins. Ithaca, NY: Cornell, 1978. 410 pp. indexed.

A wide-ranging, difficult deconstructionist study of Romantic myths of origins, which are seen as "forms of exuberance," either "accomodations with the past" or "reworkings of stories of loss into abundant recompense." The long chapter on W and most of the conclusion deal chiefly with The Prelude, analyzing six "revisionary ratios" by which Wordsworthian memory transforms the revisable past to find in it the origins of poetic power which can renovate the present. Frequently discusses W's revisions of his own myths of origins between the 1805 and 1850 Prelude.

Reviews: C. Bond, QQ 88(1981), 777; Stephen Gill, TLS, 21 Dec. 1979, p. 166; Robert F. Gleckner, SAQ 79(1980), 116; Daniel Hughes, SIR 18(1979), 316-22; Donald Reiman, KSJ 28(1979), 161-64; Mark Roberts, RES 30(1979), 478; Paul Sherwin, WC 11(1980), 137-40; L.J. Swingle, JEGP 78 (1979), 139; Stuart M. Tave, YES 11(1981), 290; George Woodcock, SR 88(1981), 298.

522. Bump, Jerome. "Science, Religion, and Personification in Poetry." Cahiers Victoriens et Edouardiens 7(1978): 123-37.

Tracing a decline in the poetic personification of nature in poems by Marvell, W, Arnold, Hopkins, Frost, and Stevens, Bump briefly discusses "Lines Written in Early Spring" and argues that even W is affected by the modern "pseudoscientific" distrust of this trope.

523. Butler, Colin. "Margaret Drabble: The Millstone and Wordsworth." English Studies 59(1978): 353-60.

Finds Drabble's 1966 introductory study of W wanting in precision and "social dimension," and compares its concerns and shortcomings with those of her 1965 novel.

524. Byrd, Max. London Transformed: Images of the City in the Eighteenth Century. New Haven, CT: Yale, 1978. x+202 pp. indexed.

Has a fine chapter on W's treatment of London, chiefly in the 1850 Prelude, book 7, discussing, with frequent comparison to Pope's Dunciad, motifs of theatrical illusion, clothing, and language, and arguing that W attempted to adapt to the city his "habitual approach to nature." More briefly discusses the city in The Excursion, book 2, and "St. Paul's" (pp. 149-56).

Reviews: J. Barnard, English 28(1979), 61; P.G. Bouce, EA 32(1979), 476; James T. Boulton, DUJ 73(1980), 114-16; Gregory Colomb, MP 78(1981), 321-24; D.J. Olsen, ECS 12(1978-79), 212; A. Parreaux, MLR 75(1980), 851; Pat Rogers, TLS, 23 June 1978, p. 689; J. Stedmond, QQ 86 (1979), 476.

525. Cohen, Philip. "Narrative and Persuasion in The Ruined Cottage." Journal of Narrative Technique 8(1978): 185-99.

Finds "The Ruined Cottage" less persuasive than book 1 of The Excursion since the former version, by omitting the history of the Wanderer, fails to "earn" its philosophical conclusion.

526. Durrant, Geoffrey. "The Elegiac Poetry of The Excursion." The Wordsworth Circle 9(1978): 155-61.

Shows how, in The Excursion, books 5, 6, and 7, tree and plant imagery and the figure of the wood-cutter work to reconfirm the explicit Christian argument about death.

527. Duthie, Elizabeth. "A Fresh Comparison of 'The Idiot Boy' and 'The Idiot.'" Notes & Queries 25(1978): 219-20.

Argues that Southey's "The Idiot" evokes condescending pity in keeping with the eighteenth-century cult of sensibility, while W's poem frustrates such conventional response.

528. Erdman, David V. "Wordsworth as Heartsworth; or, Was Regicide the Prophetic Ground of Those 'Moral Questions'?" _The Evidence of the Imagination_ (592), pp. 12-41.

A highly conjectural essay drawing parallels between W's biography and the stories of Marmaduke, Vaudracour, and _The Excursion_'s Solitary to claim "confirmative evidence" that W visited France in October, 1793.

529. Fadem, Richard. "Dorothy Wordsworth: A View from 'Tintern Abbey.'" _The Wordsworth Circle_ 9(1978): 17-32.

A vigorous rethinking of Dorothy's character along De Quincey's lines (see 91): Fadem sees Dorothy as "wild" (W's term), childlike, immersed in sensory data, either failing or refusing to become an adult, thinking being, and discusses her role as a symbol of W's childhood in _The Prelude_ and "Tintern Abbey."

530. Foakes, R.A. "'The Power of Prospect': Wordsworth's Visionary Poetry." In _The Author in His Work: Essays on a Problem in Criticism_, ed. Louis L. Martz & Aubrey Williams. New Haven, CT: Yale, 1978, pp. 123-41.

Argues against Hartman's description of W's imagination as "consciousness of self raised to apocalyptic pitch" (143) by showing that no generalization can cover "the variety of versions of vision recorded in the poems": Foakes reads the sonnets "Composed after a Journey across the Hambleton Hills" and its sequel to argue that the only constant in W's visionary experience is that the mind must be "engaged," which is not to deny the external world.

531. Friedman, Michael H. "The Princely and the Contracted Wordsworth: A Study of Wordsworth's Personality in Terms of Psychoanalytic Ego Psychology." _The Wordsworth Circle_ 9(1978): 406-12.

Analyzes W's ego in terms of "two opposite senses of self" and traces their genesis, chiefly in The Prelude, books 1-3, to the poet's psychic relationships with his mother and father.

532. Fry, Paul H. "The Absent Dead: Wordsworth, Byron, and the Epitaph." Studies in Romanticism 17(1978): 413-33.

Examining The Excursion, books 5-7, "Essays upon Epitaphs," and Byron's Childe Harold's Pilgrimage, Cantos 3-4, Fry contrasts W's epitaphic poetry, which links and mediates between living and dead, with Byron's, which emphasizes the distance between life and death, and comments in closing on the epitaph as an "assault on the sublime."

533. Gates, Barbara T. "Providential History and The Excursion." The Wordsworth Circle 9(1978): 178-81.

Finds that in The Excursion and later poems, W viewed history as providential, yet did not exclude free will.

534. Gaull, Marilyn, ed. The Wordsworth Circle 9(Autumn, 1978): 321-88.

A special issue including 31 scholars' and teachers' suggestions for teaching W, especially The Prelude. A few of these are listed separately here.

535. Gordon, Robert C. "Wordsworth and the Domestic Roots of Power." Bulletin of Research in the Humanities 81 (1978): 90-102.

Notes W's association of domestic virtue with military power in "I grieved for Buonaparte" and the Cintra pamphlet, relates this association to the tradition of eighteenth-century support for militias, and finds military undertones in poems such as "Michael" where domesticity is an issue.

536. Griffin, John. "John Keble and The Quarterly Review." Review of English Studies 29(1978): 452-56.

Attributes an 1816 review of "Wordsworth's *White Doe*" (and other works by others) to Keble, and argues that it must limit our ideas of W's influence on Keble, since much of it is "almost abusive."

537. Guest, Jenny. "Wordsworth and the Music of Humanity." *Critical Review* 20(1978): 15-30.

Argues that in varying degrees W ignores or turns away from human misery in "The Old Cumberland Beggar," *The Prelude*'s discharged-soldier episode (book 4), and *The Excursion*, book 1, though he confronts it squarely in "Michael."

538. Harris, Mason. "Arthur's Misuse of the Imagination: Sentimental Benevolence and Wordsworthian Realism in *Adam Bede*." *English Studies in Canada* 4(1978): 41-59.

Discusses Eliot's use of W, especially in making Arthur's literary taste (he calls *Lyrical Ballads* "twaddle") a cause and index of his depravity.

539. Hartman, Geoffrey H. "Blessing the Torrent: On Wordsworth's Later Style." *PMLA* 93(1978): 196-204.

Focuses on W's use of allusion and on the "elemental speech-acts of wishing, blessing, naming" in the sonnet "To the Torrent at the Devil's Bridge, North Wales, 1824," and argues that imagination is the addressee. Precipitates an exchange with Spencer Hall on Hartman's later style in *PMLA* 94(1979): 139-41.

540. Harwell, Thomas Meade. "Wordsworth and Keats: Empiricists." *Publications of the Arkansas Philological Association* 4,ii(1978): 26-36.

Not seen.

541. Heffernan, James A.W. "Reflections on Reflections in English Romantic Poetry and Painting." *Bucknell Review* 24,ii(1978): 15-37.

Paying most attention to W and Turner, shows that the Romantics, unlike their predecessors, often viewed reflections as superior to the reality.

542. Heffernan, James A.W. "The English Romantic Perception of Color." Images of Romanticism (561), 133-48.

Argues that W, C, Constable, and especially Turner share a vision of color opposed to "the Augustan principle that colors must be absolutely distinct," and depending on what W called "creation in the eye."

543. Helsinger, Elizabeth K. "Ruskin on Wordsworth: The Victorian Critic in Romantic Country." Studies in Romanticism 17(1978): 267-91.

Accounts for the increasing severity in Ruskin's assessments of W in Modern Painters, Vols. 1-3 (1843-56), which range from praise for the descriptive poetry to attack for expressionism and infidelity to visual truth, by clearly contrasting the men's epistemologies and by placing Ruskin's comments in the context of his shift from aesthetic arguments to historical and political concerns.

544. Hepworth, Brian. The Rise of Romanticism: Essential Texts. Manchester: Carcanet, 1978. vii+363 pp. not indexed.

Anthology of selections with commentary, including selections from The Excursion, books 2 and 4; Hepworth calls the poem "the most mature statement of Romantic poetic principle."

545. Herman, Judith B. "The Poet as Editor: Wordsworth's Edition of 1815." The Wordsworth Circle 9(1978): 82-87.

Treats W's classification of his poems as an editor's strategy to call attention to neglected or abused poems, examining the "Affections" and "Fancy" categories in particular. Finds the grouping "Poems of the Fancy" a "devaluation of them." Ruoff's adjacent article (594) offers an opposing view.

546. Hertz, Neil. "The Notion of Blockage in Literature of the Sublime." In Psychoanalysis and the Question of the Text, ed. Geoffrey Hartman. Baltimore, MD: Johns Hopkins, 1978, pp. 62-85.

Playfully examines a text by Thomas McFarland as a modern instance of what Kant calls the "mathematical sublime," and compares it (pp. 79-84) with both versions of The Prelude, book 7.

547. Hill, Alan G. "Wordsworth and His American Friends." Bulletin of Research in the Humanities 81(1978): 146-60.

Discusses W's views on America, presenting a sympathetic picture of the poet in his old age, and includes a helpful "select list" identifying "Wordsworth's American visitors and contacts" from 1812 to 1849.

548. Hill, James L. "The Function of the Poem in Keats's 'Ode on a Grecian Urn' and Wordsworth's 'Resolution and Independence.'" Centennial Review 22(1978): 424-44.

Contrasts the ways the poets impose order on their worlds, noting how in "Resolution and Independence" the poet struggles against the leech-gatherer's specificity and historicity in order to use him as image or symbol.

549. Holloway, Marcella M. "Hopkins' Defense of Wordsworth's Great Ode." Hopkins Quarterly 5(1978): 69-74.

Quotes Hopkins' defense, from a letter of 1886, as well as other comments on W, but does not add much to them.

550. Hugo, F.J. "Unity of Mind and the Antagonist Thought of Death in Wordsworth's Poetry." Theoria 51(1978): 15-23.

Examines W's portrayals of the recognition of death in several poems ranging from "Strange fits of passion have I known," where the recognition entails "loss of youthful unity of mind," to "Yew-Trees," in which "unity of mind" is reachieved. Briefly discusses "We are Seven," "A slumber did my spirit seal," and "Lucy Gray."

551. Jackson, Wallace. *The Probable and the Marvelous: Blake, Wordsworth, and the Eighteenth-Century Critical Tradition*. Athens: University of Georgia, 1978. 218 pp.

An informative study placing Blake and W in the context of a mid-eighteenth-century poetic of the marvelous, which they validate, argues Jackson, by grounding the marvelous in the probable and everyday life. The concluding chapter on W (incorporating Jackson's essay, 324) includes acute stylistic analysis contrasting W's treatment of emotion with that by earlier poets, and argues that Blake and W rescue the marvelous by resurrecting and internalizing Milton's theme of the fortunate fall; Jackson sees the lyrics of *Poems in Two Volumes* (1807) as songs of innocence and experience.
Reviews: Jacques Blondel, *EA* 33(1980), 215; P.M.S. Dawson, *RES* 31(1980), 112; William Edinger, *MP* 78(1980), 189-91; Laurence Goldstein, *WC* 10(1979), 256-58; Stuart M. Tave, *YES* 11(1981), 290; Joseph Wittreich, *MLQ* 40 (1979), 312.

552. Jaye, Michael C. "The Artifice of Disjunction: Book 5, *The Prelude*." *Papers on Language and Literature* 14 (1978): 32-50.

Examining the development of the 1805 *Prelude*'s book 5 from previous drafts, and arguing, for example, that the added conclusions to the drowned-man and the boy-of-Winander passages fail to assimilate them to the theme of "books," Jaye finds book 5 ununified and transitional, but denies that unity is a valid criterion of its worth.

553. Jaye, Michael C. "William Wordsworth's Alfoxdon Notebook: 1798." *The Evidence of the Imagination* (592), 42-85.

Follows the evolution of W's poetics, especially his "mode of self-apprehension," in the drafts and revisions of 1798.

554. Johnston, Kenneth R. "Wordsworth's Reckless Recluse: The Solitary." *The Wordsworth Circle* 9(1978): 131-44.

Considers the contrast between "public" and "private imagination"--i.e., between the shameless orthodoxy of some passages and the visionary character of others--in _The Excursion_, book 4.

555. Jones, Stanley. "Regency Newspaper Verse: An Anonymous Squib on Wordsworth." _Keats-Shelley Journal_ 27(1978): 87-107.

Counters Kinnaird's attribution of an 1813 satire (202) with a strong case for Moore's authorship, much of which rests on a well informed and interestingly seedy picture of Moore's activities in the period.

556. Joy, Neill R. "Two Possible Analogues for 'The Ponds' in _Walden_: Jonathan Carver and Wordsworth." _Esquire: A Journal of the American Renaissance_ 24(1978): 197-205.

Compares W's _Guide to the Lakes_.

557. Juhl, P.D. "The Appeal to the Text: What Are We Appealing To?" _Journal of Aesthetics and Art Criticism_ 36/37(1978): 277-87. Rpt. in _Interpretation: An Essay in the Philosophy of Literary Criticism_. Princeton, NJ: Princeton, 1980, pp. 66-89.

Argues elaborately, using "A slumber did my spirit seal" as a test case (but shedding little light on this poem specifically), that what critics often regard as an appeal to the text is a tacit appeal to the author's probable intention. See also 840.

558. Katz, Marilyn. "Early Dissent Between Wordsworth and Coleridge: Preface Deletion of October, 1800." _The Wordsworth Circle_ 9(1978): 50-56.

Argues from evidence in letters, Dorothy's Journal, and the Preface itself that W's and C's theoretical differences about the appropriate objects of poetry go back to 1800, and are responsible for the exclusion of "Christabel" from _Lyrical Ballads_. Essentially, what C viewed as "experiment," W seems to have taken as "a cardinal principle."

559. Ketcham, Carl H. "Dorothy Wordsworth's Journals, 1824-1835." The Wordsworth Circle 9(1978): 3-16.

Ketcham, who has been preparing the manuscripts of the later journals at Dove Cottage for publication, surveys them for information about the Wordsworths, their friends, visitors, and movements, and especially about Dorothy herself. An appendix (pp. 11-13) offers a table of dates from the journals.

560. Kissane, James. "'Michael,' 'Christabel,' and the Lyrical Ballads of 1800." The Wordsworth Circle 9(1978): 57-63.

Argues that "Christabel" was excluded because it was incomplete (not too long, or too different, as the poets have it); that "Michael," which replaced it, inspired by an image of incompletion, is both "reproach and memorial" to C's unfinished effort; and that the Ballad-Michael was a diversion, not a first draft.

561. Kroeber, Karl, and William Walling, eds. Images of Romanticism: Verbal and Visual Affinities. New Haven, CT: Yale, 1978. xv+288 pp. indexed.

Twelve articles comparing Romantic poetry and painting, including three for Wordsworthians (542, 605, and 608).
Reviews: Carl Dawson, KSJ 29(1980), 225-26; K.M. Heleniak, WC 11(1980), 162; G.P. Landow, JEGP 79(1980), 574; W.J.T. Mitchell, Criticism 21(1979), 376; Stephen Prickett, BJA 20(1980), 77; R.L. Wilson, JAAC 38(1979), 219.

562. Lane, M. Travis. "A Different 'Growth of a Poet's Mind': Derek Walcott's Another Life." Ariel 9,iv(1978): 65-78.

Compares Walcott's poem with The Prelude. See also 516.

563. Langman, F.H. "Two Wordsworth Poems." Southern Review (Adelaide) 11(1978): 247-64.

Emphasizes supernatural possibilities in "Poor Susan" (with the cancelled fifth stanza) and "To Joanna," and warns against psychological explanations which may result in "under-reading" W.

564. Lea, Sydney. "Wordsworth and His 'Michael': The Pastor Passes." ELH 45(1978): 55-68.

Relates the poem's theme of inheritance to W's anxiety, expressed in the opening lines, about transmitting a renewed pastoral tradition to "poets who...will be my second self."

565. Levin, Susan, and Robert Ready. "Unpublished Poems from Dorothy Wordsworth's Commonplace Book." The Wordsworth Circle 9(1978): 33-44.

Presents six poems and notes borrowings from W.

566. McGavran, James Holt, Jr. "The 'Home-Amusements' Scene in The Prelude and the Speaker's 'Residences.'" English Language Notes 6(1978): 94-103.

Compares W's card game in book 1 (1850 version) with Pope's in "The Rape of the Lock," and argues that the technique and tone of this scene are typical of The Prelude in providing a "confrontation of the visionary with the ordinary." See also 357.

567. McInerney, Peter F. "Natural Wisdom in Wordsworth's The Excursion." The Wordsworth Circle 9(1978): 188-99.

Attempts to explain the naturalistic logic of the poem, as well as its pious 1845 conclusion, by analyzing the Wanderer's ability to read the book of nature from a deconstructionist point of view.

568. McKie, Michael. "Shelley, Wordsworth, and the Language of Dissent." Essays in Criticism 28(1978): 184-86.

Commenting on Richard Cronin's essay, "Shelley's Language of Dissent" (EIC 27[1977]: 203-215), McKie cites W's "Essays upon Epitaphs" to show that while "the relation of thought to expression" was not a problem for Shelley, it was for W.

569. Magnuson, Paul. "Wordsworth and Spontaneity." The Evidence of the Imagination (592), pp. 101-18.

A valuable commentary on W's Preface to Lyrical Ballads, finding that poetry is "spontaneous" (i.e., "free" or "voluntary," not "unpremeditated") for W because in writing "Tintern Abbey" and early drafts of The Prelude he recognized a happy imperfection in memory, the emotion contemplated being essentially different from that produced in the act of contemplation and composition. Tentatively traces W's distinction between these emotions to John Dennis's distinctions between vulgar and enthusiastic passion.

570. Manning, Peter J. "'My former thoughts returned': Wordsworth's Resolution and Independence." The Wordsworth Circle 9(1978): 398-405.

Reads the poem for the speaker's evasion of responsibility and maturity, paying special attention to W's delay in writing it, and connecting it with "A narrow girdle of rough stones and crags."

571. Matlak, Richard E. "The Men in Wordsworth's Life." The Wordsworth Circle 9(1978): 391-97.

Reads poems from the Goslar period--especially the Matthew poems and the father's-death passage in The Prelude--in the light of W's repeated loss of male friends in his early years, and his anxiety over losing C's friendship.

572. Matlak, Richard E. "Wordsworth's Lucy Poems in Psychobiographical Context." PMLA 93(1978): 46-65.

An interesting essay agreeing with Bateson (126) that in the "Lucy Poems" W poetically kills Dorothy off, except that his motive is not incestuous passion but ambivalence: W loves Dorothy, but would rather be with C. Includes often powerful readings of all five poems as "expressions of ambivalence," taking early drafts into consideration.

573. Metzger, Lore. "Coleridge in Sicily: A Pastoral Interlude in The Prelude." Genre 11(1978): 63-81.

Discusses W's use of pastoral in the strict sense of the word, arguing, for instance, that The Prelude (1805 version) is not pastoral except in parts. One such part, the close of book 10, is examined closely for its use of pastoral topoi and allusion to Theocritus.

574. Milstead, John, and Carl Woodring. "Clarifying Wordsworthian Nature." PMLA 93(1978): 121-22.

Letters to the editor, occasioned by Woodring's "Nature and Art in the Nineteenth Century" (PMLA 92[1977]: 193-202), discussing W's humanitarianism.

575. Newmeyer, Edna. "Wordsworth on Milton and the Devil's Party." Milton Studies 11(1978): 83-98.

Pointing out that the Wordsworthian villain, especially Napoleon in the Cintra pamphlet and Robespierre in The Prelude, is lineally descended from Milton's Satan, Newmeyer argues that among all the Romantics C and W "never mistook Satan for the hero of Milton's poem."

576. Pack, Robert. "William Wordsworth and the Voice of Silence." New England Review 1(1978): 172-90.

Reflects on the importance of memory, solitude, and silence in several poems, chiefly "Tintern Abbey" and The Prelude; not a scholarly, original, or very well focused essay.

577. Parrill, Anna Sue. "Romantic Songbirds." Innisfree, 1978, pp. 44-58.

Not seen. Reportedly deals with W, Shelley, and Keats.

578. Pathak, R.S. "The Genesis and Nature of Wordsworth's 'Crisis.'" Punjab University Research Bulletin (Arts) 9(1978): 41-52.

Surveys a great number of explanations for W's decline in poetic power, but does not add anything new.

579. Patterson, Annabel. "Wordsworth's Georgic: Genre and Structure in _The Excursion_." _The Wordsworth Circle_ 9 (1978): 145-54.

Shows clearly and helpfully how _The Excursion_ adapts the topics of georgic: labor, country life, seclusion, patriotism, and education.

580. Pattison, Robert. _The Child Figure in English Literature_. Athens: University of Georgia, 1978. xi+190 pp. indexed.

Briefly (pp. 54-64) argues that, especially in the Ode, W comes close to Rousseau's "Pelagian" view of childhood innocence.

Review: David V. Erdman, _RM_, 1978, p. 55.

581. Payne, Richard. "'The Style and Spirit of the Elder Poets': The _Ancient Mariner_ and English Literary Tradition." _Modern Philology_ 75(1978): 368-84.

Argues that C's use of ancient models was parallel with W's use of more recent ones in attempting to achieve "simplicity and directness of diction," and that C's revisions were artful, "not merely a concession to W's humor." Payne also remarks that placing C's poem first in the 1798 _Lyrical Ballads_ gave the volume a structure strikingly similar to that of Percy's _Reliques of Ancient English Poetry_.

582. Peterfreund, Stuart. "'In Free Homage and Generous Subjection': Miltonic Influence on _The Excursion_." _The Wordsworth Circle_ 9(1978): 173-77.

Points to parallels between W's Wanderer and Priest, and Milton's Michael and Raphael.

583. Peterfreund, Stuart. "Structural Anthropology and the Teaching of Wordsworth." _The Wordsworth Circle_ 9 (1978): 388-90.

Suggests ways to use Levi-Strauss's studies of myth in W studies.

584. Pipkin, James W. "Wordsworth's 'Immortality Ode' and the Myth of the Fall." Renascence 30(1978): 91-98.

Discusses the Ode as W's naturalized vision of the Fall, and argues that for W this Fall is not to be described as "fortunate."

585. Pipkin, James W. "Wordsworth's 'Nutting' and Rites of Initiation." Interpretations 10(1978): 11-19.

Draws on the work of Mircea Eliade and Joseph Campbell to argue that W's poem dramatizes his initiation into a sacred view of nature.

586. Poston, Lawrence. "Wordsworth Among the Victorians: The Case of Sir Henry Taylor." Studies in Romanticism 17 (1978): 293-305.

A rather plodding and unfocused survey of the work of the minor poet, who was "Wordsworth's chief publicist in the 1830's and '40's," showing that he admired the subdued and rational rather than the mystical and imaginative aspects of W, and contrasting his Wordsworthianism with that of Aubrey De Vere.

587. Proffitt, Edward. "Romanticism, Bicamerality, and the Evolution of the Brain." The Wordsworth Circle 9 (1978): 98-105.

Attempts to relate W and C to the thesis of Julian Jaynes's The Origin of Consciousness in the Breakdown of the Bicameral Mind (1977).

588. Proffitt, Edward. "The Epic Lyric: The Long Poem in the Twentieth Century." Research Studies 46(1978): 20-27.

Argues that because of its "lyric structure" and the poet's concern with self-creation, The Prelude is "the archetypal long poem" of the modern period.

589. Ramsey, Jonathan. "The Prelusive Sounds of 'Descriptive Sketches.'" Criticism 20(1978): 31-42.

Discusses W's treatment of sound and silence in "Descriptive Sketches," and sees the more active perception and visionary silences of the later poetry as a continuous development from W's early practice.

590. Reed, Arden. "Abysmal Influence: Baudelaire, Coleridge, De Quincey, Piranesi, Wordsworth." Glyph 4(1978): 188-206.

A cryptic essay noting the association of imaginative vision with death in The Excursion, 2:834-77, a passage quoted by De Quincey, and contrasting W's control of visionary power with C's and De Quincey's subjection to it (pp. 198-201).

591. Reiman, Donald H. "Poetry of Familiarity: Wordsworth, Dorothy, and Mary Hutchinson." The Evidence of the Imagination (592), pp. 142-77.

Holds that guilt feelings, especially from his love for Dorothy, account for W's greatest poetry, and that the poetry declined as the poet's psychological conflicts were removed. Examines several poems in this light, notably "Laodamia."

592. Reiman, Donald H., Michael C. Jaye, and Betty T. Bennett, eds. The Evidence of the Imagination: Studies of Interactions between Life and Art in English Romantic Literature. New York: New York University, 1978. 409 pp. indexed.

Includes 528, 553, 569, 591, 609, and 616.

Reviews: J.H. Averill, WC 10(1979), 254; Geoffrey Little, RES 31(1980), 91; Richard E. Matlak, SIR 18 (1979), 672; L.J. Swingle, KSJ 28(1979), 164; George Woodcock, SR 88(1980), 298.

593. Roper, Derek. Reviewing before the Edinburgh, 1788-1802. Newark, DE: University of Delaware, 1978. 313 pp. indexed.

Surveys coverage of _Lyrical Ballads_ and earlier works by W and C (pp. 83-101) in the five major reviews, arguing that on the whole they were "friendly and helpful."
Reviews: J.H. Alexander, _YES_ 11(1981), 294; J.M.B., _ES_ 62(1981), 309; James T. Boulton, _DUJ_ 74(1981), 142-43; J.S. Clive, _ASch_ 49(1980), 414; Philip Flynn, _WC_ 11 (1980), 152-54; Donald A. Low, _N&Q_ 27(1980), 460-61; K.S., _CritQ_ 21(1979), 91; G.P. Tyson, _ECS_ 14(1980), 69.

594. Ruoff, Gene W. "Critical Implications of Wordsworth's 1815 Categorization, with Some Animadversions on Binaristic Commentary." _The Wordsworth Circle_ 9(1978): 75-82.

Taking W's statement that poetry should treat things "as they _seem_" ("Essay, Supplementary," 1815) as the "best guide" to his purpose, Ruoff argues convincingly that W's various classes of poems should be viewed as complementary, not dialectically opposed to one another--that W resisted scales of values that place, e.g., imagination higher than fancy. See also 545.

595. Sharp, Steven E. "Principle and Whimsey: Thomas Holcroft and _Descriptive Sketches_." _The Wordsworth Circle_ 9 (1978): 71-74.

Puzzling over his misrepresentation of "Descriptive Sketches" (see 498), Sharp argues that Holcroft, usually a principled reviewer, neglected in this case to read beyond the opening lines.

596. Sherry, Charles. "Wordsworth's Metaphors for Eternity: Appearance and Representation." _Studies in Romanticism_ 17(1978): 193-213. Rpt. in _Wordsworth's Poetry of the Imagination_ (768), pp. 32-56.

Examines nature imagery, especially of light, which W uses as "metaphors for eternity" (e.g., "Our life's star"), arguing that these metaphors differ from those of unspecified "eighteenth-century predecessors" in that W's imagination constitutes rather than discovers them.

597. Simpson, David. "Pound's Wordsworth; Or Growth of a Poet's Mind." _ELH_ 45(1978), 660-86.

Explains Pound's rudeness to W by contrasting imagism, with its implicit acceptance of "natural language," and W's more idiosyncratic symbolic mode, which rests on a nominalist view of language. Simpson finds the later Pound drawing closer to W's position.

598. Simpson, Peter. "Crisis and Recovery: Wordsworth, George Eliot, and Silas Marner." University of Toronto Quarterly 48(1978/79): 95-114.

Compares Eliot's "inward development" in the period before the novels with W's, and reads Silas Marner as, in essence, her Prelude, noting the correspondence between Marner's, Eliot's, and W's biographies. Eliot combines W's intro/retrospective gift, it is argued, with a more enduring social consciousness.

599. Smith, David Q. "The Wanderer's Silence: A Strange Reticence in Book IX of The Excursion." The Wordsworth Circle 9(1978): 162-72.

Argues that the Wanderer's closing silence does not signify his agreement with the Pastor, but is to be read dramatically as his sulking at imagination's failure to save the Solitary.

600. Smith, K.E. "Bridge Passage: A Note on The Prelude, Book VI, 1-331 (1805)." The Wordsworth Circle 9(1978): 373-75.

Suggests that critics pay more attention to the less spectacular passages, which may bring them to revise their "neater formulations about the structure" of The Prelude.

601. Solomon, Gerald. "Heaven Lies." Essays in Criticism 28 (1978): 350-52.

A weak reply to Sturrock (606).

602. Spiegelman, Willard. "Elizabeth Bishop's 'Natural Heroism.'" Centennial Review 22(1978), 28-44.

Discusses Bishop's poetry with reference to patterns and figures in W's, finding her chief movement "beyond" his achievement to be a less egotistical form of heroism.

603. Stelzig, Eugene L. "Wordsworth's Prophetic Self-Conception in _The Prelude_ and the 'Prospectus' to _The Recluse_." _Literatur in Wissenschaft und Unterricht_ 11 (1978): 14-22.

Notes that since W located the source of poetic power in his past, he necessarily foresaw the loss of his powers. For a more interesting treatment of the apparent conflict between Wordsworthian retrospection and prophecy, see 967.

604. Stephenson, William. "Wordsworth and J.M.W. Turner: A Pairing for Teaching." _The Wordsworth Circle_ 9(1978): 338-42.

Suggests that the artists be taught together, and outlines several of their more striking similarities.

605. Storch, R.F. "Abstract Idealism in English Romantic Poetry and Painting." _Images of Romanticism_ (561), pp. 189-209.

Closes a comparison of Shelley and Turner by contrasting them with the "sober realism" of W and Constable. Storch compares "Wordsworth and Constable" at greater length in _Studies in Romanticism_ 5(1966): 121-38.

606. Sturrock, June. "Heaven Lies." _Essays in Criticism_ 28 (1978): 91-93.

Rebuts Solomon's readings (500) of "We are Seven," "Anecdote for Fathers," "It is a beauteous evening," and _The Prelude_ 2:292 ff., as well as his view of W's relation to Annette and Caroline. See also 601.

607. Sturrock, J. "Wordsworth's 'Phantom of Delight' and the Development of the Imagination." _Colby Library Quarterly_ 14(1978): 213-20.

Concentrates on the imagery of light and vision to show a progress from physical sight to imaginative vision, a pattern similar to that of "Tintern Abbey," the Ode, and "Elegiac Stanzas."

608. Swingle, L.J. "Wordsworth's 'Picture of the Mind.'" _Images of Romanticism_ (561), pp. 81-90.

Discussing the Ode, "Tintern Abbey," "Elegiac Stanzas," "Two April Mornings," and other poems, Swingle argues that W's interest in mental images is not so much for the images themselves as for the power of mind they reveal.

609. Taylor, Irene. "By Peculiar Grace: Wordsworth in 1802." _The Evidence of the Imagination_ (592), pp. 119-41.

Recounts the biographical context of "Resolution and Independence," and finds the leech-gatherer W's formulation of the ideal or "true" poet--silent or not, one free from "effeminate habits of thinking and feeling" (W's phrase), and embodying human strength.

610. Thomas, Gordon K. "Whither Wordsworth on His Elfin Pinnace?" _The Wordsworth Circle_ 9(1978): 92-97.

Argues that when W revised the boat-stealing episode for the 1850 _Prelude_, he sacrificed physical for psychological realism; now the boy rows forward, toward the cliff, then turns and rows away.

611. Vann, J. Don. "The Publication of Wordsworth's 'Grace Darling.'" _Notes & Queries_ 25(1978): 223-25.

Notes that the poem did not wait until the 1845 edition for publication, but found its way into seven newspapers shortly after W had it privately printed in 1843.

612. Vendler, Helen. "Lionel Trilling and the _Immortality Ode_." _Salmagundi_ 41(1978): 66-86.

Argues impressively that the Ode must be read as poetry, not as systematic philosophy, and shows how the language, progressing from quasi-religious to metaphorical, reflects the speaker's progress. Though finding much to repudiate in Trilling (118), Vendler accepts his central insight that the poem celebrates new powers, and her reading is more complement and qualification than alternative to his. See also 846.

613. Wainwright, Jeffrey. "William Wordsworth at Briggflatts." Agenda 16,i(1978): 37-45.

Compares the style of Basil Bunting's Briggflatts with that of W's "Tintern Abbey."

614. Wolfson, Susan J. "The Speaker as Questioner in Lyrical Ballads." Journal of English and Germanic Philology 77 (1978): 546-68.

Argues that those poems in which the questioner and answerer do not quite connect dramatize the power of imagination or faith to overcome mysteries. Chiefly examines "We are Seven," "Anecdote for Fathers," "The Thorn," and "Tintern Abbey," the latter as having an implied questioner.

615. Wood, Susan A. "Resilience, Virtue and Tragic Experience: A Reading of Wordsworth's 'Michael.'" Theoria 50 (1978): 61-73.

Contrasts Michael with C's mariner as a model of simple virtue and meaningful endurance, and argues that because of his naivety he is not to blame for Luke's fate.

616. Woodring, Carl. "The New Sublimity in 'Tintern Abbey.'" The Evidence of the Imagination (592), pp. 86-100.

Explains the poem's concern with "the still, sad music of humanity" (as well as the troublesome preposition in "in the mind of man") by showing that "Tintern Abbey" describes the sublime of deprivation, "of silence in solitude," which lays emphasis on the perceiver's rather than on the landscape's powers.

617. Yip, Wai-Lim. "Aesthetic Consciousness of Landscape in Chinese and Anglo-American Poetry." Comparative Literature Studies 15(1978): 211-41.

A lucid and perceptive contrast of W's treatment of landscape with that by Chinese, chiefly Taoist, poets, noting that W places far more emphasis on the mental activity of the perceiver, so that "wise passiveness" is an unrealized ideal in his poetry.

1979

618. Arac, Jonathan. "Bounding Lines: The Prelude and Critical Revision." Boundary 2 7,iii(1979): 31-48.

An important essay identifying three major traditions in Prelude study: Abrams' (165), deriving from Arnold (98); Hartman's (143), deriving from Bradley (100); and Lindenberger's (141), deriving from Pater (96). Arac objects especially to Abrams' spatializing of The Prelude as a circular journey (see also 833), and favors Lindenberger, who stresses disruption, repetition, and incompletion in the poem.

619. Austin, Timothy R. "Stylistic Evolution in Wordsworth's Poetry: Evidence from Emendations." Language and Style 12(1979): 176-87.

Focusing chiefly on minor revisions between the 1798 version of "The Ruined Cottage" and book 1 of The Excursion (1814), Austin notes stylistic changes which are consonant with W's changing world-view: greater abstraction, fewer "spatially vivid prepositions," fewer agentless passive constructions, and a frequent shifting of agency from nature to an implied observer.

620. Bahti, Thomas. "Figures of Interpretation, The Interpretation of Figures: A Reading of Wordsworth's 'Dream of the Arab.'" Studies in Romanticism 18(1979): 601-27.

A close deconstructionist reading of the passage in the 1850 Prelude, book 5, both as illustration and as argument that "the structure of the rhetorical figure is" not "both/and" or "either/or" but "both and neither." Argues that between the poet's writing his text and his reading it, the meaning of a figure shifts between the literal and the figurative, which raises problems for a simple understanding of W in terms of the nature-imagination dialectic.

621. Barth, J. Robert, S.J. "The Poet, Death, and Immortality: The Unity of _The Prelude_, Book V." _The Wordsworth Circle_ 10(1979): 69-75.

Finds book 5, the unity of which is frequently debated (e.g., by Jaye, 552) as unified by "fear of death and the desire for immortality," and argues that W's affirmation rests not on books or on nature, but on both because of the "wiser spirit" underpinning them.

622. Barth, J. Robert, S.J. "'The Props of My Affections': A Note on _The Prelude_ II, 267-281." _The Wordsworth Circle_ 10(1979): 344-45.

Using the 1850 version, Barth argues that the "props" are the sensual stimuli of the "visible world," and that the "building" which "stood" "is W's own active mind or imagination."

623. Beer, John. "Coleridge and Wordsworth: The Vital and the Organic." In _Readings in Coleridge: Approaches and Applications_, ed. Walter B. Crawford. Ithaca, NY: Cornell, 1979, pp. 160-90.

Discusses C's concept of the interplay between organic and vital (i.e., vegetable and animate) in nature, and tenuously relates it to passages in C's and in W's poetry, especially in the two-part _Prelude_.

624. Beer, John. "Wordsworth and the Face of Things." _The Wordsworth Circle_ 10(1979): 17-29.

Examines W's use of "face" imagery, both in his descriptions of a seeing and breathing nature, and of people, to relate nature and human nature.

625. Beer, John. _Wordsworth in Time_. London: Faber & Faber, 1979. 232 pp. indexed.

Explains the visionary "undercurrent" in W's poetry by his clinging to the real world in distrust of visionary experience. This distrust, related to W's fear of madness, is the most relaxed in "periods of intimacy (or recent intimacy)" with C, whose thought is seen as a pervasive influence even (though speculatively) before the trip to Germany.

Reviews: Reviewed with Beer's *Wordsworth and the Human Heart* (517) by Averill, Baron, Gill, and Newlyn; also A.S. Byatt, *NS*, 26 Jan. 1979, pp. 118-19; G.D. Crossan, *AUMLA* 53(May, 1980), 79; Mary Wedd, *ChLB* 27(1979), 55-59.

626. Bernhardt-Kabisch, Ernest. "Wordsworth and the Simplon Revisited." *The Wordsworth Circle* 10(1979): 381-84.

An important essay pointing out that the generally accepted topography of the Simplon passage (established by Max Wildi, "Wordsworth and the Simplon Pass," *English Studies* 40[1959], 224-32) does not fit W's description of the crossing in *The Prelude*, book 6. Bernhardt-Kabisch suggests a better, but principally argues that W transformed the topography and the experience to fit his own imaginative idea. Notes too that W must have known all along that he had crossed the Simplon Pass, if not the Alps.

627. Bernstein, Gene M. "A Structuralist Reading of 'Anecdote for Fathers' and 'We Are Seven.'" *The Wordsworth Circle* 10(1979): 339-43.

Arguing that W, like Levi-Strauss, is concerned with the structure of mythic discourse, not its meaning, shows that both poems are structured on the polarity of nature and culture, child and man, which is not resolvable but is mediated by the "totemic" weather-vane and grave.

628. Bernstein, Gene M. "Levi-Strauss's *Totemism* and Wordsworth's *Lyrical Ballads*." *Studies in Romanticism* 18 (1979): 383-403.

Compares W's use of nature imagery, metaphor, and poems themselves to mediate between man and nature with the role, in Levi-Strauss's analysis, of totems in primitive societies; not much on specific poems.

629. Bowers, Frederick. "Reference and Deixis in Wordsworth's 'Yew-Trees.'" *English Studies in Canada* 5(1979): 292-300.

Argues that Riffaterre's analysis (217) is "skewed" because it fails to distinguish between reference and deixis, between words that stand for objects in general and those that "point" to specific objects. Analyzing the poem's deictic elements, Bowers finds it more "speaker-centered."

630. Buell, Lawrence. "The Question of Form in Coleridge's _Biographia Literaria_." _ELH_ 46(1979): 399-417.

Deals much with C's treatment of W; Buell follows up Whalley's suggestion that the _Biographia_ (86) is unified in terms of its treatment of W, and discusses it at length as "a kind of counter-_Prelude_."

631. Caraher, Brian G. "Lucy in Retrospect: A Late Wordsworth Manuscript of 'She dwelt among th'untrodden ways.'" _The Wordsworth Circle_ 10(1979): 353-55.

Reprints an 1848 manuscript of lines 13-16 (found in an 1800 edition of _Lyrical Ballads_) with minor variants in accidentals, and reflects on its significance.

632. Carlisle, Janice. "A Prelude to _Villette_: Charlotte Brontë's Reading, 1850-52." _Bulletin of Research in the Humanities_ 82(1979): 403-23.

Sketches the parallels between Brontë's biography and W's, and shows that _The Prelude_, especially its treatment of creative paralysis in book 1, was an important influence in shaping the theme and veiled autobiographical mode of _Villette_.

633. Cervo, Nathan. "Hazlitt, Wordsworth, Keats--A Pre-Raphaelite View." _Pre-Raphaelite Review_ 3(1979): 63-77.

Crudely contrasts W's "egotism" with the Pre-Raphaelites' "Shakespearian sympathy," adding almost nothing to extensive quotation from Hazlitt and Keats.

634. Chase, Cynthia. "The Accidents of Disfiguration: Limits to Literal and Rhetorical Reading in Book V of _The Prelude_." _Studies in Romanticism_ 18(1979): 547-65.

An impenetrable deconstructionist reading focusing on the drowned-man passage in the 1805 version.

635. Cheever, Leonard A. "Glimpses That Can Make Us Less Forlorn: Wordsworth, Borges, and Neruda." Research Studies 47(1979): 37-44.

Compares Borges' "Compass" ("Una Brujula") and Neruda's "Lazybones" ("El Perezoso") as poems that criticize the workaday world and offer imaginative alternatives.

636. Clayton, Jay. "Visionary Power and Narrative Form: Wordsworth and Adam Bede." ELH 46(1979): 645-72.

An influence-study comparing the disruption of narrative form by visionary experience in W and Adam Bede, and viewing the novel's problematic happy ending as the resultant "Wordsworthian compensation."

637. Cooke, Michael G. Acts of Inclusion: Studies Bearing on an Elementary Theory of Romanticism. New Haven, CT: Yale, 1979. xx+289 pp. indexed.

A highly readable argument that inclusiveness distinguishes Romantic poetry, though the treatment of W is piecemeal: Cooke contrasts "She dwelt among th'untrodden ways" with Pope's "Elegy to...an Unfortunate Lady" to show Romantic elegy's inclusion of satire and prophecy; examines disproportionate consequence and guilt in "A slumber did my spirit seal"; discusses relationship to the "feminine" in "Nutting"; and, for the sake of those who think it a magisterial "poetry of assertion," emphasizes "The Mode of Argument in Wordsworth's Poetry" (both in its rhetoric and in its imagery).

Reviews: J. Robert Barth, SIR 19(1980), 577; Marilyn Butler, N&Q 27(1980), 552-54; Stephen Gill, TLS, 21 Dec. 1979, 166; Alan Grob, WC 11(1980), 188-92; I. Massey, Criticism 22(1980), 176; E.B. Murray, RES 33(1982), 92-94; Stuart M. Tave, MLR 77(1982), 174; Carl Woodring, KSJ 30(1981), 191.

638. Curtis, Jared. "A Note on the Lost Manuscripts of William Wordsworth's 'Louisa' and 'I travell'd among

unknown Men.'" Yale University Library Gazette 53 (1979): 196-201.

Reasons from comments by W's nineteenth-century editors that W intended to include both poems in the 1802 edition of Lyrical Ballads, but then changed his mind.

639. D'Avanzo, Mario L. "'Expostulation and Reply' and the Gospel of Matthew." CEA Critic 41,iii(1979): 38-40.

Sees the poem as paralleling or parodying the New Testament as it promulgates its rival creed of Nature.

640. Dawson, Carl. Victorian Noon: English Literature in 1850. Baltimore, MD: Johns Hopkins, 1979. xv+268 pp. indexed.

A literary history of 1850 dealing frequently with W's place among the Victorians, especially Tennyson, Dickens, and Arnold, in the year of his death and of The Prelude's publication. Dawson challenges the view that The Prelude had to wait until the public had done with Tennyson's In Memoriam.

Reviews: J. Diedrick, MLQ 40(1979), 317; J.P. Farrell, VS 24(1980), 134; J. Haney-Peritz, SAQ 79(1980), 449; G. Joseph, WC 11(1980), 186; Neil McEwan, N&Q 27(1980), 379; J.H. Raleigh, JEGP 78(1979), 450; P. Turner, RES 32 (1981), 349.

641. de Man, Paul. "Autobiography as De-facement." Modern Language Notes 94(1979): 919-30.

Arguing that autobiography is not a genre but a "figure of reading," de Man examines W's "Essays upon Epitaphs" as though they were autobiography or "Essays upon Autobiography," and finds a fundamental ambivalence at their center: on one hand they advocate prosopopeia (literally, "to confer a mask or a face") as "the dominant figure of epitaphic or autobiographical discourse"; on the other they counsel against this trope as a dangerous abuse of language.

642. Duff, Gerald. "Tension and Counterpoise in 'Tintern Abbey.'" Structuralist Review 1,iii(1979): 57-68.

A tidy structuralist reading, presenting the poem as mediating between the oppositions of self and other, nature and culture, past and future.

643. Evans, Walter. "From Wordsworth's The Prelude to Yeats's 'The Second Coming.'" Yeats-Eliot Review 6,i(1979): 31-37.

Findings remarkably parallel to Keane's (666), though based on simple comparison of the finished texts.

644. Fergenson, Laraine. "Wordsworth and Thoreau: The Relationship Between Man and Nature." Thoreau Journal Quarterly 11,ii(1979): 3-10.

A good brief comparison of the writers' views of and metaphors for the relation of nature to the human spirit, noting that (like Huxley, 105) Thoreau, at least in his account of climbing Mt. Katahdin, laid more stress on nature's otherness.

645. Fike, Francis. "Correspondent Breeze: The Course of a Romantic Metaphor." Renascence 32(1979): 3-11.

Argues that W and C distrusted the metaphor which Abrams described in a brilliant essay of 1948, "The Correspondent Breeze: A Romantic Metaphor" (300, pp. 37-54), and traces its further deterioration in Bridges and Stevens.

646. Fleissner, Robert F. "A Road Taken: the Romantically Different Ruelle." In Robert Frost: Studies of the Poetry, ed. Kathryn Gibbs Harris. Boston: G.K. Hall, 1979, pp. 117-31.

Cites the influence of "The Lost Love" (the title Palgrave gave to "She dwelt among th'untrodden ways") on Frost's "The Road not Taken."

647. Friedman, Michael H. The Making of a Tory Humanist: William Wordsworth and the Idea of Community. New York: Columbia, 1979. ix+322 pp. indexed.

A lucid, impressive account of W's personality and social views, using Freud and Marx to show how early psychological fears were aggravated by the uncertainties of living in England's capitalist economy to make W seek stable, hierarchic community, and linking his poetic decline to socio-economic change. Includes good readings of many poems, and closes with a valuable chapter on the Cintra pamphlet.

Reviews: William H. Galperin, JEGP 80(1981), 257-59; Ronald B. Hatch, QQ 87(1980), 515-17; William Heath, SIR 20(1981), 117-21; Bishop C. Hunt, RM, 1979, p. 129; John E. Jordan, SAQ 79(1980), 451-52; Richard E. Matlak, WC 11(1980): 134-36; Lore Metzger, MLQ 41(1980), 292-95; W.J.B. Owen, YES 11(1981), 300-302.

648. Frost, Alan. "New Geographical Perspectives and the Emergence of the Romantic Imagination." In Captain James Cook and His Times, ed. Robin Fisher and Hugh Johnston. Seattle: University of Washington, 1979, pp. 5-19.

An interesting discussion of the influence of late-eighteenth-century travels and travel literature on the first-generation Romantic poets, especially as a source for the figure of the mind-traveller. Discusses W's The Borderers and his drafts for the Snowdon passage (in the 1850 Prelude, book 14).

649. Galperin, William H. "'Turns and Counter-Turns': The Crisis of Sincerity in the Final Books of The Prelude." Modern Language Quarterly 40(1979): 256-74.

Argues, somewhat obscurely, that in book 11 the 1805 Prelude turns from a private to a public poem, as W subordinates the demands of his "best self" to those of his implied reader.

650. Gaull, Marilyn. "From Wordsworth to Darwin: 'On to the Fields of Praise.'" The Wordsworth Circle 10(1979): 33-48.

A wide-ranging exploration of W's relation to contemporary science, detailing his friendship with geologist Adam Sedgwick, explaining the contemporary rage for geology, and suggesting what Charles Darwin found in W:

"that capacity for self-projection that characterizes the most creative work in modern science." Compares _The Excursion_ and _The Origin of Species_.

651. Gillham, D.G. "Five Studies in Metaphor." _English Studies in Africa_ 22(1979), 57-69.

Pages 65-68 comment on W's use of metaphor in the skating passage of _The Prelude_, book 1, and the sonnet "Whence that low voice?--A whisper from the heart," but most interesting is the contention that the sonnet presents memory as a sterile, "dead occupation."

652. Gohn, Jack Benoit. "Did Shelley Know Wordsworth's _Peter Bell_?" _Keats-Shelley Journal_ 28(1979): 20-24.

Argues that Shelley had probably read W's poem before beginning his parody.

653. Hartman, Geoffrey. "Centaur: Remarks on the Psychology of the Critic." _Salmagundi_ 43(1979), 130-39. Rpt. in _Criticism in the Wilderness: The Study of Literature Today_. New Haven, CT: Yale, 1980, pp. 214-25.

In what appears to be a digression, Hartman views "There was a Boy," with the boy's problematic search for a "living respondent," as W's self-admonition for a similar "narcissism," for his wish to give "the Mind / Some element to stamp her image on / In nature somewhat nearer to her own"--e.g., in the Dorothy of "Tintern Abbey."

654. Hartman, Geoffrey H. "Words, Wish, Worth: Wordsworth." In _Deconstruction and Criticism_, ed. Harold Bloom et al. New York: Seabury, 1979, pp. 177-216.

An impressive analysis of "A little onward lend thy guiding hand," focusing chiefly on the poem's relation to its opening lines (quoted from _Samson Agonistes_) and its "inner voice," concluding that the poem is "both a minor _poem_ and a considerable text."

655. Hayden, John O. _Polestar of the Ancients: The Aristotelian Tradition in Classical and English Literary Criticism_. Newark, DE: University of Delaware, 1979. 237 pp. indexed.

The chapter on W and C argues that their literary theory is Aristotelian--mimetic, not expressionist, stressing generality and moral purpose; W's major contribution is "his view of the _indirect_ moral working of literature." What Abrams (124) sees as a turn to expressionism is really the birth of a new interest, "creative theory," the study of the "psychology of composition." See also 810.

656. Heffernan, James A.W. "Mutilated Autobiography: Wordsworth's _Poems_ of 1815." _The Wordsworth Circle_ 10 (1979): 107-12.

Considers W's classification schemes in the 1815 _Poems_ and the 1814 Prospectus to _The Recluse_ as capitulations of imagination to the analytical and categorizing faculties.

657. Hill, Alan G. "On the Date and Significance of Wordsworth's Sonnet 'On the Extinction of the Venetian Republic.'" _Review of English Studies_ 30(1979): 441-45.

Makes a good argument for 1807 rather than 1802 as the date of composition, and suggests that the poem's "serenity" is owing to the 1806 unification of Italy, which W welcomed.

658. Hobsbaum, Philip. _Tradition and Experiment in English Poetry_. London: Macmillan, 1979. xiii+343 pp. indexed.

An "informal history of poetry in English." The chapter on "The Essential Wordsworth" (pp. 180-205) is eccentric and uninformed about scholarship of recent decades.

659. Hodgson, John A. "The Date of Wordsworth's 'It Is No Spirit Who from Heaven Hath Flown.'" _Notes & Queries_ 26(1979): 228-29. Rpt. in _Wordsworth's Philosophical Poetry, 1797-1814_ (742), pp. 174-75.

Argues that "Hesper" refers to Venus, and uses astronomy to date the poem "almost certainly...between 8 November and late December 1802, very possibly by 26 November."

660. Hughes, Kenneth J. "Troubled Tories: Theory of History and Didactic Function of Wordsworth's Ecclesiastical Sonnets." CIEFL Bulletin 15,i(1979): 29-44.

Against Moorman (79), who sees the sonnets as even-handed, Hughes argues that they are skillful propaganda, on behalf of the landed Tories, against Catholic emancipation.

661. Hugo, F.J. "Wordsworth's Perspectives of Unity and Diversity." Theoria 52(1979): 50-62.

On W's imaginative treatment of space, examining his use of optical illusion in "A Night-Piece" and of multiple perspectives in "Tintern Abbey."

662. Jackson, Geoffrey. "Moral Dimensions of 'The Thorn.'" The Wordsworth Circle 10(1979): 91-96.

Argues that when read as a dramatic monologue, the poem implicates the narrator--and the reader--as scandal-mongers.

663. Jacobus, Mary. "Wordsworth and the Language of the Dream." ELH 46(1979): 618-44.

Extremely difficult deconstructionist reading of the dream passage in the 1805 Prelude, book 5, hoping to trace "the process by which meaning is at once generated and unsettled in The Prelude."

664. Johnson, Lee M. "Virgil, Wordsworth, and the Power of Sound." Mosaic 13,i(1979): 93-109.

Argues that Virgil's Fourth Eclogue and W's Ode are both structured as golden sections, and comments on both poets' use of sound-patterns and golden sections as expressions of idealism. See also Johnson's book-length study (889). (For those interested in portraits, an

1848 medallion of W, from a life drawing by L.C. Wyon, is reproduced facing Johnson's title page.)

665. Jordan, John E. "'Wordsworth's Most Wonderful as well as Admirable Poem.'" _The Wordsworth Circle_ 10(1979): 49-58.

Surveys a very broad range of critical comment on "Peter Bell," from W's to modern times, and argues that the poem is a mock epic spoken by "a sort of village Milton."

666. Keane, Patrick J. "Revolutions French and Russian: Burke, Wordsworth, and the Genesis of Yeats's 'The Second Coming.'" _Bulletin of Research in the Humanities_ 83(1979): 18-52.

An impressive and important study establishing W's direct, if limited, influence on Yeats, citing both Yeats's drafts of "The Second Coming" and his marginalia to _The Prelude_, books 10 and 11. See also 643.

667. Ketterer, David. "'Glimpses' in Wordsworth's 'The World Is Too Much With Us.'" _The Wordsworth Circle_ 10(1979): 122-23.

Argues that the poem describes the inception and birth of Triton and Proteus, and that Proteus's birth is W's rebirth. Perhaps more important is the introductory note pointing out that the poem does _not_ pit Christianity against paganism or choose the latter over the former.

668. Kishel, Joseph F. "The 'Analogy Passage' from Wordsworth's Five-Book _Prelude_." _Studies in Romanticism_ 18 (1979): 271-85.

Arguing against Hartman (143) that W was more unsure of his abilities than afraid of his imagination, Kishel holds that the excised passage originally following the ascent of Snowdon (see Norton _Prelude_, 17, pp. 496-9) shows this uncertainty and is relevant to his decision to expand _The Prelude_. Compares the passage with Milton's battle in heaven (_Paradise Lost_, book 6) and with the spots of time.

669. Kramer, Lawrence. "The Other Will: The Daemonic in Coleridge and Wordsworth." Philological Quarterly 58 (1979): 298-320.

An illuminating exploration of alternating sublime and beautiful passages in The Prelude as the "rhythms" of repressed, "demonic imagination," and "healing," idealizing, "romantic imagination." Pages 313-20 discuss the drowned-man and beacon passages of the 1805 Prelude, books 5 and 11, noting that neither C nor most later poets "can admit and overcome as much darkness as W."

670. McClellan, Jane. "Auden's Creative Relationship to Blake, Coleridge, and Wordsworth." North Dakota Quarterly 47,i(1979), 41-54.

Briefly (pp. 49-54) compares the poets' use of landscape to depict mind, and their beliefs in reform of the heart rather than social reform, and argues that W, whom Auden called "a bleak old bore," was "both model and warning" to the later poet.

671. MacDonell, Diane C. "The Place of the Device of Expectation, or 'Seeing through a Medium,' in Book I of The Excursion." Studies in Romanticism 18(1979): 427-51.

A structuralist reading, replete with jargon, arguing that the tale of the Pedlar teaches us how to read the tale of Margaret.

672. Mainusch, Herbert. "William Wordsworth's Theory of Literature." Unisa English Studies 17,ii(1979): 8-20.

Sees W's 1800 Preface as mainly in the tradition of the eighteenth-century, drawing parallels especially among German theorists.

673. Mellown, Muriel J. "Images of Fancy and Imagination: A Reading of The Prelude, Book III." Durham University Journal 71(1979): 245-51.

Discusses the alternating subject matter and style of book 3 as the alternation between the two poetic faculties, arguing that the book is not disunified but reflects the nature of W's experience at Cambridge.

674. Miller, J. Hillis. "On Edge: The Crossways of Contemporary Criticism." Bulletin of the American Academy of Arts and Sciences 32,iv(1979): 13-32.

Urges us to discover "the inexhaustible strangeness of literary texts" with a long exemplary discussion of "A slumber did my spirit seal" (pp. 20-31), intended to show that dialectical criticism is impossible because of the poem's "oscillation in meaning." Miller fails to acknowledge the many non-deconstructionist readings of this poem which have made discoveries similar to his own.

675. Morris, Brian. "Mr. Wordsworth's Ear." The Wordsworth Circle 10(1979): 113-21.

A fascinating essay comparing W's indifference to music with the attitudes of some contemporaries. Morris lists other treatments of the topic, gives excellent analyses of sound in "Resolution and Independence" and "The Solitary Reaper," and discusses musical settings of W's poems (especially the Ode), which are rarer than for other great poets.

676. Owen, W.J.B. "The Perfect Image of a Mighty Mind." The Wordsworth Circle 10 (1979): 3-16.

Attempts to show how Snowdon is an "image of a mighty mind" in the 1805 Prelude, book 13, by considering W's revisions, arguing that in earlier versions the scene on Snowdon represented the processes or products of the mind, not the mind itself.

677. Pipkin, James W. "The Borderers and the Genesis of Wordsworth's Spots of Time." Tennessee Studies in Literature 24(1979): 111-19.

Much the same as Pipkin's previous essay (409), treating Oswald as W's chief spokesman, and Oswald's island experience as a "spot of time."

678. Plotz, Judith. "The Perpetual Messiah: Romanticism, Childhood, and the Paradoxes of Human Development." In _Regulated Children/Liberated Children: Education in Psychohistorical Perspective_, ed. Barbara Finkelstein. New York: Psychohistory Press, 1979, pp. 63-95.

A good essay on the Romantic reevaluation of childhood, with much on C, Blake, and W (chiefly citing _The Prelude_). As Plotz argues, the child is the central Romantic symbol, but still flesh and blood; and the Romantic ideal of organic or (in Rousseau's term) "negative education" was sane and influential in presenting imagination as a help rather than hindrance to mental growth.

679. Priestman, Donald G. "An Early Imitation and a Parody of Wordsworth." _Notes & Queries_ 26(1979): 229-31.

Reprints and comments on Southey's interesting imitation and parody of "Lines Left upon a Seat in a Yew Tree," both dating from 1799.

680. Ridenour, George M. "Justification by Faith in Two Romantic Poems." _The Wordsworth Circle_ 10(1979): 351-52.

On "Tintern Abbey" and C's "Limbo." Agrees with Brantley (304) that "Tintern Abbey" describes a "mature experience of grace" and points out an echo of Matthew 16:18.

681. Roberts, David. _Paternalism in Early Victorian England._ New Brunswick, NJ: Rutgers, 1979. x+337 pp. indexed.

Mentions of W are infrequent and he is nowhere discussed at length, but the book provides a helpful context for understanding the later W's social views and influence.
Reviews: Alan Heesom, _DUJ_ 74(1982), 291-92; Julia D. Pappageorge, _RM_, 1979, pp. 57-58.

682. Ruoff, Gene W. "The Sense of a Beginning: _Mansfield Park_." _The Wordsworth Circle_ 10(1979), 174-86.

Discusses the implications for Romantic narrative of W's belief that a thought "Hath no beginning," and compares _The Prelude_'s narrative art with that of Austen's _Mansfield Park_.

683. Simpson, David. Irony and Authority in Romantic Poetry. London: Macmillan, 1979. xiv + 267 pp. indexed.

Acute readings of some W poems as well as a discussion of the child-figure as "Romantic ironist" play a large part in Simpson's argument that Romantic irony occurs when the poet undercuts his own authority in the dramatic lyric, such undercutting stemming from Romantic anticipation of modern hermeneutics.

Reviews: Marshall Brown, ELN 18(1980), 148-50; Marilyn Butler, N&Q 27(1980), 552-54; David Erdman, RM, 1980, p. 63; W. Keach, SIR 20(1981), 539; I. McGilchrist, TLS, 31 Oct. 1980, p. 1238; Anne K. Mellor, WC 12(1981), 196; Mark Storey, English 29(1980), 153-59; Stuart M. Tave, MLR 77(1982), 174; Peter L. Thorslev, Jr., KSJ 31(1982), 202.

684. Simpson, Peter. "Hardy's 'The Self-Unseeing' and the Romantic Problem of Consciousness." Victorian Poetry 17(1979): 45-50.

Contrasts the "gleam/dream" rhyme in W's Ode and in his "Elegiac Stanzas," arguing that Hardy's poem, which uses the same rhyme, achieves "a kind of synthesis" of W's poems, but that Hardy is more optimistic than W.

685. Siskin, Clifford. "Wordsworth's Gothic Endeavor: From Esthwaite to the Great Decade." The Wordsworth Circle 10(1979): 161-73.

Convincingly relates W's practice in "The Vale of Esthwaite" and later poems to the aims of Romantic Gothicism as enunciated by Walpole; interesting observations on the genesis and function of the "spot of time," and on W's relation to his audience.

686. Stelzig, Eugene L. "Mutability, Ageing, and Permanence in Wordsworth's Later Poetry." Studies in English Literature, 1500-1900 19(1979): 623-44.

Discusses several of the later poems briefly to suggest that the personal, retrospective mode of the great decade gives way to more objective and traditional concerns with mutability and "the permanence of process."

687. Stewart, Annette. "Wordsworth and Coleridge and 'The Ancient Mariner.'" Quadrant 143(1979): 54-57.

Argues that the key event in the poets' decision to publish Lyrical Ballads rather than their tragedies or "Salibury Plain" was C's completion of "The Rime of the Ancient Mariner," which inspired W's ballads.

688. Storey, Mark. Poetry and Humour from Cowper to Clough. London: Macmillan, 1979. xii+192 pp. indexed.

The discussion of humor and its relation to pathos in Lyrical Ballads and "Peter Bell" is able, but admittedly does not go much beyond previous studies (see 162, 213, and 390); more important is the brief look at mock-epic elements in The Prelude.

689. Strickland, Edward. "The Context of 'The Mad Monk.'" The Wordsworth Circle 10(1979): 229-33.

Argues that C wrote the poem after "Christabel" was cut from Lyrical Ballads, not as a parody of W, but as a statement of disappointment and jealousy.

690. Stuart, Simon. New Phoenix Wings: Reparation in Literature. London: Routledge & Kegan Paul, 1979. viii+189 pp. indexed.

The work of Melanie Klein and Hanna Segal suggesting that artistic creation originates in infantile aggression and reparation provides the basis for shrewd psychological readings (pp. 99-138) of the opening and beacon passages of The Prelude, "Tintern Abbey," the "Lucy Poems," and the Ode.

Reviews: Thomas R. Frosch, BlakeQ 14(1981), 224-28; L.C. Knights, TLS, 15 Feb. 1980, p. 163; Peter J. Manning, MLR 75(1980), 823.

691. Sturrock, J. "Wordsworth's Translations of Ariosto." Notes & Queries 26(1979): 227-28.

Prints a new stanza translating Orlando Furioso i, 38, and corrects a reading in de Selincourt (1).

692. Taylor, Anya. Magic and English Romanticism. Athens: University of Georgia, 1979. 278 pp. indexed.

The long chapter on "Wordsworth's Arguments against Magical Words" presents the "dialogue" between W and C on language as an aspect of their differences on the supernatural. Taylor sees W as responding to the "Ancient Mariner" with "Peter Bell" and to C's debility in the 1805 Prelude, so that "passages previously thought to refer to Wordsworth's internal struggles refer at once or instead to discussions with Coleridge."

Reviews: James Benziger, WC 11(1980), 148-49; D. Degrois, EA 35(1982), 219; Barbara Fauss Leavy, JEGP 79 (1980), 256-59; Geoffrey Little, RES 32(1981), 339-40; Elizabeth Sewell, SIR 19(1980), 442-45; Stuart M. Tave, MLR 77(1982), 174.

693. Thomson, Douglass H. "Wordsworth's Lucy of 'Nutting.'" Studies in Romanticism 18(1979): 287-98.

Considers the threatening character of Lucy in a "Nutting" draft (Dove Cottage MS. 16) in relation to "Wordsworth's deliberate 'elision' of her presence" here and in the "Lucy Poems."

694. Vann, J. Don. "Wordsworth and the Burns Festival: An Uncollected Letter." Modern Philology 77(1979): 57-58.

Prints a short letter of 7 July 1844 in which W declines to attend the festival.

695. Watson, J.R. "A Note on the Date in the Title of 'Tintern Abbey.'" The Wordsworth Circle 10(1979): 379-80.

Suggests that W chose July 13 to commemorate his landing in France in 1790 and the murder of Marat in 1793.

696. Westbrook, Sue Weaver. "A Note on Hartley's Theory of 'the Sensation of Chilliness' in Wordsworth's 'Goody Blake and Harry Gill.'" The Wordsworth Circle 10 (1979): 124-26.

Quotes Hartley to show that Harry's fate is psychologically plausible--or was for W.

697. Woodman, Ross G. "Milton's Urania and Her Romantic Descendants." University of Toronto Quarterly 48(1979): 189-208.

Using Blake's comments on W, presents Blake's Milton and W's Prospectus to The Recluse as "the two poles of possible interpretation" of Milton's inspiration, W rejecting Milton's myth-making as pagan and emphasizing Milton's natural religion instead, which Blake abhorred (199-201).

698. Young, Robert. "The Eye and Progress of His Song: A Lacanian Reading of The Prelude." Oxford Literary Review 3,iii(1979): 79-98.

Indubitably Lacanian, but dubious as a reading of poetry.

699. Zall, P.M. "The Cool World of Samuel Taylor Coleridge: Vicesimus Knox, Elegant Activist." The Wordsworth Circle 10(1979): 345-47.

Traces the variant of "The Babes in the Wood" quoted in W's 1800 Preface to Lyrical Ballads to Knox's Elegant Extracts in Poetry (ca. 1780); gives a brief biographical sketch of Knox.

1980

700. Aarsleff, Hans. "Wordsworth, Language, and Romanticism." Essays in Criticism 30(1980): 215-26. Rpt. in From Locke to Saussure: Essays on the Study of Language and Intellectual History. Minneapolis: University of Minnesota, 1982, pp. 372-81.

An important argument, against the "Mirror-and-the-Lamp" school (see 124), that W's expressionist theory of language and creative epistemology do not derive from Germany and break with the French Enlightenment, but find their roots in Locke and Condillac.

701. Alexander, Meena. The Poetic Self: Towards a Phenomenology of Romanticism. Atlantic Highlands, NJ: Humanities Press, 1980. 280 pp. not indexed.

A 1973 University of Nottingham dissertation, first published in India in 1979, examining the "Romantic" writer's establishment of a "poetic self" through his bodily relation to the world. Attention paid to W is divided between "Tintern Abbey" (pp. 51-71) and the 1805 Prelude (pp. 72-120).

Reviews: Roger Asselineau, EA 33(1980), 471; Christopher Clausen, SR 91(1983), 672.

702. Arac, Jonathan. "Romanticism, the Self, and the City: The Secret Agent in Literary History." Boundary 2 9 (1980): 75-90.

Sees the continuity between W and Conrad not so much in terms of Conrad's Romanticism (see 230) as of W's modernity, comparing the view of urban life in the Preface to Lyrical Ballads with that of Baudelaire, and finding an anticipation of Walter Benjamin's distinction between Erlebnis and Erfahrung in W's descriptions of modern time-consciousness.

703. Averill, James H. "A Fragment of a Late Wordsworth Notebook (1835)." Modern Philology 78(1980): 158-61.

Prints and comments on drafts for poems on Robert Burns and James Hogg from a half-page now at Princeton, and notes "how much of W we do not have."

704. Averill, James H. Wordsworth and the Poetry of Human Suffering. Ithaca, NY: Cornell, 1980. 291 pp. indexed.

A valuable study of W's indebtedness to the literature of sensibility and of his search for an adequate, non-exploitative literary response to human misery. Averill finds the movement of "The Ruined Cottage," from a tale of suffering to catharctic calm, a characteristic pattern in the early poetry, comparing it to sublime passages which culminate in meditative tranquillity. Chapter 4 discusses W's attempt to moralize "the pleasures of tragedy," chiefly in "The Old Cumberland Beggar" and "Ruined Cottage" revisions; chapters 5 and 6 distinguish between responses to suffering in the two volumes of Lyrical Ballads; and chapter 7 sees W reformulating his "pathetic response" in the two-part, five-book, and thirteen-book Preludes.

Reviews: Jonathan Arac, SIR 22(1983), 136-46; Don Bialostosky, MP 79(1981), 92-96; James A. Butler, WC 11 (1980), 132-33; William Galperin, Criticism 23(1981), 185-87; Frederick Garber, MLQ 42(1981), 392-94; Bishop C. Hunt, RM, 1980, pp. 133-34; Zachary Leader, TLS, 30 Jan. 1981, p. 120; Kerry McSweeney, QQ 89(1982), 113-20; W.J.B. Owen, RES 34(1983), 346-50.

705. Baker, Jeffrey. Time and Mind in Wordsworth's Poetry. Detroit: Wayne State University, 1980. 212 pp. indexed.

Baker's focus on W's imaginative freedoms with clock-time yields useful readings of many poems, leading him to discussion of the mystical experiences and visionary states in the 1850 Prelude. But on Baker's inaccuracies (chiefly in chronology), see Butler's review.

Reviews: James A. Butler, WC 12(1981), 153-54; P.M.S. Dawson, TLS, 12 Dec. 1980, p. 1423; Geoffrey Durrant, ESC 8(1982), 509-13; James A.W. Heffernan, SIR 21(1982), 253-58; A. McWhir, UTQ 50(1981), 122; W.J.B. Owen, RES 34(1983), 346-50.

706. Benston, Kimberly W. "'I Wandered Lonely as a Cloud': Can We Know the Dancer from the Dance?" CEA Critic 42, iv(1980): 10-14.

Comments on memory's capacity to involve the poet imaginatively in the remembered experience or scene.

707. Bialostosky, Don H. "Narrative Point of View in 'The Last of the Flock' and 'Old Man Travelling.'" The Wordsworth Circle 11(1980): 207-11.

Argues for the unity in each poem of narrative lead-in and interlocutor's speech. In each, as in "Simon Lee," the poet disrupts conventional expectations to involve the reader. Most interesting is the reading of "Old Man Travelling."

708. Binns, J.W. "The Title-Page Epigraph of the Lyrical Ballads, 1800." The Library 2(1980): 222-24.

Finds the source of the epigraph in a poem lamenting the failure of poetic powers, by the Dutch poet Jan Dousa the Elder (1545-1604).

709. Bose, Mandakranta. "Nature and the Creative Mind in Wordsworth and Tagore." Commonwealth Quarterly 4,xv (1980): 33-48.

Compares W's view of nature with that of the Hindu poet, finding them similar except that for W mind and nature are intimately related, while for Tagore they are unified.

710. Boulger, James D. The Calvinist Temper in English Poetry. The Hague: Mouton, 1980. xii+498 pp. indexed.

The chapter on W (pp. 383-424) traces elements of Puritan and Quaker traditions, particularly their "rhetoric of the spirit" and of "inner light," in poems of the great decade. The connection is suggestive rather than compelling (one problem, Boulger notes, is showing W's sources), but yields some illuminating insights.
Review: Mason I. Lowance, Jr., WC 13(1982), 157-58.

711. Brennan, Pegeen. "'Michael' and the 'Preface.'" The Wordsworth Circle 11(1980): 204-206.

Argues in Michaelic verse that "Michael" vindicates the poetic of the Preface.

712. Briesmaster, Allan. "Wordsworth as a Teacher of 'Thought.'" The Wordsworth Circle 11(1980): 19-23.

Explains W's classification of poems as a means to elicit reader interaction, or "thought"; considering W's reiteration of "thought" in the poems, Briesmaster suggests that the term may be as crucial as "imagination," though "it could also prove as problematic."

713. Brisman, Susan Hawk, and Leslie Brisman. "Lies Against Solitude: Symbolic, Imaginary, and Real." In The Literary Freud: Mechanisms of Defense and the Poetic Will, ed. Joseph H. Smith. New Haven, CT: Yale, 1980, pp. 29-65.

An excellent study of poetry's relation to audience, using terms and concepts of Lacan and comparing the poetic act to psychoanalysis: the analysand and poem, it is argued, both seek "recognition," creating myths of presence or "lies against solitude." Especially interesting on W's myth of the child in the Ode and The Prelude, and on C's relation to W in C's "Dejection."

714. Chandler, James K. "Wordsworth and Burke." ELH 47(1980): 741-71.

Surveys W's attitudes toward Burke, from scorn in the Letter to Llandaff (1793) to respect in the 1818 Addresses and the apostrophe to Burke in Prelude 7 (ca. 1820); finds W's "change of heart" as early as "The Old Cumberland Beggar" (ca. 1797), and with this challenges the Abrams portrait of early W as an apocalyptic poet, as well as Bloom's humanistic W. See also Chandler's book-length study, 1010.

715. Christensen, Jerome. "Wordsworth's Misery, Coleridge's Woe: Reading 'The Thorn.'" Papers on Language and Literature 16(1980): 268-86.

Using C's criticisms, Christensen reads the poem as a demonstration of W's poetic as expressed in the 1800 Preface: the narrator, especially in using repetition and fabrication in his expressions of passion to the interlocutor (who, for all his rationalism, seems "more superstitious" than the narrator himself), is not so much the speaker of a dramatic monologue (see 213) as an analogue of the poet.

716. Clarke, Bruce. "Wordsworth's Departed Swans: Sublimation and Sublimity in _Home at Grasmere_." _Studies in Romanticism_ 19(1980): 355-74.

Discussing the sublime and sublimation as (roughly) obstacle and bridge in desire's path, Clarke makes this poem an exemplum of W's "counter-sublime" poetic of sublimation by focusing on its hidden frustrations and "currents of regret," and on the great rhetorical pains the poet was at to achieve that "complacency" for which the poem has often been criticized.

717. Cooke, Michael G. "Byron and Wordsworth: The Complementary of a Rock and the Sea." _The Wordsworth Circle_ 11 (1980): 10-18. Rpt. in _Lord Byron and His Contemporaries: Essays from the Sixth International Byron Seminar_, ed. Charles E. Robinson. Newark, DE: University of Delaware, 1982, pp. 19-42.

States the poets' personal and poetic polarity within the same movement in terms of Freud's distinction between primary and secondary processes of imagination. Byron, identifying with the sea and idealizing youth, and W, identifying with the mountain and idealizing age and endurance, find in one another "a sort of measure and check."

718. Cosgrove, Brian. "Wordsworth and the Arcadian Imagination." _Durham University Journal_ 73(1980): 37-43.

A good essay showing "the realist bias of W's temperament" by citing numerous poems which critique Arcadian ideals or move from fanciful hopes to a recognition of reality and death.

719. Cox, Charles. "Harriette Harrison's Grasmere Journal." The Wordsworth Circle 11(1980): 239-42.

On the journal of an 1847 visitor to Grasmere with little bearing on W, though it furnishes a glimpse of him at Dora's funeral.

720. Curtis, Jared. "Charles A. Elton and Wordsworth's 'New Poem': A Study in Taste." The Wordsworth Circle 11 (1980): 36-42.

Gives a brief sketch of the life and opinions of Elton, in whose letters "The Barberry-Tree" was found, discusses his imitations of W, and considers W the probable author of the poem.

721. Curtis, Jared. "The Wellesley Copy of Wordsworth's Poetical Works, 1832." Harvard Library Bulletin 23(1980): 5-15.

An important consideration of the copy W revised for his 1836 edition, showing the care he took with his texts in this period and suggesting that even the changes in accidentals are to be attributed to W, not to publishing-house practice. Includes four full-page photos.

722. Damrosch, David. "Peter Bell Revised." The Wordsworth Circle 11 (1980): 232-38.

Parodies "Peter Bell," surveys other parodies and studies of them in a preface which parodies W's prose, and laments the state of W criticism.

723. Dann, Joanne. "Some Notes on the Relationship between the Wordsworth and the Lowther Families." The Wordsworth Circle 11(1980): 80-82.

Covers W's father's services for Lowther in a "land-grab," a mass eviction of tenants, and the unpopular 1768 election, and questions whether W's own relations with the Lowthers merely reflect, or influence, W's changing political stance.

724. Davies, Hunter. William Wordsworth: A Biography. London: Weidenfeld & Nicolson, 1980. xiii+367 pp. indexed.

No new research, but addresses the need for a brief, popular biography. For others, see Section 3.

Reviews: P. Beer, Li, 31 July 1980, 150; A. Broyard, NYT, 29 Oct. 1980, p. C27; D. Grumbach, NYT, 14 Dec. 1980, p. 11; J. Hunter, HudR 34(1981), 135; VQR 57 (1981), 48.

725. Devlin, D[avid] D[ouglas]. Wordsworth and the Poetry of Epitaphs. London: Macmillan, 1980. lx+143 pp. indexed.

A mistitled and poorly organized study of W's critical statements, not his poetry, presenting its thesis only on p. 109: "Wordsworth, especially in his Essays upon Epitaphs, saw reconcilement of opposites as the aim and purpose of his poetry," and valued the epitaph for its unifying capability.

Review: James A.W. Heffernan, SIR 21(1982), 253-58; Karen Horowitz, EIC 32(1982), 74-81.

726. Durrant, Geoffrey. "The Prophetic Vision in Wordsworth's 'Resolution and Independence.'" Generous Converse (734), pp. 88-101.

Argues plausibly that the leech-gatherer is Tiresias, representing the burden of visionary power. Cites the poem's cancelled stanzas, and compares Tiresias in Pope's Homer, in Ovid, and in Dante.

727. Easson, Angus. "'The Idiot Boy': Wordsworth Serves Out His Poetic Indentures." Critical Quarterly 22,iii (1980): 3-18.

Argues that "The Idiot Boy" is a major poem in Lyrical Ballads, and reads it as a statement on poetry and the task of the poet.

728. Ellis, David. "Autobiography and Reminiscence in the First Two Books of The Prelude." Critical Quarterly 22,i(1980): 21-29.

Attempts to distinguish passages of nostalgic reminiscence, especially the skating scene (book 1) from passages of true autobiography, in which W interrogates his past, in the 1805 _Prelude_.

729. Erdman, David V. "Leonora, Laodamia, and the Dead Ardours." _Blake: An Illustrated Quarterly_ 14(1980): 96-98.

Briefly notes Bürger's "Leonora" as a source for W's "Laodamia," particularly Laodamia's uxoriousness.

730. Finch, G.J. "Wordsworth, Keats, and 'the language of the sense.'" _Ariel_ 11,ii(1980): 23-36.

Gives W's famous phrase in "Tintern Abbey" a more literal and precise sense than usual, discussing the poets' "languages of the sense" as having linguistic structure and meaning. Includes incisive short comment on "Tintern Abbey" and the Ode, and explores the implications of the incompleteness of each poet's "language"--W being conversant in sight and sound, Keats in taste and touch.

731. Fry, Paul H. _The Poet's Calling in the English Ode_. New Haven, CT: Yale, 1980. viii+328 pp. indexed.

Difficult reading, but the chapter on W's Ode (pp. 133-61) is valuable for its close consideration of the importance of form. Fry sees W's ambivalence between natural and supernatural, as expressed in the phrase "natural piety," as ultimately decided in favor of the natural, the adult, "intimations of death." Though this "betrays" odal logic, it "recovers humanity." Also considers "Ode to Duty" and W's relation to C's "Dejection: an Ode."

Reviews: M. Brown, _SIR_ 20(1981), 249; Douglas Bush, _JEGP_ 80(1981), 133-35; Anne Elliott, _RES_ 34(1983), 120-21; Pat Rogers, _TLS_, 8 Aug. 1980, p. 891; Helen Vendler, _MLQ_ 42(1981), 87-90; Carl Woodring, _KSJ_ 30(1981), 191.

732. Galperin, William. "'Imperfect While Unshared': The Role of the Implied Reader in Wordsworth's 'Excursion.'" _Criticism_ 22(1980): 193-213.

Discusses the shifting roles of the Poet-narrator and their effect of engaging the implied reader, who more than the Wanderer or Pastor is the poem's "chief arbiter."

733. Gillham, D.G. "Wordsworth's Hidden Figures of Speech." Generous Converse (734), pp. 79-87.

Interesting examination of W's art in making literal description double as metaphor, especially in The Prelude and "Tintern Abbey."

734. Green, Brian, ed. Generous Converse: English Essays in Memory of Edward Davis. Cape Town: Oxford, 1980. 160 pp. not indexed.

Includes 726, 733, 738, and 751.

735. Hartman, Geoffrey H. "Diction and Defense in Wordsworth." In The Literary Freud: Mechanisms of Defense and The Poetic Will, ed. Joseph H. Smith. New Haven, CT: Yale, 1980, pp. 205-15.

Explains the poetic diction and allusions to Milton, Shakespeare, and Sophocles in "A little onward lend thy guiding hand" as defensive strategy against the "pressure of imagination" rather than as signs of poetic decline. See also 654.

736. Hartshorne, Charles. "In Defense of Wordsworth's View of Nature." Philosophy and Literature 4(1980): 80-91.

Argues that W's view of nature, especially his animism as exemplified in "The Simplon Pass," is more in keeping with modern science than with the science of W's day.

737. Harvey, A.D. English Poetry in a Changing Society 1780-1825. London: Allison & Busby, 1980. 195 pp. indexed.

Taking the enormous task of assessing Romanticism in relation to popular readership and the work of lesser poets, Harvey succeeds at the cost of assertions and generalizations that are at times blunt and hackneyed,

at times arbitrary and ill-defended. Interestingly places the Romantics' break with tradition not with Lyrical Ballads and the Preface (cf. 128), but with Scott (pp. 62-70, 101).
Reviews: P.M.S. Dawson, CritQ 25(1983), 85; E.B. Murray, RES 35(1984), 96-98.

738. Harvey, C.J.D. "Wordsworth and the Young Romantics: An Analysis of 'To a Skylark.'" Generous Converse (734), pp. 64-70.

Reads W's second poem "To a Skylark" as a resentful comparison between himself and the younger Romantic poets.

739. Heinzelman, Kurt. The Economics of the Imagination. Amherst: University of Massachusetts, 1980. xiv+328 pp. indexed.

"Wordsworth's Labor Theory" (pp. 196-233) is an excellent discussion of W's view/justification of his economic role, arguing that he actually had two labor theories--one for material labor; and, underlying his economic tropes for the poet's job, a more ideal "poetic economics," wherein poet and reader cooperate to create (rather than exchange) value. Incisive readings of "Resolution and Independence," "Michael," and "Home at Grasmere" develop the close relations between the two.

740. Helms, Alan. "The Sense of Punctuation." Yale Review 69 (1980): 177-96.

Distinguishes between the punctuation of prose and of poetry, the latter serving rhythmic and rhetorical rather than grammatical or logical purposes; gives a few pages to W's practice in the "Lucy Poems" and the sonnet "Not hurled precipitous from steep to steep."

741. Hill, Alan G. "Wordsworth and the Two Faces of Machiavelli." Review of English Studies 31(1980): 285-304.

A well informed essay suggesting that Machiavelli was a considerable influence on W's political views, especially affecting his view of Napoleon.

742. Hodgson, John A. Wordsworth's Philosophical Poetry, 1797-1814. Lincoln: University of Nebraska, 1980. xxi+216 pp. indexed.

On W as a religious poet, tracing his views from belief in "one life" to orthodoxy in four stages of his "emblematic" vision, from The Borderers to The Excursion (but dealing chiefly with the period 1797-1805). Hodgson sees "philosophical naivete" as responsible for W's decline as a poet. Much on W's versions and revisions, which are used to reveal his changing views. For philosophical contexts, Grob (193) is far more helpful.

Reviews: Jonathan Arac, SIR 22(1983), 136-46; James H. Averill, JEGP 81(1982), 119; Bishop C. Hunt, RM, 1981, pp. 149-50; David McCracken, MP 80(1983), 430; Peter J. Manning, WC 12(1981), 151-53; David Profumo, TLS, 20 Feb. 1981, p. 209; VQR 57(1981), 16.

743. Jackson, J[ames] R[obert] de J. Poetry of the Romantic Period. Routledge History of English Poetry, Vol. 4. London: Routledge & Kegan Paul, 1980. xvi+334 pp. indexed.

Juxtaposes the work of major and minor writers in ways that are occasionally revealing, treating a dozen or so W poems plus The Prelude and The Excursion in discussions that alternate between extended quotation, quick paraphrase, and too-brief comment.

Reviews: David Bromwich, TLS, 4 July 1980, p. 753; Marilyn Butler, English 29(1980), 239; Michael G. Cooke, KSJ 31(1982), 206; G. Dekker, WC 12(1981), 186; John E. Jordan, ELN 18(1981), 307; Donald H. Reiman, SIR 20 (1981), 254; Jack Stillinger, JEGP 80(1981), 581.

744. Kalinevitch, Karen. "Apparelled in Celestial Light/ Bathed in So Pure a Light: Verbal Echoes in Wordsworth's and Thoreau's Works." Thoreau Journal Quarterly 12,ii(1980): 27-30.

Cites echoes of W's poems in Walden evincing Thoreau's Wordsworthian sense of diminished spirituality.

745. Keith, W[illiam] J[ohn]. The Poetry of Nature: Rural Perspectives in Poetry from Wordsworth to the Present.

Toronto: University of Toronto, 1980. xi+219 pp. indexed.

Presents W as the founder of a tradition, comparing and contrasting him with Clare, William Barnes, Hardy, Frost, Edward Thomas, and R.S. Thomas. As the first chapter argues, W's influence lies not in his concept of nature (which is summarily dismissed), but in his dramatic mode: by viewing landscape through fictional speakers, W highlights its relation to the human.

Reviews: Peter J. Casagrande, JEGP 81(1982), 122; Christopher Clausen, DR 60(1980-81), 760; J.E.J., RM, 1980, pp. 58-59; April London, RES 34(1983), 89-90; A. McWhir, ArielE 13(1982), 122; Lore Metzger, ELN 19 (1981), 148-49; W.J.B. Owen, ESC 8(1982), 507-509; Max Keith Sutton, WC 12(1981), 187-90.

746. Kelley, Theresa M. "Deluge and Buried Treasure in Wordsworth's Arab Dream." Notes & Queries 27(1980): 70-71.

Offers a source for the dream in The Prelude, book 5, in Josephus's A History of the Jews, and sketches its implications, which are treated more fully in Kelley's later essay (893).

747. Kelley, Theresa M. "Proteus, Nature, and Romantic Mythography." The Wordsworth Circle 11(1980): 78-79.

Argues that in "The world is too much with us" W uses Proteus "to subvert, not celebrate, nature."

748. King, Everard H. "Beattie's The Minstrel and Wordsworth's The Excursion: What the Critics Overlook." Bulletin of Research in the Humanities 83(1980): 339-59.

Makes large claims for the influence of The Minstrel on The Excursion, books 1-4, on The Prelude, and on W himself.

749. Kramer, Lawrence. "Ocean and Vision: Imaginative Dilemma in Wordsworth, Whitman, and Stevens." Journal of English and Germanic Philology 79(1980): 210-30.

Includes a fine reading of the Snowdon passage (1850 Prelude, book 14) as a description of nature's temporary usurpation of the imaginative role.

750. Kramer, Lawrence. "The 'Intimations' Ode and Victorian Romanticism." Victorian Poetry 18(1980): 315-35.

Examines poems of loss and consolation by Tennyson, Arnold, and Browning to argue that the Victorians distrust W's self-reliance, and seek consolation outside themselves instead.

751. Langman, F.H. "Wordsworth's 'The Mad Mother,'" in Generous Converse (734), pp. 71-78.

Discusses "The Mad Mother" and W's other deserted women, focusing on the "mutual support" of mother and child.

752. Lea, Sydney. "From Sublime to Rigamarole: Relations of Frost to Wordsworth." Studies in Romanticism 19(1980): 83-108.

Contrasts W's sublimity with Frosts's lowly wisdom (not to Frost's disadvantage), commenting on "Tintern Abbey," "Michael," and "Ode to Duty." Especially astute on the latter, a favorite of Frost's, praising it for its renunciation of pretensions.

753. Lechay, Daniel. "Wordsworth's 'The Two April Mornings': A Note on the Blooming Girl." The Wordsworth Circle 11 (1980): 206.

A Freudian explanation for the girl's appearance to Matthew.

754. McNally, Paul. "Milton and the Immortality Ode." The Wordsworth Circle 11(1980): 28-33.

Relying in part on Jared Curtis's study of manuscript variants ("The Best Philosopher: New Variants," YULG 44[1970]: 139-47), McNally convincingly shows that Milton's invocation in Paradise Lost, book 3, lies behind the Ode's concern with light and failing vision, and examines W's sonnets on Milton to suggest that the Ode's conclusion alludes to Milton himself.

755. Mann, Karen B. "George Eliot and Wordsworth: The Power of Sound and the Power of Mind." _Studies in English Literature, 1500-1900_ 20(1980): 675-94.

Examines W's influence on Eliot in terms of their "similar conception of imagination as the crucial faculty," comparing their depictions of imagination as responsiveness to sound or music, especially in W's "On the Power of Sound" and Eliot's "The Legend of Jubal."

756. Manning, Peter J. "Keats's and Wordsworth's Nightingales." _English Language Notes_ 17(1980): 189-92.

Notes echoes in Keats's ode of W's "O Nightingale! thou surely art...," and contrasts the poets' uses of the bird.

757. Miller, Nan. "A Bout with Duty: Wordsworth's Transient Ode." _The Wordsworth Circle_ 11(1980): 224-27.

Follows other commentators in seeing the polarization of "duty" and "imagination," but argues that the "Ode to Duty" does not represent "a turning point in W's thought." For the correct form of p. 224, see _WC_ 12 (1981), p. 3.

758. Nabholtz, John R. "Romantic Prose and Classical Rhetoric." _The Wordsworth Circle_ 11(1980): 119-26.

Correlates the Romantics' grammar-school grounding in classical rhetoric with the persuasive temper of much of their prose. Though Nabholtz examines the works of C, not W, to show this influence, the background and method are germane to W as well.

759. Owen, W.J.B. "Two Wordsworthian Ambivalences." _The Wordsworth Circle_ 11(1980): 2-9.

Cites two cases in which W's ambivalence is not "either," but "both." Though in _The Prelude_, book 8, W contrasts the Lake District with literary pastoral to exalt the former, he respects both forms of pastoral. Similarly, W's views of the city, negative in book 7, positive in book 8, are not mutually exclusive but complementary.

760. Patterson, Charles I., Jr. "The Still Sad Music of Humanity in The Excursion: Wordsworth's Tragic View of Man." Milton and the Romantics 4(1980): 33-41.

Points out how many of the tales embody themes of man's interdependence and endurance.

761. Proffitt, Edward. "Samson and the Intimations Ode: Further Evidence of Milton's Influence." The Wordsworth Circle 11(1980): 197.

Points out verbal and thematic similarities between the Ode and Samson Agonistes, especially between the child and Samson.

762. Proffitt, Edward. "'This Pleasant Lea': Waning Vision in 'The World Is Too Much With Us.'" The Wordsworth Circle 11(1980): 75-77.

Finds the sonnet "an impassioned lament over waning vision."

763. Rackin, Donald. "'God's Grandeur': Hopkins' Sermon to Wordsworth." The Wordsworth Circle 11(1980): 66-73.

A close and convincing reading of "God's Grandeur" as response to "The World Is Too Much With Us."

764. Rajan, Tilottama. Dark Interpreter: The Discourse of Romanticism. Ithaca, NY: Cornell, 1980. 281 pp. indexed.

Argues that deconstruction, though not always applicable, is an historically valid approach to Romantic poetry, since the poetry, as well as the theory of Schiller, Schopenhauer, and Nietzsche, similarly questions the "surface content" of language. Does not deal at length with W, but his works are implicated in the general argument, and he figures prominently in chapter 5, on C, where the "dialectic of absence and presence" is analyzed in "Two April Mornings" and "Tintern Abbey."

Reviews: R. Ashton, TLS, 9 Jan. 1981, p. 38; Stuart Curran, Review 4(1982), 135-57; Geoffrey Durrant, UTQ 50 (1981), 117; Helen Regueiro Elam, WC 12(1981), 197-99; Nancy M. Goslee, KSJ 31(1982), 204; L.J. Swingle, MLQ 43 (1982), 89.

765. Ross, Donald, Jr. "A Map of Mental Faculties." The Wordsworth Circle 11(1980): 221-23.

Diagrams various nineteenth-century systems of mental faculties, such as W's in the 1815 Preface, in order to reveal both their surface disagreements and their deeper similarities. Suggests that "intuition" was the received term for what W and C call "imagination."

766. Rylestone, Anne. "Violence and the Abandoned Woman in Wordsworth's Poetry." Massachussetts Studies in English 7,iii(1980): 40-56.

Balanced but inconclusive speculation on W's biography, based on his expressions of guilt and shame in the 1805 Prelude, books 9 and 10, and on the recurrence of abandoned women in his poetry.

767. Schneider, Lisa Efimov. "An Examination of Shevchenko's Romanticism." In Shevchenko and the Critics, 1861-1980, ed. George S.N. Luckyj. Toronto: University of Toronto, 1980, pp. 430-53.

Compares "The Emigrant Mother" and "The Mad Mother" with Shevchenko's "Kateryna" (pp. 445-48), but the discussion of W is rather obtuse.

768. Sherry, Charles. Wordsworth's Poetry of the Imagination. Oxford: Clarendon, 1980. 115 pp. indexed.

Sees the anamnesis described in the Ode as the source of Wordsworthian imagination, and argues that all W's "poetry of the imagination" follows the pattern of the Ode: the speaker is displaced and visited by "imagination as anamnestic repetition," the divine significance of which he understands only in recollection.

Reviews: Jonathan Arac, SIR 22(1983), 136-46; James H. Averill, JEGP 81(1982), 119; P.M.S. Dawson, TLS, 12 Dec. 1980, p. 1423; Frances Ferguson, WC 12(1981), 149-51; Bishop C. Hunt, RM, 1981, 152-54; W.J.B. Owen, RES 34 (1983), 346-50; Judith W. Page, MP 80(1982), 205; Susan Wolfson, MLN 96(1981), 1221.

769. Spengemann, William C. The Forms of Autobiography: Episodes in the History of a Literary Genre. New Haven, CT: Yale, 1980. xvii+254 pp. indexed.

Includes a sensitive discussion of the 1850 Prelude (pp. 72-91), arguing that W fails as a "philosophical" autobiographer because he cannot bridge the cultural experiences which divide his past and present selves, but that he succeeds poetically by re-experiencing his earlier self in the spots of time.

Reviews: Gay Wilson Allen, GaR 35(1981), 411-15; Peter Hollingdale, RES 34(1983), 117-18; John N. Morris, ELN 18(1981), 229-33.

770. Stoddard, Eve Walsh. "The Borderers: A Critique of Both Reason and Feeling as Moral Agents." The Wordsworth Circle 11(1980): 93-97.

Views the play in political and biographical context, arguing that it represents "the nadir of W's hope for man" since it critiques "both moral agencies of the eighteenth century"--reason in Oswald, and feeling in Marmaduke--and that, avoiding simple solutions, W locates the source of evil "in human nature itself."

771. Sturrock, J. "Wordsworth: An Early Borrowing from Dante." Notes & Queries 27(1980): 204-205.

Finds that "Salisbury Plain," lines 19-22, echo Francesca's lament, which is "the earliest evidence of W's acquaintance with Dante."

772. Varney, Andrew. "Wordsworth and 'Those Italian Clocks.'" Notes & Queries 27(1980): 69-70.

Enlarges on Havens' explanation (115) for W's confusion in the 1805 Prelude, 6:622-24, and prefers the irritable tone of the 1805 version to the 1850 revision.

773. Vlasopolos, Anca. "Clouds of Glory: The Ruling Passion as Key to the Artist." Literature/Film Quarterly 8 (1980): 2-13.

Descriptive review of Ken Russell's film biographies of W and C, Clouds of Glory (BBC TV, July 1978); the slant of the former is aptly described by its subtitle, "William and Dorothy: The Love Story of the Poet and His Sister."

774. Wedd, Mary R. "Wordsworth's Stolen Boat." The Wordsworth Circle 11(1980): 243-48.

Gives two possible locations on Ullswater for the scene in The Prelude, book 1, with photographs.

775. Wittreich, Joseph. "'The Illustrious Dead': Milton's Legacy and Romantic Prophecy." Milton and the Romantics 4(1980): 17-32.

Argues that with Milton as exemplar, the Romantics--expecially Blake, W, and Shelley--developed a genre of secular prophecy, which offers a public rather than a personal vision, urges renovation of the individual, and is the less apocalyptic in that it seeks to alter history rather than threatening it. W's chief prophecies are The Prelude and "Home at Grasmere."

776. Woodman, Ross. "Child and Patriot: Shifting Perspectives in The Prelude. The Wordsworth Circle 11(1980): 83-92.

Focusing chiefly on books 8 to 10, Woodman argues that in forming the 1850 Prelude from the earlier versions W moves from innocence to experience, from patriotism to humanity.

777. Wordsworth, Jonathan. "On Man, on Nature, and on Human Life." Review of English Studies 31(1980): 17-29.

Argues that "'Home at Grasmere' is, almost in its entirety, a poem of 1800" (not 1806), and that the Prospectus to The Recluse was written first, then moved to the end of the poem.

778. Wordsworth, Jonathan. "That Wordsworth 'Epic.'" The Wordsworth Circle 11(1980): 34-35.

A note on the chronology of the long poems, suggesting that W's hope for a "narrative poem of Epic proportions" in June, 1805, refers merely to The Excursion.

779. Wüscher, Hermann J. Liberty, Equality, and Fraternity in Wordsworth, 1791-1800. Stockholm: Almqvist & Wiksell, 1980. 204 pp. indexed.

With close attention to vocabulary and sometimes cumbersome stylistic analysis, this careful study traces the growth of W's political acumen alongside the ripening of his poetic powers, from vocal radicalism to somewhat more moderate reticence. Wüscher is anxious to show how W's political ideals, especially of "brotherhood," find implicit expression in his poetry ("The Ruined Cottage," for instance, "is political dynamite"), and to reveal the chronological development of W's politics from his writings of the period.

Reviews: Michael Friedman, WC 13(1982), 133-35; Bishop C. Hunt, RM, 1980, pp. 141-42; Mary Moorman, DUJ 74 (1982), 312-14; Nicholas Roe, N&Q 30(1983), 86.

1981

780. Adams, Anthony. Wordsworth. Authors in their Age Series. London: Blackie & Son, 1981. 166 pp. indexed.

An elementary general introduction to the poet, his age, and his work, along the same lines as the American Monarch Notes.

781. Aers, David. "Wordsworth's Model of Man in 'The Prelude.'" Romanticism and Ideology (782), pp. 64-81.

A remarkably hostile look at W's "love of man," charging that by writing off social circumstances as mere "outside marks" of man (Prelude 12:217), W winds up loving a mere abstraction, which vitiates his poetry, ethics, politics, religion, everything.

782. Aers, David, Jonathan Cook, and David Punter. Romanticism and Ideology: Studies in English Writing 1765-1830. London: Routledge & Kegan Paul, 1981. v+194 pp. indexed.

Includes two feisty assessments of W's dismissal of social factors in his vision of man, 781 and 797.

Reviews: Terry Eagleton, L&H 8(1982), 255; P.M.S. Dawson, CritQ 26(1984), 139; Theresa M. Kelley, WC 14 (1983), 127-29; Clifford Siskin, CLS 21(1984), 228.

783. Alexander, J.H. "The Treatment of Scott in Reviews of the English Romantics." Yearbook of English Studies 11 (1981): 67-86.

Cites a number of reviews which compare W and Scott, not always to Scott's disadvantage.

784. Armstrong, Isobel. "Wordsworth's Complexity: Repetition and Doubled Syntax in The Prelude Book VI." Oxford Literary Review 4(1981): 20-42.

Intricate analysis of W's ambiguities, centering in W's use of different syntaxes and looking in particular at passages in which idealist and naturalist views are balanced. An important essay.

785. Averill, James H. "The Shape of _Lyrical Ballads_ (1798)." _Philological Quarterly_ 60(1981): 387-407.

Follows up C's suggestion that the volume is structured as an ode, remarking on the relations between contiguous poems and especially on the significance of the opening and closing poems, but without arguing for the volume's entire unity or perfect organization. Cf. 341, 517.

786. Avni, Abraham. "Wordsworth and Ecclesiastes: A 'Skeptical' Affinity." _Research Studies_ 49(1981): 66-71.

Notes three of W's allusions to Ecclesiastes 12:6, and compares the Solitary of _The Excursion_ with the preacher of Ecclesiastes.

787. Beck, Charlotte H. "'Something of a Dramatic Form': 'The Ruined Cottage' and _The Excursion_." _University of Mississippi Studies in English_ 2(1981): 98-108.

A judicious mini-reading of _The Excursion_ arguing that "The Ruined Cottage" provided not just a beginning, but also a paradigm for the poem's dramatic structure.

788. Beckham, Sabina. "'Star-Gazers': The Carnival-Urban Man and the Poetic Imagination." _College Language Association Journal_ 24(1981): 321-28.

Discusses the theme of city life's dulling effects on the imagination.

789. Brinkley, Robert A. "The Incident in the Simplon Pass: A Note on Wordsworth's Revisions." _The Wordsworth Circle_ 12(1981): 122-25.

Argues that between 1805 and 1850 W changes the focus in the Simplon passage from the past event to the present act of narration.

790. Brooks, Elmer. "Tintern Abbey: Neoclassic and Romantic." CEA Critic 43(1981): 3-8.

Prints Sneyd Davies's poem, "A Voyage to Tinterne Abbey in Monmouthshire, from Whitminister in Gloucestershire" (1745), and contrasts it with W's "Tintern Abbey" to point up differences between Neoclassic and Romantic.

791. Bushnell, John P. "'Where Is The Lamb for a Burnt Offering?': Michael's Covenant and Sacrifice." The Wordsworth Circle 12(1981): 246-52.

An excellent essay developing the similarity of Michael and Luke to Abraham and Isaac, arguing that Michael sacrifices Luke because his love for the land outweighs his familial love.

792. Butler, Marilyn. Romantics, Rebels, and Reactionaries: English Literature and its Background, 1760-1830. London: Oxford, 1981. 213 pp. indexed.

An attempt to place Romanticism in the context of political and social currents. Without treating W at great length or depth, Butler discusses his allegiance to Enlightenment ideals, the sociological factors in his reception by reviewers, and his fortunes at the hands of the younger Romantics (chapters 2, 6).

Reviews: R. Ashton, TLS, 9 Oct. 1981, p. 1177; T. Boorman, English 31(1982), 150; Karl Kroeber, WC 16 (1983), 126-27; M. Scrivener, Criticism 24(1982), 286; A. Ward, KSJ 32(1983), 204; Carl Woodring, BlakeQ 16 (1983), 232-33.

793. Caraher, Brian G. "Metaphor as Contradiction: A Grammar and Epistemology of Poetic Metaphor." Philosophy and Rhetoric 14(1981): 69-88.

Examines W's assimilation of men to natural objects in "The Old Cumberland Beggar" and "Resolution and Independence" (pp. 76-82) to demonstrate that in metaphor a human "vehicle" may be used to convey a natural "tenor," and that the nature of metaphor is to join contradictory rather than synonymous terms (in this case, the human and the natural).

794. Carney, Raymond. "Making the Most of a Mess." Georgia Review 35(1981): 631-42

Notes that the Cornell Editions (see Section 1.2) will have profound implications for our concepts of the text and of the compositional process, and briefly examines early drafts of "The Ruined Cottage."

795. Carothers, Yvonne M. "Alastor: Shelley Corrects Wordsworth." Modern Language Quarterly 42(1981): 21-47.

Reads Alastor as a depiction, in response to The Excursion, of W's estrangement from his youthful self which "allows W to identify and correct his faults."

796. Christensen, Jerome. "'Thoughts That Do Often Lie Too Deep for Tears': Toward a Romantic Concept of Lyrical Drama." The Wordsworth Circle 12(1981): 52-64.

Taking the last two lines and stanzas 7-9 as his text, Christensen argues that the poem stages the Oedipal urges of the child toward his divine father, and of the man toward his child/father, that are repressed in "piety" and find no resolution. W thus avoids tragedy in favor of "lyrical drama," a "drama of the mind" leading to "meditative pathos." Difficult reading.

797. Cook, Jonathan. "Romantic Literature and Childhood." Romanticism and Ideology (782), pp. 44-63.

A penetrating Marxist analysis of the child-figure in Blake and W; W comes off badly for sidestepping social in favor of natural determinants. Discusses The Excursion, books 8 and 9; "Alice Fell" (failing to take W's irony into account); The Prelude, book 1; and the Ode.

798. Dudley, Edward. "Cervantes and Wordsworth: Literary History as Literature and Literature as Literary History." In Cervantes: Su Obra Y Su Mundo: Actas Del I Congreso Internacional Sobre Cervantes, ed. Manuel Criado de Val. Madrid, 1981, pp. 1097-1104.

Argues that in the Arab Dream (1805 Prelude, book 5) W combines the figures of Cide Hamete and Quixote: he not only equates madness and vision, like the former, but, like the latter, produces literature from "literary history," or his reading (as Quixote read chivalry, W read Quixote).

799. Enani, M.M. Dialectic of Memory: A Critical Study of Wordsworth's Two-Part Prelude Incorporating Texts of the 1798-1799 Manuscripts. Cairo: Egyptian State Publishing House, 1981. 77 pp.

Poorly printed text, prefaced by an essay on the "dialectic" between poet and persona.

800. Engell, James. The Creative Imagination: Enlightenment to Romanticism. Cambridge, MA: Harvard, 1981. xix+416 pp. indexed.

An excellent source on the heritage of W's multivalent concept of imagination. A chapter specifically on W (pp. 265-76) focuses on the 1805 Prelude and the criticism, and finds W's contribution to be the idea of reciprocity between imagination and nature.

Reviews: Alex Page, WC 13(1982): 150-51; L.J. Swingle, MLQ 43(1982), 89-97.

801. Erdman, David V. "The Man Who Was Not Napoleon." The Wordsworth Circle 12(1981): 92-96. Revised article from Worldview, 23 Sept. 1980.

Presents John Oswald, a Jacobin Scot who was in Paris when W arrived, as the prototype for Oswald of "The Borderers," and conjectures that in autumn, 1792, W briefly considered one of Oswald's schemes, a naval attack on London. Retracted in 881.

802. Essick, Robert N. "Wordsworth and Leech-Lore." The Wordsworth Circle 12(1981): 100-102.

Sharing some of the leech-gatherer's trade-secrets, Essick points out parallels of leech-gathering to poem-writing, gatherer to poet, leech to poem, to argue that the leech-gatherer is, especially in point of his dwindling quarry, chosen as an analogue of the poet.

803. Gates, Barbara T. "Wordsworth's Mirror of Morality: Distortions of Church History." The Wordsworth Circle 12(1981): 129-32.

Outlines several factors which made W slight historical accuracy in Ecclesiastical Sonnets, especially his instinct for moral exempla, which he selected to the exclusion of less exemplary incidents and characters, and his greater interest in individuals than in institutions.

804. Gottlieb, Erika. Lost Angels of a Ruined Paradise: Themes of Cosmic Strife in Romantic Tragedy. Victoria, BC: Sono Nis, 1981.

Reads The Borderers as an allegorical "quest for Paradise," drawing parallels with The Faerie Queene and Paradise Lost, especially the former (pp. 14-44).
Reviews: A. McWhir, UTQ 51(1982), 420; Carl Woodring, CompD 17(1983), 85.

805. Greer, Germaine. "Wordsworth and Winchilsea: The Progress of an Error." The Nature of Identity (865), pp. 1-13.

On W's misrepresentation of Anne Finch, Countess of Winchilsea, arguing that in excerpting her poetry for an album presented to Lady Lowther in 1819, he arrogantly cut out everything that did not sound like his own.

806. Halliburton, David. "From Poetic Thinking to Concrete Interpretation." Papers on Language and Literature 17 (1981): 71-79.

An opaque essay attempting a "concrete interpretation"--i.e., one that "focuses on the relevance to literature of social, economic, and political concerns"--of "Michael," with particular attention to the importance of news, work, and memory.

807. Haney, David P. "The Emergence of the Autobiographical Figure in The Prelude, Book I." Studies in Romanticism 20(1981): 33-63.

A good deconstructionist study of the rhetorical strategies enabling W to get under way with his poem (in the 1805 version), paying special attention to problems of temporality such as the text's shift from a present-tense lyrical beginning (lines 1-55) to past-tense autobiographical narrative.

808. Hartman, Geoffrey. "The Poetics of Prophecy." _High Romantic Argument_ (824), pp. 15-40.

Explores the relationship between poet and prophet, seeking "a poetics of prophecy," and examining the father's-death and Snowdon passages in the 1850 _Prelude_, books 11 and 14. W's re-vision of "let there be light" on Snowdon moves us away from "the dichotomizing of religious and nonreligious" thought. Comparing the passages treating the deaths of W's mother and father, and "A slumber did my spirit seal," Hartman argues that the causally unrelated death in each case "corrects" the speaker's apocalyptic wish to end time; the chastened poet then works _in_ time to bond the events in a prophetic "blast of harmony." A stimulating discussion.

809. Hayden, John O. "The Road to Tintern Abbey." _The Wordsworth Circle_ 12(1981): 211-16.

Presents a cento of eighteenth-century blank verse, strikingly parallel in many passages to "Tintern Abbey," to demonstrate the unBloomian nature of W's borrowings, many of which (Hayden argues) are unconsciously lifted, and to show the affinity between W's and earlier eighteenth-century verse.

810. Hayden, John O. "Wordsworth and Coleridge: Shattered Mirrors, Shining Lamps?" _The Wordsworth Circle_ 12 (1981): 71-81.

Argues against Abrams (124) that W and C are Aristotelians, not expressionists; most of this is reprinted from Hayden's _Polestar of the Ancients_ (655).

811. Hollander, John. _The Figure of Echo: A Mode of Allusion in Milton and After_. Berkeley and Los Angeles: University of California, 1981. x+155 pp. indexed.

Includes a number of brief but sensitive examinations of echoes (which Hollander distinguishes from intentional allusions) in poems by W.

Reviews: John Bayley, TLS, 7 May 1982, p. 499; Christopher Ricks, YR 72(1983), 439; Joseph Wittreich, JEGP 83(1984), 237-39.

812. Homans, Margaret. "Eliot, Wordsworth, and the Scenes of the Sisters' Instruction." Critical Inquiry 8(1981): 223-41.

A sensitive feminist influence-study noting George Eliot's "ambivalent response to the authority of a text."

813. Hopkins, Brooke. "Pear-Stealing and Other Faults: An Essay on Confessional Autobiography." South Atlantic Quarterly 80(1981), 305-21.

Contrasts W's boat-stealing episode (Prelude 1) with theft episodes in Augustine and Rousseau, focusing on the writers' dissimilar interpretations of their similar actions (pp. 316-21).

814. Hopkins, Brooke. "Reading, and Believing in, Autobiography." Soundings 64(1981): 93-111.

Compares and contrasts W's relation to a public audience in the 1805 Prelude with Augustine's and Rousseau's in their Confessions, focusing on the problem of sincerity.

815. Hopkins, Brooke. "The Mystical Dimensions of Wordsworth's Poetry." Studia Mystica 4(1981): 49-62.

Sees "The Idiot Boy" as exemplifying both W's project of defamiliarization in Lyrical Ballads, and the ineffable experience of what Rudolph Otto calls the numinous.

816. Hugo, F.J. "Wordsworth's Blank Misgivings." Theoria 57 (1981): 51-62.

Unimpressive comparison of "Tintern Abbey" and "Resolution and Independence" as poems of crisis leading to "broader insight."

817. Jackson, Geoffrey. "Nominal and Actual Audiences: Some Strategies of Communication in Wordsworth's Poetry." The Wordsworth Circle 12(1981): 226-31.

Carefully considers the rhetorical effect of assuming various sorts of audiences in several W poems, and suggests that in The Prelude W nominally addresses C to justify the poem's intimacy and didacticism.

818. Jarvis, Robin J. "The Five-Book Prelude: A Reconsideration." Journal of English and Germanic Philology 80 (1981): 528-51.

Takes issue with Jonathan Wordsworth's conjectural reconstruction of the five-book Prelude (512), arguing that this version was never completed. In particular, Jarvis considers chronology and examines MSS. W and WW to argue that book 4 cannot be reconstructed with anything like certainty, and holds that W never finished book 5 before deciding on the much longer thirteen-book version of 1805.

819. Keach, William. "Obstinate Questionings: The Immortality Ode and Alastor." The Wordsworth Circle 12(1981): 36-44.

Finds Shelley restating the loss and rejecting the consolation of the Ode, and argues that it is a more important source for Alastor than is The Excursion.

820. Kelley, Paul. "Wordsworth and Pope's Epistle to Cobham." Notes & Queries 28(1981): 314-15.

Finds a source for W's line, "We murder to dissect" ("The Tables Turned"), and similar lines in The Borderers and The Prelude, in Pope's poem, which is called "a seminal influence" for the period 1794-97.

821. Kelley, Theresa M. "The Economics of the Heart: Wordsworth's Sublime and Beautiful." Romanticism Past and Present 5,i(1981): 15-32.

Shrewd psychological analysis of the Wordsworthian sublime and beautiful, arguing that W's sublime involves conscious suppression rather than unconscious repression of anxiety; that confronted with the ineffable guilt and anxiety that ground his sublime passages, W consistently and consciously reverts to the rhetoric of the beautiful. Making good sense of W's revisions, Kelley illustrates her thesis in sensitive readings of the spots of time in book 11 of the 1805 _Prelude_.

822. Kishel, Joseph F. "Wordsworth and the Grande Chartreuse." _The Wordsworth Circle_ 12(1981): 82-88.

Considers W's refinement of the lines on the Grande Chartreuse in their successive contexts--"Descriptive Sketches," "The Tuft of Primroses," the "Essay, Supplementary," and the 1850 _Prelude_, book 6--so that they come to express doubt in the efficacy of revolution, and faith in imaginative power.

823. Larkin, Peter. "Wordsworth's 'After-Sojourn': Revision and Unself-Rivalry in the Later Poetry." _Studies in Romanticism_ 20(1981): 409-36.

Interesting but difficult examination of "deliberate discontinuity" in W's later poetry, stressing his "belatedness" in relation to the great decade and examining a dozen or so later lyrics for three "stances" or "temperaments": "counter-sublime," "sufficient mutuality," and "prevenience." Not on revision in the traditional sense.

824. Lipking, Lawrence, ed. _High Romantic Argument: Essays for M.H. Abrams_. Ithaca, NY: Cornell, 1981. 182 pp. not indexed.

Includes 808 and 869.

Reviews: Jonathan Arac, _WC_ 13(1982): 147-49; Jerome C. Christensen, _RM_, 1981, pp. 63-64; Kerry McSweeney, _QQ_ 89 (1982), 113-20; Donald H. Reiman, _ELN_ 19(1981), 133-40; Christopher Salvesen, _TLS_, 26 Feb. 1982, p. 231.

825. Luther, Susan. "Wordsworth's _Prelude_: VI, 592-616 (1850)." _The Wordsworth Circle_ 12(1981): 253-61.

Lacking a thesis, Luther considers almost everything the passage might mean, and locates its greatness in its "argumentative surface discourse with semantic and syntactic ambiguity."

826. McFarland, Thomas. Romanticism and the Forms of Ruin: Wordsworth, Coleridge, and Modalities of Fragmentation. Princeton, 1981. xxxiv+432 pp.

A wide-ranging scholarly study defining Romanticism in terms of "diasparactive awareness," to which McFarland traces many of the Romanticist topoi--organicism, unity, symbolism, lyricism, the relation of poetry to philosophy. More on C than on W, but deals at length with "The Symbiosis of Coleridge and Wordsworth" (ch. 1), W's egotism, stoicism, and politics (ch. 3), the variety and unevenness of his style (ch. 4), and his ideal of unity ("Second Landing Place").

Reviews: Stuart Curran, Review 4(1982), 135-57; David V. Erdman, RM, 1981, pp. 64-65; Lilian R. Furst, CL 34 (1982), 281-83; Robert Ginsberg, JAAC 40(1981), 218-20; A.C. Goodson, ELN 20(1982), 70; J.H. Haeger, RP&P 5,ii (1981), 45-50; James A.W. Heffernan, WC 13(1982), 125-28; Anne K. Mellor, MLQ 42(1981), 194-96; Christopher Salvesen, TLS, 17 July 1981, p. 806.

827. McGavran, James Holt, Jr. "'Alone Seeking the Visible World': The Wordsworths, Virginia Woolf, and The Waves." Modern Language Quarterly 42(1981): 265-91.

An excellent study of Woolf's complex relation to W as both precursor and "literary father-figure," comparing and contrasting their sensibilities with special reference to their Romantic shore-symbolism. McGavran sees The Waves as a "revisionary effort."

828. McNulty, J. Bard. "Self-Awareness in the Making of 'Tintern Abbey.'" The Wordsworth Circle 12(1981): 97-100.

Argues that the period referred to in the poem is 1791, seven years before, not five, and reads the poem as an impromptu ode by stressing its contradictions and discontinuities.

829. Magnuson, Paul. "The Genesis of Wordsworth's 'Ode.'" The Wordsworth Circle 12(1981): 23-30.

Views the first four stanzas as fragments which express an anxiety better glossed by W's previous and contemporary projects than by the 1804 conclusion: as two _Prelude_ fragments (_ca._ spring, 1799) show, W worried about his ability to shape spontaneous fragments into a "perfect form." The ode form was a partial solution to his dilemma, but progress still waited till 1804, when such doubts subsided.

830. Manning, Peter J. "Tales and Politics: _The Corsair_, _Lara_, and _The White Doe of Rylstone_." _Byron: Poetry and Politics_ (860), pp. 204-30.

Focuses not only on politics in the usual sense, but also on the poems' "politics of presentation," examining such things as dedications and pricing to contrast Byron's cheap, popular tales with W's expensive and slow-selling "White Doe." But, Manning argues, the political implications of the poems themselves are strikingly similar.

831. Marder, Daniel. "The Picturesque in Wordsworth's Imagination: His _Guide to the Lakes_." _The Nature of Identity_ (865), pp. 27-35.

Notes the _Guide_'s alternation between the language of the picturesque and of more imaginative ways of seeing.

832. Marsden-Smedley, Hester. "Beginning at Racedown." _The Wordsworth Circle_ 12(1981): 141-42.

A chatty account of the W's move to Racedown by a descendent of the Pinneys, who owned it; nothing much new.

833. Mitchell, W.J.T. "Diagrammatology." _Critical Inquiry_ 7 (1981): 622-33.

Arguing for the critical usefulness of spatializing literary form, Mitchell briefly discusses W's images for the form of _The Prelude_. Written in response to Leon Surette's "Rational Form in Literature" (_CritI_ 7[1981]: 612-21), which is a reply to Mitchell's "Spatial Form in Literature: Toward a General Theory" (_CritI_ 6[1980]: 539-67). See also 618.

834. Miyagawa, Kiyoshi. "Sound and Vision in Wordsworth's Poetry." Studies in English Literature (Tokyo), English Number, 1981, pp. 25-42.

Good criticism on the interrelation of sound and sight in several poems, especially "To the Cuckoo" ("O blithe newcomer!"), "Resolution and Independence," and the Snowdon passage of the 1850 Prelude, book 14.

835. Newby, Peter T. "Literature and the Fashioning of Tourist Taste." In Humanistic Geography and Literature: Essays on the Experience of Place, ed. Douglas C.D. Pocock. London: Groom Helm, 1981, pp. 130-41.

Discusses literature's "ability to influence styles of tourism," but the treatment of W and the Lake District (pp. 130-35) is vague and provides no evidence that W's descriptive poetry or his Guide to the Lakes indeed had any effect on tourism.

836. Newlyn, Lucy. "'In City Pent': Echo and Allusion in Wordsworth, Coleridge, and Lamb." Review of English Studies 32(1981): 408-28.

A good discussion of W's and C's uses of the city as a symbol for imprisonment and "imaginative deadness," and of Lamb's rebuttals. Cites "To Joanna," "Tintern Abbey," The Prelude, and other poems.

837. Newlyn, Lucy. "Wordsworth, Coleridge, and the 'Castle of Indolence' Stanzas." The Wordsworth Circle 12(1981): 106-113.

Argues that W idealizes the portraits of himself and C in an effort to reconstitute their early relationship, and in particular that the portrait of C is "a projection of W himself." Helpful on literary sources of the poem.

838. O'Brien, Darcy. "Seamus Heaney and Wordsworth, A Correspondent Breeze." The Nature of Identity (865), pp. 37-46.

Does little more of service than list Heaney's mentions of W in poems and epigraphs.

839. Peterfreund, Stuart. "*The Prelude*: Wordsworth's Metamorphic Epic." *Genre* 14(1981): 441-72.

Comparing the Virgilian model of the poetic career, wherein a poet works up a ladder of genres to epic, and eighteenth-century biology's idea that each organism "recapitulates the evolutionary history leading up to it," Peterfreund ingeniously argues that *The Prelude* "*becomes* an epic" by moving through pastoral and satire in the earlier books. Cf. 899.

840. Phelan, James. *Worlds from Words: A Theory of Language in Fiction*. Chicago: University of Chicago, 1981. xi+259 pp. indexed.

Five pages on "A slumber did my spirit seal" respond to Hirsch's discussion in *Validity in Interpretation* (New Haven, CT: Yale, 1967), agreeing that interpretation must refer to the author's intention, but arguing that this can be inferred only from the text itself. (See also 557.) Phelan believes that in stanza 2 the speaker has moved "beyond grief" to acceptance, not of death, but of the "difference between human life and other forms."

841. Prickett, Stephen, ed. *The Romantics*. The Context of English Literature Series. London: Methuen, 1981. 267 pp. indexed.

This multi-disciplinary book of five essays on historical, religious, and philosophical contexts, as well as on art and literature, provides a good introduction to the period. The final essay, Prickett's "Romantic Literature" (pp. 202-57), contains much on W and is helpful for understanding his ties to the eighteenth century.

Reviews: G. Cavaliero, *TLS*, 11 Dec. 1981, p. 1449; P.M.S. Dawson, *CritQ* 24(1982), 91; A. Rodway, *BJA* 22 (1982), 281.

842. Prickett, Stephen. "'Types and Symbols of Eternity': The Poet as Prophet." *Centrum* 1,i(1981): 19-35.

An informative essay stressing the importance of Bishop Robert Lowth's Biblical Study, The Sacred Poetry of the Hebrews (first published in English in 1787), in making the Bible rather than the classics "the central poetic tradition of the Romantics," since Lowth not only associates poet and prophet but also makes the Bible "a model of sublimity" and of natural language. Discusses W's typology in the crossing of the Alps and on Snowdon (1805 Prelude, books 6 and 13) as both Biblical and secular.

843. Raschke, Carl, and Donna Gregory. "Revelation, the Poetic Imagination, and the Archaeology of the Feminine." The Archaeology of the Imagination, ed. Charles E. Windquist. Journal of the American Academy of Religion: Thematic Studies 48,ii(1981): 89-104.

Reflecting on the possibility and meaning of "revelation" in modern times, the authors briefly examine The Prelude and find W's use of imagination to achieve revelation, and his reliance on the "feminine" (Dorothy) to preserve his imaginative powers, heuristic. But in general the Romantics' "eternal feminine" is a mere "construct of the patriarchal consciousness."

844. Rehder, Robert. Wordsworth and the Beginnings of Modern Poetry. Totowa, N.J.: Barnes & Noble, 1981. 245 pp. indexed.

Uses W to mark the beginning of modern poetry, focusing on aspects of his work which have been central for subsequent writers, especially the emphasis on subjectivity and psychology, but without shedding much new light on W specifically.

Reviews: David McCracken, MP 80(1983), 430; Lachlan Mackinnon, TLS, 19 June 1981, p. 704; Lucy Newlyn, RES 35(1984), 243; W.J.B. Owen, MLR 79(1984), 675; P. Swaab, EIC 33(1983), 55.

845. Reiman, Donald H. "Wordsworth, Shelley, and the Romantic Inheritance." Romanticism Past and Present 5,ii(1981): 1-22.

Sees W and Shelley as representing opposite poles of Romanticism, "pastoral" and "gothic," the one accepting the natural world, the other crying out against it. Locates Auden and Stevens in W's camp, Eliot and Yeats in Shelley's.

846. Robinson, Jeffrey C. "The Immortality Ode: Lionel Trilling and Helen Vendler." The Wordsworth Circle 12 (1981): 64-70.

Though too easily assuming that concerns of W's contemporary poems are the Ode's concerns, this is an intelligent defense of Trilling's reading (118), finding the Ode naturalistic, not theological, tragic, not elegiac, ambivalent rather than conclusive. But Robinson's strength lies in defense of Trilling, not in critique of Vendler (612).

847. Roe, Nicholas. "Leigh Hunt and Wordsworth's Poems, 1815." The Wordsworth Circle 12(1981): 89-91.

Corrects Moorman (79) regarding the date Hunt received a presentation copy--about April 15, not February 12.

848. Ross, Donald. "Poems 'Bound Each to Each' in the 1815 Edition of Wordsworth." The Wordsworth Circle 12 (1981): 133-40.

Points out that the 1815 edition, in which W first tried out his famous classification of poems, was meant to be read through as an "integrated work." Ross argues that the poems "follow a person's history," that of "a British lad," though not W's. Includes charts which will be helpful for surveying W's organization and reorganization.

849. Ruoff, Gene W. "'Fields of Sheep': The Obscurities of the Ode, I-IV." The Wordsworth Circle 12(1981): 45-51.

Offers a fresh perspective on the Ode: surveying critics' ways "not to read a line" in the Note & Queries exchange of 1889-90 over "fields of sleep," Ruoff explains the obscurities of stanzas 1-4 as resulting from W's reluctance to alter an early draft to which C had already responded in "Dejection," and sketches the implications for W's post-"Dejection" continuation in stanzas 5-9. Succinct and entertainingly written.

850. Schippers, J.G. "On Persuading (Some Notes on the Implied Author in Critical Discourse)." Dutch Quarterly Review 11,i(1981): 34-54.

Nothing on W himself, but interesting rhetorical analysis of three essays on W, taken as random examples to demonstrate the importance of the authorial persona in criticism: Arnold's (98), Leavis's (111), and Cleanth Brooks's "Wordsworth and the Paradox of the Imagination" (in 165).

851. Schofield, Mary Anne. "Wordsworth and the Philadelphia Port Folio." English Language Notes 18(1981): 186-91.

Lists the poems "quoted" and concisely surveys the criticism in America's "most popular and definitive literary magazine of the first quarter of the nineteenth century," as an indicator of W's early American reputation.

852. Schopf, Sue Weaver. "Wordsworth's Exploration of Geriatric Psychology: Another Look at the Narrator of 'The Thorn.'" English Language Notes 19(1981): 33-40.

Suggests sources in Hartley for the narrator's "senility, his flawed memory, and his excitement," and finds the poem an "engaging attempt at geriatric psychological analysis."

853. Schulman, Samuel E. "The Spenserian Enchantments of Wordsworth's 'Resolution and Independence.'" Modern Philology 79(1981): 24-44.

Citing important sources in both Thomson and Spenser, Schulman argues that "Resolution and Independence" is one in a series of W's Spenserian poems, and shows that in revising it W brought it closer not just to Spenserian style or verse form, but also to what W saw as Spenserian strategy, giving "the universality and permanence of abstractions to human beings."

854. Schulman, Samuel E. "The Spenser of the Intimations Ode." The Wordsworth Circle 12(1981): 31-35.

Suggests that it is W's "role as poet, his sense of vocation," that alienates him from the celebrations in the Ode, considering sources in Spenser's "Maye AEclogue" and Prothalamion.

855. Smith, K.E. "Love in The Borderers." Durham University Journal 74 (1981): 97-102.

Presents Godwin's opposition of rational benevolence to love as a central issue in the play.

856. Spivak, Gayatri Chakravorty. "Sex and History in The Prelude (1805), Books Nine to Thirteen." Texas Studies in Literature and Language 23 (1981): 324-60.

Argues that in occluding women (Annette and Dorothy), transforming history into "an iconic text," and substituting poetry for revolutionary action as a cure for social ills, The Prelude's later books reveal "the sexual-political program of the Great Tradition."

857. Springer, Carolyn. "Far From the Madding Crowd: Wordsworth and the News of Robespierre's Death." The Wordsworth Circle 12(1981): 243-45.

A close reading pointing out that even this important event (book 10) has greater private than public significance in The Prelude.

858. Staley, Thomas F. "The Shaping of the Artificer: Reflections on Wordsworth and Joyce in France," in The Nature of Identity (865), pp. 47-55.

A contrived comparison with nothing new on W.

859. Stempel, Daniel. "Wordsworth and the Phenomenology of Textual Constitution." Philosophy and Literature 5 (1981): 150-75.

Attempts to use the terms of Husserlian phenomenology to analyze the workings of the imagination in "Tintern Abbey" and the 1805 Prelude.

860. Stürzl, Erwin A., and James Hogg, eds. Byron: Poetry and Politics. 7th International Byron Symposium, Salzburg, 1980. Salzburg: Institut für Anglistik und Amerikanistik, Universität Salzburg, 1981. x+427 pp. not indexed. pbk.

Includes two essays, 830 and 862, stressing the similarity of W's and Byron's politics.

861. Thomas, Gordon K. "'Christabel,' 'The Idiot Boy,' and Paraphasia." Encyclia 58(1981): 63-68.

Argues that the poems are "companion pieces" since both deal with speech disorders.

862. Thomas, Gordon K. "Strange Political Bedfellows: Inkel and Wordswords in Iberia." Byron: Poetry and Politics (860), pp. 231-42. Rpt. as "Allies and Guerrillas: The Peninsular Campaigns of Wordsworth and Byron." The Wordsworth Circle 14(1983): 56-61.

Argues that Byron's attacks on W for political apostacy are provoked not by W's politics, of which Byron was ignorant, but by W's association with Southey. Finds Byron's and W's views on the peninsular campaigns essentially the same.

863. Thomson, Douglass H. "Wordsworth's Warning Voice: A Miltonic Echo in Book II of The Prelude." The Wordsworth Circle 12(1981): 132.

Finds a line from Paradise Lost echoed and secularized in the 1850 Prelude, 2:19-21.

864. Ward, William S. "Laying Bricks and Squaring a Circle: Wordsworth and Two of His Literary Friends--Barron Field and Thomas Noon Talfourd." The Wordsworth Circle 12(1981): 12-22.

Arguing for study of minor literary figures, Ward gives brief lives of Field (see 332) and Talfourd (lawyer, playwright, important early champion of W), and anecdotes of their relations with W, Lamb, and Hunt.

865. Weathers, William, ed. The Nature of Identity: Essays Presented to Donald E. Hayden by the Graduate Faculty of Modern Letters, the University of Tulsa. Tulsa: University of Oklahoma, 1981. viii+96 pp.

Includes 805, 831, 838, and 858, none but perhaps the first containing much of importance.

866. Wellens, Oskar. "Henry Crabb Robinson, Reviewer of Wordsworth, Coleridge, and Byron in the Critical Review: Some New Attributions." Bulletin of Research in the Humanities 84(1981): 98-120.

Among nineteen attributions the only review of W is the favorable review (July, 1816) of W's "Letter to a Friend of Robert Burns." Sketches Robinson's admiration of W, and reprints an engraving of Robinson (pp. 98-101, 105-107).

867. Williams, Anne. "The Intimations Ode: Wordsworth's Fortunate Fall." Romanticism Past and Present 5,i(1981): 1-13.

Finds the theme of Paradise Lost at the heart of the Ode, and seeks to justify the poem's "disunity" by arguing that its modulation from elegy (stanzas 1-4) to ode reflects this theme.

868. Woolford, John. "Wordsworth Agonistes." Essays in Criticism 31(1981): 27-40.

Fascinating analysis of Milton's positive influence in the opening of The Prelude: Woolford traces "Was it for this" to Samson Agonistes, and argues that it determines the poem's direction and method.

869. Wordsworth, Jonathan. "As with the Silence of the Thought." High Romantic Argument (824), pp. 41-76.

Discusses W's distrust of language, citing the 1805 _Prelude_ and "Essays upon Epitaphs." For W, it is argued, thought is prior to the word--the word is at best its "incarnation," at worst its dress. Hence W's wish we could circumvent words (_The Prelude_, book 5), and his interest in a "silent poetry" of impressions, and in the thoughts and feelings a healthy mind associates with them.

870. Wu, Qian-zhi. "Another Possible Influence on Wordsworth's Lyrical Ballads." _The Wordsworth Circle_ 12 (1981): 269-70.

Presents the nursery rhyme, "O dear, what can the matter be?" as a source for "The Idiot Boy" and "Goody Blake and Harry Gill."

871. Zall, P.M. "The Cool World of Samuel Taylor Coleridge: Charles MacKay Visits Samuel Rogers and William Wordsworth." _The Wordsworth Circle_ 12(1981): 113-15.

Anecdotes of W in his seventies.

1982

872. Baker, Jeffrey. "Prelude and Prejudice." The Wordsworth Circle 13(1982): 79-86.

Challenges the view, especially as stated in the Norton Prelude (17), that W's revisions are "normally for the worse," and attempts to justify many changes by arguing that W conceived the 1850 version not as autobiography but as his philosophical poem. A reply by Robert Young, pp. 87-88, takes issue with Baker's assumption that anyone can "see [The Prelude] as it really is."

873. Barth, J. Robert, S.J. "A Moment on a Mountaintop." Literature and Belief 2(1982): 51-53.

Sermon delivered at the tenth annual Wordsworth Conference, stressing the power of vision, as in "Tintern Abbey," to sustain us in everyday life.

874. Bement, Peter. "Simon Lee and Ivor Hall: A Possible Source." The Wordsworth Circle 13(1982): 35-36.

Suggests that W encountered the ruins of "Ivor's lofty hall" in a Welsh poem by Evan Evans.

875. Bialostosky, Don. "Narrative Diction in Wordsworth's Poetics of Speech." Comparative Literature 34(1982): 305-29.

Traces C's disagreements with W on diction (see also 1009) to a fundamental difference in poetics, arguing that C, with his "Aristotelian poetics of artificially imitated action," failed to appreciate W's Platonic "poetics of speech." For W, the point of narrative is not to describe action, but to "report the speech of his characters"--whence the poets' differences on diction.

876. Bidlake, Stephen. "'Hidden Dialog' in 'The Mad Mother' and 'The Complaint of a Forsaken Indian Woman.'" The Wordsworth Circle 13(1982): 188-93.

Reads both monologues as "hidden dialogues" (Bakhtin's term) between speaker and internalized voices; stresses the mad mother's madness.

877. Bromwich, David. "Wordsworth, Frost, Stevens and the Poetic Vocation." Studies in Romanticism 21(1982): 87-100.

Calling W "the first lyric allegorist of the poetic career," Bromwich focuses on "Resolution and Independence" as the archetype in this kind, comparing it with Frost's "Two Tramps in Mud Time" and Stevens' "The Course of a Particular," and noting the greater tension in W between the poetic and the other career, the poet/speaker and the other.

878. Cappon, Alexander P. About Wordsworth and Whitehead: A Prelude to Philosophy. New York: Philosophical Library, 1982. xi+190 pp. indexed.

Works through the 1805 Prelude, books 1-6, in sequence to point out parallels between W and Whitehead, using both to moralize about life in general. Eccentric and loosely written, with occasional errors and few references to previous scholarship.

879. Cosgrove, Brian. "Wordsworth's Moonlight-Poetry and the Sense of the 'Uncanny.'" Ariel 13,ii(1982): 19-32.

Suggests the terms "preternatural" and "uncanny" to describe the effects of W's mediation between "the strange and the familiar, the supernatural and the actual," briefly examining "The Idiot Boy," "Peter Bell," and the discharged-soldier passage of Prelude 4.

880. Dawson, William P. "The Perceptual Bond in 'Strange Fits of Passion.'" The Wordsworth Circle 13(1982): 96-97.

Argues that since the poem describes an illusion based on the speaker's shifting perspective--as does The Prelude's boat-stealing passage--its subject is the "interaction of man and nature in perception."

881. Erdman, David V. "Oops! My Misprision!" The Wordsworth Circle 13(1982): 201-202.

Retracts the reading set forth in 801 on the basis of a more careful reading.

882. Frosch, Thomas R. "Wordsworth's 'Beggars' and a Brief Instance of 'Writer's Block.'" Studies in Romanticism 21(1982): 619-36.

Relates W's difficulties in shaping "Beggars" from Dorothy's journal entry, and his minimal divergence from her account, to the tale's evocation of W's loss of his mother, and to his need to navigate a fictional path between the plain fact and the outright lie.

883. Garber, Frederick. The Autonomy of the Self from Richardson to Huysmans. Princeton, NJ: Princeton, 1982. xiii+326 pp. indexed.

Chapter four discusses the egotism of W's relation to nature in comparison with Blake, Hölderlin, and Emerson; chapter seven, "The Landscape of Desire," compares and contrasts W's "Home at Grasmere" with Rousseau's Edens as a search for a "paradisal context for the self" which fails but is even thus discovered to be unnecessary.

Review: J. Black, CLS 20(1983), 450; Lilian R. Furst, CL 35(1983), 182; Mark Kipperman, WC 14(1983), 149-51; P. Parrinder, MLR 79(1984), 403; J. Sitter, ECS 17 (1984), 189; Peter L. Thorslev, Jr., MLQ 43(1982), 302-304.

884. Garner, Margaret. "The Anapestic Lyrical Ballads: New Sympathies." The Wordsworth Circle 13(1982): 183-88.

Does not discuss meter (beyond noting that W puts the anapest to serious purpose), but interestingly shows how all the anapestic poems reveal their speakers' various abilities to sympathize with suffering.

885. Gould, Timothy. "The Audience of Originality: Kant and Wordsworth on the Reception of Genius." In *Essays in Kant's Aesthetics*, ed. Ted Cohen and Paul Guyer. Chicago: University of Chicago, 1982, pp. 179-93.

Compares Kant's observations on the relation of originality to genius with W's dictum that the original artist "must create the taste by which he is to be relished." More on Kant than on W.

886. Gravil, Richard. "*Lyrical Ballads* (1798): Wordsworth as Ironist." *Critical Quarterly* 24,iv(1982): 39-57.

Explains the conventional appearance of the *Lyrical Ballads* (see 128) by suggesting that the poems subtly parody contemporary poetic fashions.

887. Heldrith, Leonard G. "Ascending the Depths: Wordsworth's Vision on Mt. Snowdon." In *Essays on the Literature of Mountaineering*, ed. Armand E. Singer. Morgantown: West Virginia University, 1982, pp. 35-45.

A Jungian interpretation of the ascent of Snowdon as a dream, in which W "looks into his own depths." Uses the 1850 text.

888. Hill, Alan G. "Lamb and Wordsworth: The Story of a Remarkable Friendship." *Charles Lamb Bulletin* 37 (1982): 85-92.

Interesting brief biography of the long-lasting friendship.

889. Johnson, Lee M. *Wordsworth's Metaphysical Verse: Geometry, Nature, and Form*. Toronto: University of Toronto, 1982. ix+241 pp. indexed.

Original and useful formal analysis, most notable for its documentation of W's use of golden sections and blank-verse sonnets at "special moments" in his poetry as expressions of idealism. Primarily examining *The Prelude*, *The Excursion* (on which the commentary is especially incisive), the Ode, and "Tintern Abbey," Johnson also offers shrewd insights on the more conventional elements of W's art, such as his use of meter. See also 664.

Reviews: John A. Hodgson, SIR 23(1984), 121-27; R. Lessa, UTQ 52(1983), 422; George Woodcock, SR 91(1983), 664.

890. Johnston, Kenneth R. "Wordsworth and The Recluse: The University of Imagination." PMLA 97(1982): 60-82.

Describes three major stages in W's work on The Recluse, arguing that the poem is more substantial than is commonly thought, and describing a dynamic between the public, Recluse work and the private, Prelude work.

891. Kelley, Paul. "Charlotte Smith and An Evening Walk." Notes & Queries 29(1982): 220.

Identifies quotations in "An Evening Walk" from Smith's sonnet, "To the South Downs."

892. Kelley, Theresa M. "Proteus and Romantic Allegory." ELH 49(1982): 623-52.

Argues cogently, against de Man's "The Rhetoric of Temporality" (in Interpretation: Theory and Practice, ed. Charles Singleton. Baltimore, MD: Johns Hopkins, 1969), that Romantic poetry is frequently symbolic and allegorical both at once. Chiefly uses W in illustration, examining Proteus figures in "The World is Too Much with Us," "Nutting," "Resolution and Independence," Excursion 4, and the Arab Dream (Prelude 5).

893. Kelley, Theresa M. "Spirit and Geometric Form: The Stone and the Shell in Wordsworth's Arab Dream." Studies in English Literature, 1500-1900 22(1982): 563-82.

An excellent discussion of the symbolism of the dream in Prelude 5, challenging the view that in the stone and shell W opposes science to poetry, and viewing the dream as marking an important shift in W's response to science.

894. Kelliher, Hilton. "Thomas Wilkinson of Yanwath, Friend of Wordsworth and Coleridge." British Library Journal 8(1982): 147-67.

Biographical essay including texts of two W letters (with minor variants) and "To the Spade of a Friend," from manuscripts in the British Museum; a photo of a holograph of "The Solitary Reaper"; and the text of the poem by Wilkinson which W praises in the Fenwick note on "To the Spade of a Friend."

895. Ketcham, Carl H. "'That "Stone of Rowe"': Prelude (1805) II: 33-47." The Wordsworth Circle 13(1982): 174-75.

Points out that W's revision of line 38 in MS. A is not "Stone of Rowe," but "Stone of Power," which means a stone that supernaturally rocks at the touch of a guilty man.

896. Korshin, Paul. Typologies in England, 1650-1820. Princeton, NJ: Princeton, 1982. xvii+437 pp. indexed.

Includes a few scattered pages on W's "types."
Review: Pat Rogers, TLS, 6 Jan. 1984, p. 10.

897. Lamb, Jonathan. "Hartley and Wordsworth: Philosophical Language and Figures of the Sublime." Modern Language Notes 97(1982): 1064-85.

Compares W's statements on language, chiefly in the Preface, with eighteenth-century natural-language theories, and suggests that what C objected to as "matter-of-factness" and "laborious minuteness" are really figures of a little-regarded species of the sublime, in his use of which W was influenced by Longinus, Robert Lowth, and David Hartley, and which achieve sublimity by virtue of their very proximity to the contemptible and ordinary.

898. Langbaum, Robert. "Wordsworth's Lyrical Characterizations." Studies in Romanticism 21(1982): 319-39.

Distinguishes between W's dramatic characterization, and his more successful, quasi-symbolic, "lyrical characterization," the art by which his solitaries are made to "approximate pure being." Examines "The Thorn," "The Idiot Boy," "Resolution and Independence," "The Old Cumberland Beggar," "The White Doe of Rylstone," and others.

899. Liu, Alan. "'Shapeless Eagerness': The Genre of Revolution in Books 9-10 of The Prelude." Modern Language Quarterly 43(1982): 3-28.

An interesting analysis, arguing that W's movement through the genres of travel poetry, romance, drama, and epic, toward epitaphic calm, shows his difficulty in coming to grips with the revolution's historical reality. (Uses 1805 version.) Cf. 839.

900. McCracken, David. "Wordsworth's Doctrine of 'Things as They Seem.'" The Wordsworth Circle 13(1982): 179-83.

Argues that the groupings in the 1800 Lyrical Ballads demonstrate W's dictum that poetry should treat things "as they appear" ("Essay, Supplementary," 1815), each poem in a group giving a different perspective on a similar object. A good article.

901. McCracken, David. "Wordsworth on Human Wishes and Poetic Borrowing." Modern Philology 79(1982): 386-99.

An interesting discussion of W's views on literary theft and borrowing, including C's, is brought to bear on a reading of W's "The Wishing Gate," which echoes Pope, Gray, and Johnson.

902. McFarland, Thomas. "Wordsworth on Man, on Nature, and on Human Life." Studies in Romanticism 21(1982): 601-18.

Notes W's anxieties about C's and Milton's influence in the Prospectus to The Recluse, and finds its famous first line confused: the truly systematic and philosophical triad, McFarland argues, is Man, Nature, and God. Though ill-fated as the first line of a philosophical poem, the line is characteristic of W in putting "Nature" before "Human Life" ("Man," it is argued, being W himself).

903. McFarland, Thomas. "Wordsworth's Best Philosopher." The Wordsworth Circle 13(1982): 59-68.

Uses the concept of "blockage" to explain lapses and irrelevancies in W's greatest poetry, especially in the Ode, and argues that the Ode's "best philosopher" passage escapes such defects because here W's deepest beliefs coincide rather than conflict with C's influence.

904. McReynolds, Ronald W. "Primitivism in Wordsworth's 'We Are Seven.'" Publications of the Missouri Philological Association 7(1982): 34-37.

Not seen.

905. Magnuson, Paul. "The Articulation of 'Michael': or, Could Michael Talk?" The Wordsworth Circle 13(1982): 72-79.

Argues interestingly that "Michael," being the last piece composed for the 1800 Lyrical Ballads, was shaped to fit its context; Michael's relationship to language complements the treatment of language in the Preface, "The Brothers," and "Hart-Leap Well."

906. Manning, Peter J. "Wordsworth and Gray's Sonnet on the Death of West." Studies in English Literature, 1500-1900 22(1982): 505-18.

Contrasts Gray's poem which W criticized in the Preface for inflated diction with W's "Lucy Poems," noting especially W's ability to move beyond Lucy to the self, and beyond the self to a "cosmic vantage."

907. Memmott, A. James. "Wordsworth in the Bleachers: The Baseball Essays of Roger Angell." Journal of American Culture 5,iv(1982): 52-56.

Documents one of the further reaches of W's influence, comparing Angell's retrospective mode with W's use of the "spots of time."

908. Morse, David. Romanticism: A Structural Analysis. London: Macmillan, 1982. x+306 pp. indexed.

Little on W, but pages 246-59 discuss the figure of the poet in several W poems, including "Resolution and Independence," "Peter Bell," and the Ode, arguing that "it is W who institutionalizes the poet as teacher and sage."

909. Morton, Lionel. "Books and Drowned Men: Unconscious Mourning in Book V of The Prelude." English Studies in Canada 8(1982): 23-37.

Argues that the events of book 5 (in the 1850 version) are unified by a common but repressed sense of loss, and points to the number of male solitaries and wanderers in W's poetry to suggest the importance of the death of his father (as opposed to that of his mother, which has been extensively discussed, e.g., by Onorato, 80).

910. Nixon, David. "Wordsworth's 'A Slumber Did My Spirit Seal.'" Explicator 41,i(1982): 25-26.

Brief explication emphasizing irony; nothing new.

911. Owen, W.J.B. "The Charm More Superficial." The Wordsworth Circle 13 (1982): 8-16.

Discusses W's theory of the fancy and compares his practice in several poems, examining in particular two mentions of fancy in the 1805 Prelude, books 8 and 13.

912. Owen, W.J.B. "Two Addenda." The Wordsworth Circle 13 (1982): 98.

Addenda to 482 and 483: reprints a passage from Joseph Cottle's Malvern Hills (1798) as a source for "The Thorn," and notes a possible echo of Lear in "The Old Cumberland Beggar."

913. Piper, David. The Image of the Poet: British Poets and their Portraits. Oxford: Clarendon, 1982. xxi+219 pp. indexed. 225 illustrations.

Reprints and criticism of six W portraits: R. Carruthers, 1817; B.R. Haydon, 1817 and 1842; H.W. Pickersgill, ca. 1850; the marble bust by Sir Francis Chantrey, 1820; and the life-mask by B.R. Haydon, 1815. A more complete treatment to which Piper refers is Frances Blanshard's Portraits of Wordsworth (Ithaca, NY: Cornell, 1959), 208 pp., 82 illustrations.

914. Pirie, David B. William Wordsworth: The Poetry of Grandeur and of Tenderness. New York and London: Methuen, 1982. 301 pp. indexed.

Finds W's power in his refusal to resolve the tensions between man and nature, giving close readings that range from original to hackneyed. Always interesting, but somewhat cranky, given to summarily dismissing large tracts of criticism and of W himself. Manning's review is just in protesting that while Pirie attacks W criticism and flaunts his own originality, he is oblivious to recent developments and much in debt to the not-so-recent (e.g., to Ferry, 131).

Reviews: Don H. Bialostosky, MLQ 44(1983), 305-10; Theresa Kelley, SIR 23(1984), 128-32; Peter J. Manning, WC 14(1983), 120-21; R. Sharrock, N&Q 31(1984), 143; Stuart M. Sperry, JEGP 82(1983), 564; Kathryn Sutherland, CritQ 24(1982), 77; C. Watts, TLS, 24 Sept. 1982, p. 1046.

915. Plank, Jeffrey. "Literary Criticism as an Autobiographical Form." The Wordsworth Circle 13(1982): 168-74.

Describes Hartman's critical practice and points to shortcomings: Hartman interprets W as W interprets nature, i.e., by stressing the interpreter's role and tracing his own development. Not only does this preclude shared interpretations, it undermines any given interpretation as temporary; and since it substitutes terms describing continuous psychological development for formal literary terms, it is inadequate for Hartman's project of describing "radical literary change," which is discontinuous.

916. Proffitt, Edward. "'Though Inland Far We Be': Intimations of Evolution in the Great Ode." The Wordsworth Circle 13(1982): 88-90.

Compares lines 162-68 of the Ode with the sea-shell passage of _Excursion_ 4 (lines 1132-40), suggesting that W is alluding to our natural, rather than divine, origins.

917. Reed, Mark. "Constable, Wordsworth, and Beaumont: A New Constable Letter in Evidence." _Art Bulletin_ 64(1982): 481-83.

Prints a letter from Constable to W, 15 June 1836, presenting a copy of Constable's _English Landscape_ (1833), and draws conclusions for the chronology of their friendship--notably that Constable had probably read _Lyrical Ballads_ by 1801.

918. Roe, Nicholas. "Wordsworth, Samuel Nicholson, and the Society for Constitutional Information." _The Wordsworth Circle_ 13(1982): 197-201.

Offers some information, but chiefly conjectures, on W's friend of the early 1790s, discussing Nicholson's membership in the radical SCI, where he may have come to know Joseph Johnson, his influence on W's early radicalism during the pamphlet war with Burke, and his possible role in introducing W and Johnson. See also 984.

919. Schneider, Steven. "An Interview with Louis Simpson." _The Wordsworth Circle_ 13(1982): 99-104.

Simpson answers questions about W's influence on American poetry and on Simpson's own.

920. Simpson, David. _Wordsworth and the Figurings of the Real_. London: Macmillan, 1982. xxvii+183 pp. indexed.

Traces epistemological problems through several poems by C and W, arguing that W concedes the necessity of "figurative attribution" of reality for the sake of common perception, but that he is also aware of its dangers as "it comes to be what we call 'ideology.'" The final chapter uses this insight to explain W's preference of rural to urban life and labor.

Reviews: Don H. Bialostosky, _MLQ_ 44(1983), 305-10; E.

Neill, TLS 3 Dec. 1982, p. 1340; Tilottama Rajan, WC 14 (1983), 122-24 (Reply by Simpson, 124-26).

921. Sinclair, John. "Lines about 'Lines.'" In Language and Literature: An Introductory Reader in Stylistics, ed. Ronald Carter. London: Allen & Unwin, 1982, pp. 161-76.

Technical stylistic analysis of "Tintern Abbey," attempting to narrow the distance between literary and linguistic interpretation by focusing on points of interest to both.

922. Stevenson, Warren. "Wordsworth and the Stone of Night." The Wordsworth Circle 13(1982): 175-78.

Comparing W's use of the stone symbol in connection with the old dame and the discharged soldier of The Prelude, books 2 and 4, with Blake's use of the stone (as interpreted by Damon and Frye), Stevenson points to "tension between the surface connotations and the archetypal symbolism involved" in W's passages.

923. Sutton, Max Keith. "The Prelude and Lorna Doone." The Wordsworth Circle 13(1982): 193-97.

Suggests that The Prelude is a source for Blackmore's 1869 novel, citing similarities in the rural narration, landscape, and certain scenes, as well as Wordsworthian themes such as the power of fear and of early memories.

924. Thesing, William B. The London Muse: Victorian Poetic Responses to the City. Athens: University of Georgia, 1982. xviii+230 pp. indexed.

The section on "Wordsworth's Urban Vision" (pp. 12-24) examines the "pastoral cityscape" of several lyrics, explains what may seem "elitist and snobbish" in Prelude 7 as W's self-defensive attitude toward urban confusion, and notes The Excursion's ambivalence toward the city.

925. Thomas, Gordon K. "New Worlds Viewed from the Shore." Literature and Belief 2(1982): 43-49.

Objects to criticisms of the Christian elements in the 1850 Prelude, and notes another possible allusion to Paradise Lost in the Snowdon passage.

926. Thomas, Gordon K. "Wordsworth's Iberian Sonnets: Turncoat's Creed?" The Wordsworth Circle 13(1982): 31-34.

Argues that the Iberian sonnets (among the "Poems Dedicated to National Independence and Liberty") do not show W turning to conservatism and hero-worship, but are democratic in tendency.

927. Thompson, Denys. "Anne Finch." PN Review 8,vi(1982): 35-38.

Argues that W and Gosse were wrong in finding the poetry of Anne Finch, Countess of Winchilsea (1661-1720) uncharacteristic of her age.

928. Watson, J[ohn] R[ichard]. Wordsworth's Vital Soul: The Sacred and Profane in Wordsworth's Poetry. London: Methuen, 1982. x+259 pp. indexed.

Using Mircea Eliade's terms, and quoting Eliade and Buber too often, Watson stresses the importance of "fundamental, even primitive, ideas of the sacred" in W's poetry, from which the later orthodoxy is seen as a natural development. Readings are not critically incisive or startling.

Review: R. Sharrock, N&Q 31(1984), 143.

929. Wordsworth, Jonathan. William Wordsworth: The Borders of Vision. Oxford: Clarendon, 1982. xviii+496 pp. indexed. pbk.

A major study which focuses on various forms of "border vision" in the poetry composed between 1798 and 1805, especially in the successive recastings of The Prelude. Pays close attention to chronology in order to show W's changing beliefs and poetics. See also Wordsworth's earlier study (300, pp. 170-87).

Reviews: Michael Baron, English 33(1984), 71; David Bromwich, TLS, 9 Sept. 1983, 963-64.

1983

930. Baron, Michael. "Speaking and Writing: Wordsworth's 'Fit Audience.'" English 32(1983): 217-50.

A rather diffuse essay discussing W's relation to audience and arguing that he succeeds in bridging "the deep gulf between private and public communication," especially in The Prelude. Sees an analogy between the "familiar conversation" depicted in the "Lucy Poems" and "Poems on the Naming of Places," and the poet's project of communication with his audience.

931. Beer, John. "Nature and Liberty: The Linking of Unstable Concepts." The Wordsworth Circle 14(1983): 201-213.

Traces the Romantic poets', especially W's, attempts to correlate nature and human liberty, showing W's movement in "Poems Dedicated to National Independence and Liberty" and the 1805 Prelude toward the view that liberty does not come naturally to a people but is cultivated by the individual.

932. Bewell, Alan J. "Wordsworth's Primal Scene: Retrospective Tales of Idiots, Wild Children, and Savages." ELH 50(1983): 321-46.

Sees the story of John Walford's murder of his idiot-wife Jenny as a powerful influence on W's poetry, and suggests that W's interest in idiots and savages, e.g., in "The Idiot Boy" and Peter Bell, is intellectual rather than sentimental; like many eighteenth-century thinkers, W found that idiots provided insights into the origins of human perception and memory.

933. Blondel, Jacques. "Wordsworth and Solitude." An Infinite Complexity (1000), 26-45.

Discusses the "dual aspect of solitude"--blissful and frightening--in W's poetry, drawing a rather tenuous connection with light and dark imagery which is examined at length in the Ode.

934. Brennan, Matthew. "The Light of Wordsworth's Desire for Darkness in The Prelude." Romanticism Past and Present 7,ii(1983): 27-40.

Draws attention to the importance of darkness and blindness in W's descriptions of imagination in the 1805 Prelude, and argues that W values imagination not just for its power to illuminate the invisible world, but also for its its obliteration of the visible, "real" world.

935. Brown, Stephen W. "'The Tide Returns Again': Change, Repetition, and the Structure of The Prelude, Book X." University of Windsor Review 17(1983): 5-16.

Argues that book 10 of the 1805 Prelude is composed of two parallel sequences (which become books 10 and 11 in the 1850 version) testifying to W's inability to achieve closure in dealing with his experience of the revolution.

936. Butler, James A. "Wordsworth's Descriptive Sketches: The Huntington and Cornell Copies." Huntington Library Quarterly 46(1983): 175-80.

Establishes the provenance of two important and problematic copies of Descriptive Sketches, both of which at one time belonged to Henry Reed, W's first American editor.

937. Byrd, Max. "Metamorphosis and Tintern Abbey: Two Notes." Modern Philology 81(1983): 24-37.

Noting the strangely literal quality of Wordsworthian metaphor, Byrd finds W's mentions of change in the poem suggestive of Ovidian metamorphosis, and relates them to eighteenth-century questions regarding the meaningfulness of changes in man and nature.

938. Cappon, Alexander P. _Aspects of Wordsworth and Whitehead: Philosophy and Continuing Life-Problems_. New York: Philosophical Library, 1983. 283 pp. indexed.

Much in the same vein as Cappon's earlier book (878), which is recapitulated in chapters 1-6. In this volume Cappon continues his chatty, moralizing commentary on the 1805 _Prelude_ through book 11.

939. Chavkin, Allan. "_Humboldt's Gift_ and the Romantic Imagination." _Philological Quarterly_ 62(1983): 1-19.

Discusses the role of English Romantic poetry--especially W's--in providing Saul Bellow an alternative to Modernist pessimism.

940. Chavkin, Allan. "Wordsworth's Secular Imagination and 'Spots of Time.'" _College Language Association Journal_ 26(1983): 452-64.

Examines the discharged-soldier passage of the 1850 _Prelude_, book 4, and "Resolution and Independence" as dramatizations of the "secular imagination," i.e., that which "half creates," participating in rather than transcending nature.

941. Christian, Henry A., Marylou Motto, Carl R. Sonn, and Ann C. Watts. _The City and Literature: An Introduction_. Newark, NJ: Rutgers, 1983. ii+160 pp. indexed. pbk.

Includes brief discussions of the blind-beggar episode and "Westminster Bridge" (pp. 53-59), but does not break any new ground.

942. Christie, Will. "Wordsworth and the Language of Nature." _The Wordsworth Circle_ 14(1983): 40-47.

Distinguishes two ideals of "natural language" in W's Preface and poetry: that which perfectly represents or signifies nature, and that (always tending toward silence) which "transcends art altogether by _being_ rather than _representing_ nature." Helpfully sketches the precedents of each ideal, philosophical and theological.

943. Clubbe, John, and Ernest J. Lovell, Jr. English Romanticism: The Grounds of Belief. DeKalb: University of Northern Illinois, 1983. xv+195 pp. indexed.

Stresses W's Anglican background and upbringing, and devotes most attention to his "sympathies" with Blake's and C's fundamental beliefs, seeing the three poets as essentially agreed on the nature and importance of imaginative perception as profoundly moral.

944. Crucefix, Martyn. "Wordsworth, Superstition, and Shelley's Alastor." Essays in Criticism 33(1983): 126-47.

Argues that Shelley critiques W in the figures of both the narrator and the visionary, both of whom fail to recognize the primacy of their own mental powers over externals such as nature and supernatural spirits.

945. Davis, Norma S. "Stone as Metaphor: Wordsworth and Moore." The Wordsworth Circle 14(1983): 264-68.

Compares W's and the sculptor Henry Moore's use of stone as a figure for human endurance.

946. Devlin, D[avid] D[ouglas]. De Quincey, Wordsworth and the Art of Prose. London: Macmillan, 1983. 132 pp. indexed.

Finds W a formidable influence on De Quincey's critical principles and prose--a source for the younger writer's use of "power" as a critical standard, a sanction for his subjective writing, etc. All Devlin's insights into W himself are repeated from his earlier study (725).

947. Fleishman, Avrom. Figures of Autobiography: The Language of Self-Writing in Victorian and Modern England. Berkeley: University of California, 1983. xiv+486 pp. indexed.

Includes a brief description (pp. 95-104) of The Prelude as a variation on the Christian peregrinatio, following Abrams (161) and Harold Bloom's "The Internalization of Quest Romance," in Romanticism and Consciousness (New York: Norton, 1970), pp. 3-24.

948. Foot, Michael, MP. "Hazlitt's Revenge on the Lakers." The Wordsworth Circle 14(1983): 61-68.

Attributes Hazlitt's break with W to Christopher Wordsworth's attack on Hazlitt's Principles of Human Action in 1806; bestowing high praise on Hazlitt's writing and politics, Foot applauds the constancy of his criticism of W's poetry.

949. Gill, Stephen. "Wordsworth's Poems: The Question of Text." Review of English Studies 34(1983): 172-90.

A good statement by one of the Cornell editors (see 21) of the dilemmas facing W's readers and editors in light of his revisions, reflecting thoughtfully also on the implications of the recent "editorial creation" of poems not published as such by the poet. See also Gill's selection of W's poems (29).

950. Glen, Heather. Vision and Disenchantment: Blake's Songs and Wordsworth's Lyrical Ballads. London: Cambridge, 1983. ix+399 pp. indexed.

Compares the social criticism in Blake's and W's works, beginning with a consideration of the genres--children's and magazine literature--which they subvert, proceeding through perceptive close readings, and finding that W's vision, in the end, is "deeply pessimistic as to human possibility."

Reviews: C. Baldick, TLS, 19 Aug. 1983, p. 884; P.M.S. Dawson, CritQ 26(1984), 139; S. Matthews, English 33 (1984), 66.

951. Goodman, Alice. "Wordsworth and the Sucking Babe." Essays in Criticism 33(1983): 108-25.

Excellent rebuttal to Shelley's description of W as "unsexual," pointing out the eroticism, and stressing the perfect reprocity, in his portrayals of suckling mothers and infants.

952. Gravil, Richard. "Wordsworth's Last Retreat." Charles Lamb Bulletin 43(1983): 54-67.

Surveys the many explanations which have been offered for W's decline, and suggests that it begins with his "Grasmere embowerment" in 1800. Criticizes "Home at Grasmere" and The Excursion, but praises The Convention of Cintra as "perhaps W's last poem on the grand scale."

953. Gravil, Richard. "Wordsworth's Second Selves?" The Wordsworth Circle 14(1983): 191-201.

Discusses W's "hauntings of contemporary poetry"--in particular, that of Geoffrey Hill, W.S. Graham, R.S. Thomas, Seamus Heaney, and Ted Hughes.

954. Hay, Samuel H. "Wordsworth's Solitary: The Struggle with Despondency." The Wordsworth Circle 14(1983): 243-45.

Relates the Wanderer's failure to console the Solitary to W's movement toward orthodox Anglicanism.

955. Hayden, Donald E. Wordsworth's Walking Tour of 1790. Tulsa, OK: University of Tulsa, 1983. x+129 pp. pbk.

Hayden has not only drawn on all the pertinent biographical materials, but has even traced the steps of W and Robert Jones to provide a full account of their European tour with a plentiful accompaniment of maps and photographs.

956. Holt, Ted, and John Gilroy. A Commentary on Wordsworth's Prelude, Books I-V. London: Routledge and Kegan Paul, 1983. xi+124 pp. not indexed. pbk.

A consecutive commentary on the 1805 version, designed to present the beginning student with more than the poem's great lyric moments.

957. Hugo, F.J. "Wordsworth's Imagination of Contrary States." Theoria 60(1983): 13-25.

Compares W and Blake by noting W's depictions of opposites, especially "violent energy and peaceful stillness," in "creative tension"; focuses chiefly on "The Simplon Pass."

958. Jacobus, Mary. "'That Great Stage Where Senators Perform': Macbeth and the Politics of Romantic Theatre." Studies in Romanticism 22(1983): 353-87.

An essay on W, Burke, C, Lamb, and De Quincey which is not to be summarized but is chiefly on the uses and limitations of aesthetic modes as patterns for seeing the French Revolution. Deals with the 1805 Prelude, books 7, 10, and 11, and The Borderers.

959. Johnston, Kenneth R. "The Politics of Tintern Abbey." The Wordsworth Circle 14(1983): 6-14.

Contains observations on W's attitude to the picturesque, but is really about the limits of the poem's political vision, the narrow range of social ills W adduces as "the still, sad music of humanity." Johnston argues, for example, that W moved two miles upstream to avoid beggars at the abbey and industry on the Wye, and suggests by the way (contra Moorman, 78) that W had a hand in the Godwinian Philanthropist of 1795-96.

960. Kelley, Paul. "Wordsworth and Lucretius' De Rerum Natura." Notes & Queries 30(1983): 219-22.

Notes references and allusions to Lucretius in W's letters and poetry to argue that his "knowledge of De Rerum Natura was indeed intimate."

961. Kestner, Joseph. "A Manchester Woman's Wordsworth: Elisabeth Stone and The Horn of Egremont Castle." The Wordsworth Circle 14(1983): 107-108.

A note on the novelist's use of W's poem in Sir Eustace de Lucie (1844).

962. Kishel, Joseph. "Wordsworth's 'To the Clouds.'" The Wordsworth Circle 14(1983): 92-94.

A brief history of W's "To the Clouds," begun in 1808, it is argued, as part of The Recluse.

963. Kroeber, Karl. "Constable: Millais / Wordsworth: Tennyson." In _Articulate Images: The Sister Arts from Hogarth to Tennyson,_ ed. Richard Wendorf. Minneapolis: University of Minnesota, 1983, pp. 216-42.

Distinguishes Romantic from Victorian and Modernist art through parallel contrasts between Constable's _Salisbury Cathedral, from the Meadows_ and Millais's _The Blind Girl,_ W's "Michael" and Tennyson's "Enoch Arden," paying special attention to ambivalences, indeterminateness, and reader-participation in W's poem. See also 329.

964. Langbaum, Robert. "The Epiphanic Mode in Wordsworth and Modern Literature." _New Literary History_ 14(1983): 335-58.

Distinguishing "epiphany" from traditional "vision" and arguing that the _Prelude_'s "spots of time" as well as many of W's ballads and lyrics are essentially epiphanic (contrast 329, ch. 1), Langbaum sees W as founding a mode in modern poetry, and argues that he invented the epiphanic (as opposed to Miltonic) sonnet.

965. Leyda, Seraphia D. "A Letter to the Editor." _The Wordsworth Circle_ 14(1983): 82.

Indignant objection to Bushnell's reading (791).

966. Leyda, Seraphia D. "Wordsworth's _Sonnets Upon the Punishment of Death_." _The Wordsworth Circle_ 14(1983): 48-53.

A sympathetic reading of W's argument, with some historical background.

967. McFarland, Thomas. "Wordsworth: Prophet of the Past." _The Wordsworth Circle_ 14(1983): 251-55.

Sees W as firmly in the prophetic tradition, arguing that "_gravitas_," "a certain indistinctness," and "an attempt to integrate human existence" are surer earmarks of prophecy than its reference to the future.

968. McGann, Jerome J. The Romantic Ideology: A Critical Investigation. Chicago: University of Chicago, 1983. x+172 pp. indexed.

Pleads for the recognition of Romanticism as socially and historically specific, urging critics to cease taking the Romantics' self-representations at face value. Devotes a chapter to showing W's "elision" of social contexts in "The Ruined Cottage," "Tintern Abbey," and the Ode.

Reviews: William H. Galperin, JEGP 84(1985), 135-38; Peter L. Thorslev, Jr., KSJ 33(1984), 205.

969. Malekin, Peter. "Wordsworth and the Mind of Man." An Infinite Complexity (1000), pp. 1-25.

Compares W's descriptions of mystical experience in "Tintern Abbey," the Ode, and The Prelude with those provided by W.T. Stace (Mysticism and Philosophy, 1960), Boehme, and others, viewing W's inconsistencies and revisions sympathetically as evidence of his difficulty interpreting experience which was not recognized by western models of the mind.

970. Manning, Peter J. "Reading Wordsworth's Revisions: Othello and the Drowned Man." Studies in Romanticism 22(1983): 3-28.

Superb demonstration of the method in W's revisions and re-orderings, tracing the dispersal of the spots of time, and especially the development of the drowned-man passage, from the two-part to the 1805 Prelude and beyond. In the early version the passage, with its allusion to Othello, suggests the violence and guilt of the story-teller, a suggestion which is reversed by the 1805 context and by removal of the Othello allusions.

971. Manning, Peter J. "Wordsworth's Intimations Ode and its Epigraphs." Journal of English and Germanic Philology 82(1983): 526-40.

An excellent article demonstrating the importance both of exact texts and of interpretive presuppositions by arguing that tensions and ambivalences which are central to the Ode under its original Vergilian epigraph and its original title, "Ode," are disarmed by the interpretive title and epigraph which the poet added in 1815.

972. Morland, Kjell. "The Disturbing 'Presence': A Central Problem in Wordsworth's 'Tintern Abbey.'" In The Romantic Heritage: A Collection of Critical Essays, ed. Karsten Engelberg. Copenhagen: University of Copenhagen, 1983, pp. 33-52.

Not seen.

973. Newlyn, Lucy. "The Little Actor and his Mock Apparel." The Wordsworth Circle 14(1983): 30-39.

Taking the child of the Ode and of some Prelude passages to be Hartley Coleridge, Newlyn compares these with "To H.C." to argue that W's fear for the child leads him to "embalm" or freeze it in the childhood state--with the mortifying result for Hartley memorialized in his own "Longtime a Child..." sonnet.

974. Nichols, Ashton. "Towards 'Spots of Time': 'Visionary Dreariness' in 'An Evening Walk.'" The Wordsworth Circle 14(1983): 233-37.

Contrasts W's poem with Dyer's "A Country Walk" (1726), emphasizing W's descriptions of bleak, barren landscapes and his shift in emphasis from landscape to perceiver.

975. Oguro, Kazuko. "Wordsworth to Kagaku." In Igirisu Bungaku ni okeru Kagau Shiso, ed. Masao Watanabe. Tokyo: Kenkyusha, 1983, pp. 187-215.

Not seen.

976. Owen, W.J.B. "The Object, the Eye, and the Imagination." The Wordsworth Circle 14(1983): 15-21.

Distinguishes three types of description--simple ("A Night-Piece"), unifying ("Nutting"), and symbolic ("The Old Cumberland Beggar")--in an unfruitful search for evaluative criteria.

977. Owen, W.J.B. "Wordsworth's Imaginations." The Wordsworth Circle 14(1983): 213-24.

A careful survey of W's uses of the term "imagination," especially in the prose, the "Poems of the Imagination," and the various states of The Prelude, attempting to explain why he did not distinguish between the mind's active and passive states or between C's "primary" and "secondary" imagination.

978. Page, Judith W. "Style and Rhetorical Intention in Wordsworth's Lyrical Ballads." Philological Quarterly 62(1983): 293-313.

Sound but unstartling discussion of W's modification of the traditional ballad, examining the "Matthew" and "Lucy" poems in particular.

979. Parrish, Stephen Maxfield. "The Editor as Archaeologist." Kentucky Review 4(1983): 3-14.

Paper read at the dedication of the W. Hugh Peal Collection (see 1012), offering an apologetic for the Cornell Editions (sec. 1.2; see also 408, 949) and describing their methodology. Parrish also describes the recent discovery of W's love letters (43).

980. Paulson, Ronald. Representations of Revolution (1789-1820). New Haven, CT: Yale, 1983. xviii+398 pp. indexed.

Chapter 8, on "Wordsworth's Prelude" (pp. 248-85), emphasizes the poet's relation to patriarchy in the spots of time, with their recurrent motifs of crime and punishment, and sees them as W's "internalization" of his account of the French Revolution.

Reviews: D. Carrier, JAAC 42(1983), 223; R. Gagnier, Criticism 26(1984), 201; Laurence Goldstein, MQR 23 (1984), 455; N. Hampson, TLS, 4 Nov. 1983, p. 1225; R. King, KR 5(1983), 128.

981. Petersen, Per Serritslev. "The Inner Spirit of the Lotos-Eater: Romantic Primitivism and Its Psychodynamics." In The Romantic Heritage: A Collection of Criti-

cal Essays, ed. Karsten Engelberg. Copenhagen: University of Copenhagen, 1983, pp. 123-138.

Not seen.

982. Priestman, Martin. Cowper's Task: Structure and Influence. Cambridge: Cambridge, 1983. vi+217 pp. indexed.

The concluding chapter is a pedestrian but thorough book-by-book detailing of the structural and verbal parallels between The Task and the 1805 Prelude.

983. Primeau, John K. "The Influence of Gottfried August Bürger on the 'Lyrical Ballads' of William Wordsworth: The Supernatural vs. the Natural." Germanic Review 58 (1983): 89-96.

Compares "The Idiot Boy," "Simon Lee," "Hart Leap Well," and "The Thorn" with Bürger's ballads to emphasize W's avoidance of the supernatural, presenting the first two as parodies of the German poet's sensationalism.

984. Roe, Nicholas. "Citizen Wordsworth." The Wordsworth Circle 14(1983): 21-30.

Argues informatively that W was sympathetic with the English Democratic reform movement--especially the Society for Constitutional Information--in 1791-95. See also 918.

985. Rogers, David. "Wordsworth's Late Echo of 'My Heart Leaps Up.'" Greyfriar 24(1983): 47-52.

Compares "Glad sight wherever new with old" (ca. 1845), stressing the importance of continuity between the early and late poetry.

986. Roy, G. Ross. "The British Poetical Miscellany." Notes & Queries 30(1983): 222-23.

Notes that "Goody Blake and Harry Gill" is included but not credited to W in a rare 1818 fourth edition of the Miscellany.

987. Sales, Roger. English Literature in History, 1780-1830: Pastoral and Politics. London: Hutchinson, 1983. 247 pp. indexed.

A brief chapter, "William Wordsworth and the Real Estate" (pp. 52-69), argues that the sympathy W shows with "local gentry" in his 1818 Freeholders is implicit in much earlier works, especially "Michael" and "The Female Vagrant."

988. Sambrook, James. English Pastoral Poetry. Boston: Twayne, 1983. 160 pp. indexed.

Includes a brief discussion of pastoral in W's Excursion, book 1, "Michael," and The Prelude, arguing that "W completes the eighteenth-century naturalization of pastoral."

989. Schapiro, Barbara A. The Romantic Mother: Narcissistic Patterns in Romantic Poetry. Baltimore: Johns Hopkins, 1983. xvi+143 pp. indexed.

The concluding chapter on W offers Kleinian psychological readings of several poems, stressing not the death of W's mother (as does Onorato, 80) but W's "ambivalent relations with the mother imago," which have much earlier origins; unlike other poets considered, W is seen as able to resolve his ambivalence, and to "accept the mother as a whole reality." Though Schapiro tends to patronize without really refuting Onorato and Trilling (118), her view of W's ability to find "goodness and love in the mother, in the self, and, by extension, in humanity," is a refreshing counter to views of the misanthropic W (see, e.g., Ferry, 131, and Aers, 781).

Reviews: Thomas R. Frosch, KSJ 33(1984), 208; Alan Liu, Criticism 26(1984), 115.

990. Schell, John F. "Prose Prefaces and Romantic Poets: Insinuation and Ethos." Journal of Narrative Technique 13(1983): 86-99.

Interesting examination of the Romantic poets' experiments with narrative, focusing on their innovative use of prose prefaces, such as W's 1800 preface to "The Thorn," to present and develop fictional speakers.

991. Siskin, Clifford. "Revision Romanticized: A Study in Literary Change." Romanticism Past and Present 7 (1983): 1-16.

A highly abstract and difficult comparison-and-contrast essay on Young's "Conjectures on Original Composition" (1759) and W's Prefaces.

992. Sprinker, Michael. "Aesthetic Criticism: Geoffrey Hartman." In The Yale Critics: Deconstruction in America, ed. Jonathan Arac et al. Minneapolis: University of Minnesota, 1983, pp. 53-65.

Discusses Hartman on W, and especially on W's relation to Milton and Shakespeare (pp. 47-54).

993. Sutherland, Kathryn. "Defining the Self in the Poetry of Scott and Wordsworth." In Scott and His Influence, ed. J.H. Alexander and David Hewitt. Aberdeen: Association for Scottish Literary Studies, 1983, pp. 51-62.

Compares the poets' use of history to define the present self, and, conversely, their interest in how history is affected by the identity of the perceiver or narrator. Cf. 419.

994. Thomas, Gordon K. "Rueful Woes, Joyous Hap: The Associate Labors of 'The Idiot Boy' and 'Christabel.'" The Wordsworth Circle 14(1983): 94-96.

Argues that the poems share the theme of language and its perversion, their "complementarity" lying "at the heart of the original plan for the Lyrical Ballads."

995. Thomas, Gordon K. "'The Thorn' in the Flesh of English Romanticism." The Wordsworth Circle 14(1983): 237-42.

Comments informatively on Byron's view of W, and suggests that the mention of "The Thorn" in the Preface to Don Juan is really an acknowledgment, since Byron's poem follows W's in taking the narrator as its topic.

996. Thomas, Gordon K. "Wordsworth, Byron, and 'Our Friend, the Storyteller.'" Dutch Quarterly Review 13(1983): 200-212.

Makes the same argument as 995.

997. Trickett, Rachel. "Cowper, Wordsworth, and the Animal Fable." Review of English Studies 34(1983): 471-80.

Includes a brief but appreciative view of several of W's more seldom discussed poems (especially among "Poems of the Fancy"), arguing that they are influenced by Cowper's serious and realistic development of the animal-fable tradition.

998. Twitchell, James B. Romantic Horizons: Aspects of the Sublime in English Poetry and Painting, 1770-1850. Columbia: University of Missouri, 1983. xi+232 pp. indexed.

Investigating the Romantic sublime's involvement with horizons, borders between land and sky, light and dark, conscious and supraconscious, Twitchell discusses W's theory and compares his "Yew-Trees" with Joseph Wright of Derby's A Cavern: Evening (pp. 60-84).

999. Ware, Tracy. "Remembering It All Well: 'The Tantramar Revisited.'" Studies in Canadian Literature 8(1983): 221-37.

Traces the influence of "Tintern Abbey" on "The Tantramar Revisited" by the Canadian poet Charles G.D. Roberts.

1000. Watson, J[ohn] R[ichard], ed. An Infinite Complexity: Essays in Romanticism. Edinburgh: University of Durham, 1983. xv+248 pp. indexed.

Includes 933 and 969.

1001. Wedd, Mary R. "Lamb as a Critic of Wordsworth." Charles Lamb Bulletin 41(1983): 1-16.

Finds Lamb a sensitive and perceptive critic, much as Ades (434) does.

1002. Wedd, Mary R. "Light on Landscape in Wordsworth's 'Spots of Time.'" _The Wordsworth Circle_ 14(1983): 224-32.

Comments on W's art of idealizing landscape while conveying a sense of particular place, and provides literary and historical background for the raven's-nesting passage in _The Prelude_, book 1.

1003. Williams, John. "_Salisbury Plain_: Politics in Wordsworth's Poetry." _Literature and History_ 9(1983): 164-93.

Argues that W's radicalism in the 1790s is rooted in the tradition of Commonwealth or "Old Whig" thought rather than, like Paine's, repudiating tradition. Williams sees W's ideal of retreat (e.g., in the _Recluse_ project) as deriving from this tradition, and puts unconvincing "political" constructions on several poems (pp. 182-90) including "The Idiot Boy," "Anecdote for Fathers," and especially "Benjamin the Waggoner."

1004. Wilson, Milton. "Bodies in Motion: Wordsworth's Myths of Natural Philosophy." In _Centre and Labyrinth: Essays in Honour of Northrop Frye_, ed. Eleanor Cook et al. Toronto: University of Toronto, 1983, pp. 197-209.

Comments on W's use of the language of physics and physiology in his poetry, especially in the skating-scene (1850 _Prelude_, book 1) and "Tintern Abbey."

1005. Wordsworth, Jonathan. "The Mind as Lord and Master: Wordsworth and Wallace Stevens." _The Wordsworth Circle_ 14(1983): 183-91.

Finds the poets similar in their relationships to imagination and reality, comparing "The Solitary Reaper" with "The Idea of Order at Key West."

1006. Yost, George. "Existence Precedes Dramatic Essence: Wordsworth and Shaw." In _From Pen to Performance: Drama as Conceived and Performed_, Vol. 3, ed. Karelisa V. Hartigan. Lanham, MD: University Press of America, 1983, pp. 135-44.

Notes that _The Borderers_ is an early "drama of ideas," briefly discusses its relation to Godwinian rationalism, and compares W's and Shaw's movements "beyond their first doctrinaire bases."

1984

1007. Abrams, M[eyer] H. The Correspondent Breeze: Essays on English Romanticism. New York: Norton, 1984. xii+296 pp. indexed.

Collects nine previously published essays, including five of special importance for W studies: "Wordsworth and Coleridge on Diction and Figures" (1952), "The Correspondent Breeze: A Romantic Metaphor" (1960), "English Romanticism: The Spirit of the Age" (1963), "Structure and Style in the Greater Romantic Lyric" (1965), and "Two Roads to Wordsworth" (1972).

1008. Bahti, Timothy. "Wordsworth's Rhetorical Theft." Romanticism and Language (1029), pp. 86-124.

Impressive deconstructionist analysis of the preamble and the three theft-scenes (particularly of the boat-stealing) in the 1805 Prelude, book 1. For Bahti, book 1 is an "allegory of metaphor," the theft scenes enacting the "structure of metaphor as the dispossession, transfer, and appropriation of properties" (cf. 1059) and recapitulating W's initial failed efforts to effect the "appropriation of the self" that might ground his autobiographical narrative.

1009. Bialostosky, Don H. Making Tales: The Poetics of Wordsworth's Narrative Experiments. Chicago: University of Chicago, 1984. xii+208 pp. indexed. pbk.

An important rethinking of W's poetics as stated in the Preface, arguing that W's is a Platonic "poetics of speech" which has been misunderstood by C and subsequent subscribers to Aristotelian poetics of imitated action. Uses Barbara Herrnstein Smith's and Mikhail Bakhtin's work on poetics of speech to reexamine W's narrative experiments, chiefly the "tales" in Lyrical Ballads, but also the "dialogic anecdotes," from "Anecdote for Fathers" to the discharged-soldier passage in Prelude 4.

1010. Chandler, James K. Wordsworth's Second Nature: A Study of the Poetry and Politics. Chicago: University of Chicago, 1984. xxiv+313 pp. indexed. pbk.

A superb study attacking the "assumption that W's idea of the natural is essentially Rousseauist" and finding the Burkean "second nature" of habit, custom, and tradition implicit in W's writings as early as 1797. Illuminating the less obvious ideological grounds of much of W's major poetry, Chandler focuses largely on W's ideal of "natural" education, which he sees as synonymous with oral tradition and as responding to Rousseauist educational theory, not just in book 5 of The Prelude, but also in "The Ruined Cottage," "Michael," and the five-book Prelude; considers the French ideologues rather than Godwin the target of The Borderers; and argues that in The Prelude C figures as a symbol of England's unhealthy rationalism. See also 714.

1011. Chase, Cynthia. "The Ring of Gyges and the Coat of Darkness: Reading Rousseau with Wordsworth." Romanticism and Language (1029), pp. 50-85.

Offers parallel deconstructions of Rousseau's Sixième Promenade and of W's descriptions of the theater at Sadler's Wells and the blind beggar (1850 Prelude, book 7). The examination of W, which is heavily indebted to de Man (641), makes much of W's casual allusion to Samson Agonistes and interprets W's stress on sense-deprivation as showing the impossibility of meaning.

1012. Clubbe, John. "The W. Hugh Peal Collection at the University of Kentucky." The Wordsworth Circle 15 (1984): 73-74.

Notes the existence of "about a hundred letters, some unpublished," and of early editions in a recently donated collection.

1013. Davis, Philip. Memory and Writing: From Wordsworth to Lawrence. Liverpool: Liverpool University, 1984. 511 pp.

Not seen. According to Mackinnon's review, the book is "most impressive" in its treatment of W.
Review: Lachlan Mackinnon, _TLS_, 3 Aug. 1984, p. 862.

1014. de Man, Paul. _The Rhetoric of Romanticism_. New York: Columbia, 1984. ix+327 pp. indexed.

A posthumous collection with four essays on W, including one not previously published, "Wordsworth and the Victorians," commenting on the shift in critical interest from W's moral philosophy (see 97 and 98) to his "phenomenology of mind."

1015. Gleckner, Robert F. "Coleridge and Wordsworth Together in America." _The Wordsworth Circle_ 15(1984): 17-19.

Notes an American journal which printed poems by both C and W in one issue in 1822, and remarks on W's unpopularity in America between 1802 and 1829.

1016. Gravil, Richard. "Coleridge's Wordsworth." _The Wordsworth Circle_ 15(1984): 38-46.

Argues that C's criticism of W--primarily in the _Biographia_ (86)--is highly misleading, and attributes C's blind spots to resentment and to his early idealization of W. See also Bialostosky, 518 and 1009.

1017. Hinchliffe, Keith. "Wordsworth and the Kinds of Metaphor." _Studies in Romanticism_ 23(1984): 81-100.

Argues that in general W shuns metaphor of the tenor-vehicle variety, which implies a clear distinction between concrete and abstract, in favor of what Max Black terms the "focus," a word or word-cluster for which the meanings "turn." W "is, as it were, punning his way back towards a pre-dualistic way of thinking and talking about mind and world."

1018. Jacobus, Mary. "The Art of Managing Books: Romantic Prose and the Writing of the Past." _Romanticism and Language_ (1029), pp. 215-46.

A murky deconstructionist exploration of essays by De Quincey, Hazlitt, and Lamb in comparison with W's _Prelude_, books 4 and 5.

1019. Jay, Paul. _Being in the Text: Self-Representation from Wordsworth to Roland Barthes_. Ithaca, NY: Cornell, 1984. 189 pp. indexed. pbk.

Reads _The Prelude_ along the lines and in the language of Hartman and de Man, noting problematic self-consciousness, forgetting, unsettled revision, and the darkness of insight.

1020. Johnston, Kenneth R. _Wordsworth and_ The Recluse. New Haven, CT: Yale, 1984. xxxi+397 pp. indexed.

A major study of W's life-long project. Johnston argues that _The Recluse_ exists in fragmentary but readable form as a series of poems written toward it in three major stages, each stage repeating a movement from _Recluse_ composition toward more autobiographical work. Provides both clear accounts of composition and illuminating close readings of _The Recluse_'s component poems.
Review: Keith Hanley, _TLS_, 3 Aug. 1984, p. 862.

1021. Kelley, Theresa M. "Wordsworth and the Rhinefall." _Studies in Romanticism_ 23(1984): 61-79.

Attempting to refute the idea that "signs refer only to texts," Kelley shows in detail how W's perception of the falls evolved, between 1790 and his fragmentary essay on "The Sublime and the Beautiful" (_ca._ 1811-12), into an image both of aesthetic and of political events.

1022. Kelley, Theresa. "Wordsworth, Kant, and the Romantic Sublime." _Philological Quarterly_ 63(1984): 130-40.

Appeals to W's essay on "The Sublime and the Beautiful" (30, vol. 2) in order to distinguish between Kant's and W's concepts of the sublime, and questions a recent critical disposition to see W in terms of an aesthetic of the sublime rather than of the beautiful.

1023. McCracken, David. Wordsworth and the Lake District: A Guide to the Poems and their Places. Oxford: Oxford, 1984. xiv+300 pp. indexed.

"Explores the connections between W's poetry and its sources in Lake District places," including seventeen maps with walking guides, and eighteen excellent reproductions of contemporary illustrations.

Review: Jonathan Keates, TLS, 22 June 1984, p. 690.

1024. Milstead, John. "Wordsworth's Non-Privileged Ungrammaticality: A Failed Semiosis." The Wordsworth Circle 15 (1984): 32-35.

Parodic deconstructionist argument that "'Lines Written in Early Spring' is not a poem," since it contains two scientific references which "blow all mythic systems to smithereens."

1025. Parker, Reeve. "'Oh Could You Hear His Voice!': Wordsworth, Coleridge, and Ventriloquism." Romanticism and Language (1029), pp. 125-43.

Argues that a writer's self-creation may inform not just the work in which it occurs, but also his subsequent works and life; the situations and attitudes of W's The Borderers are recapitulated in W's and C's later works, as well as in their relations to one another.

1026. Pinion, F.B. A Wordsworth Companion. Survey and Assessment Series. London: Macmillan, 1984. x+351 pp. indexed.

Combined biography and introduction to the poet's works.

1027. Proffitt, Edward. "Book V in The Prelude: A Developmental Reading." Romanticism Past and Present 8,i (1984): 1-16.

Reading book 5 in the context of the larger poem (1805 version), argues that since it is a part of a larger whole its unity as a book is irrelevant. Pays special attention to themes of education and solipsism, and enlarges on what Michael Jaye has called, in the same context, W's "artifice of disjunction" (552).

1028. Radcliffe, Evan. "'In Dreams Begins Responsibility': Wordsworth's Ruined Cottage Story." _Studies in Romanticism_ 23(1984): 101-119.

Argues that Wordsworth added the story of the Pedlar, in which he elaborates his conception of the dreamer-as-poet, as self-justification for his own projected retirement.

1029. Reed, Arden, ed. _Romanticism and Language_. Ithaca, NY: Cornell, 1984. 327 pp. indexed. pbk.

Includes four deconstructionist and intertextualist essays on W: 1008, 1011, 1018, and 1025.

1030. Reiman, Donald H. "The Beauty of Buttermere as Fact and Romantic Symbol." _Criticism_ 26(1984): 139-70.

Providing a useful history of the 1802 seduction of Mary Robinson ("the Beauty of Buttermere"), Reiman ponders the great popular interest in her story, contrasting the comparatively sensational and sentimental accounts of C and De Quincey with W's in _The Prelude_, book 7, which stresses the saving power of Mary's "family ties, local attachments, and familiar traditions." Suggests by the way that the fourteen-book _Prelude_ is structured as a "macrosonnet" (pp. 148-51).

1031. Riffaterre, Michael. "Intertextual Representation: On Mimesis as Interpretive Discourse." _Critical Inquiry_ 11(1984): 141-62.

Arguing that texts refer not to objects but to other texts (cf. 217), so that "intertextuality is the agent both of the mimesis and of the hermeneutic constructions on the mimesis," but helpfully distinguishing between "intertextuality" and source-study, Riffaterre offers an excellent reading of "Composed Upon Westminster Bridge" (pp. 149-50) showing that the poem succeeds as poetry not by representing the city but by "negating the intertext," our sociolect for the city.

1032. Roe, Nicholas. "Who was Spy Nosy?" The Wordsworth Circle 15(1984): 46-50.

Identifies the spy noticed by W and C at Stowey in 1797 as James Walsh, and attempts to explain how W's name was known to government spies in this period.

1033. Sampson, David. "Wordsworth and the Poor: The Poetry of Survival." Studies in Romanticism 23(1984): 31-59.

As opposed to Averill (704), Sampson finds W's treatment of suffering at variance with "any category of sentimental poetry": it is impersonal, stressing not sympathy but the "dynamic and unmediated interaction" between nature and humanity. Examines "Goody Blake and Harry Gill," "The Old Cumberland Beggar," "Resolution and Independence," and "Michael."

1034. Simpson, David. "Criticism, Politics, and Style in Wordsworth's Poetry." Critical Inquiry 11(1984): 52-81.

Reading "Alice Fell" and "Gypsies" to point at their "referentiality" to contemporary political problems (poor-relief and alienation), and noting our lack of a vocabulary to explain or assess this, Simpson calls for unification of academic factions, suggesting that greater historical and political consciousness may help achieve this.

1035. Stevenson, Warren. "Wordsworth's 'Satanism.'" The Wordsworth Circle 15(1984): 82-84.

Cites three passages in which the poet may be comparing himself with Milton's Satan.

1036. Thorslev, Peter L., Jr. Romantic Contraries: Freedom versus Design. New Haven, CT: Yale, 1984. ix+225 pp. indexed.

Literary history of the Romantics' obsession with the concepts of "Freedom and Destiny," with an excellent long chapter exploring the implications of the organicist world-view (pp. 84-125) devoted almost entirely to W. Most valuable is Thorslev's discussion of the Romantics' discovery of the unconscious in their "retreat from consciousness," but he also builds on Abrams' comparison (161) of The Prelude with Hegel's Phenomenology of Spirit as "biodicy," and discusses the amorality of the "organic sublime" in "The Ruined Cottage."

1037. Versluys, Kristiaan. "Western Wordsworthianism: Cities Reviled and Cities Idealized." The Wordsworth Circle 15(1984): 20-22.

Argues that W's views of urban and rural life influenced the poetry of nineteenth-century California.

1038. Ward, J.P. Wordsworth's Language of Men. Brighton, Sussex: Harvester, 1984. xii+235 pp. indexed.

Attempts to relate W's original use of language, especially regarding nominals, to shifts in western civilization's world-view, a task for which Ward's own unnecessarily vague and evasive language is not well suited.

1039. Werner, Brette Charlene. "Romantic Lyrics in Landscape: Constable and Wordsworth." Comparative Literature 36 (1984): 110-29.

Compares and contrasts "The Solitary Reaper" with Constable's The Gleaners, Brighton.

1040. Wolfson, Susan J. "The Illusion of Mastery: Wordsworth's Revisions of 'The Drowned Man of Esthwaite': 1798, 1805, 1850." PMLA 99(1984): 917-35.

A sensitive comparison of the three versions of this "spot of time" available in the Norton Prelude (17), taking full account of the implications in its change in context (from the two-part poem to book 5 of the later versions). Wolfson celebrates the "autobiographical drama" of W's revision itself as an "interpretive effort," arguing that his alterations show his continuing sense of his past's mystery, on which he is reluctant to impose any settled viewpoint.

1041. Woodman, Ross. "Milton's Satan in Wordsworth's 'Vale of Soul-Making.'" _Studies in Romanticism_ 23(1984): 3-30.

Sees _The Prelude_ as re-presenting the myth of _Paradise Lost_ and _Paradise Regained_, W finally overcoming the Satanic self-hood as this is represented in the revolutionary books. Woodman argues, against Hartman (143), that W is not simply prevented "from becoming a visionary poet," but, like Milton's Christ, renounces the "satanic nature of apocalyptic imagination."

APPENDIX: SUPPLEMENTARY LISTINGS FOR 1971-1972

David Stam's *Wordsworthian Criticism 1964-1973* (64), being published in 1974, was unable to cover 1973 thoroughly, so we have begun our comprehensive listing with 1973, even though this means repeating his few listings for that year. In addition, the list below supplements his for the two previous years. But this listing is *not* designed to guarantee that the years before 1973 are covered comprehensively.

1971

1042. Asselineau, Roger, et al., eds. *Le romantisme anglo-americain: Melanges offerts à Louis Bonnerot*. Paris: Didier, 1971. 421 pp. not indexed. pbk.

Includes 1043, 1044, and 1047.

1043. Danchin, Pierre. "Poetry as Speech: Some Reflections on the Poetic Style of William Cowper and William Wordsworth." *Le romantism anglo-americain* (1042), pp. 69-84.

Notes that W designed most of his verse for oral delivery, and attributes to this his gift for capturing the rhythms of living speech.

1044. King-Hele, Desmond. "The Influence of Erasmus Darwin on Wordsworth, Coleridge, Keats, and Shelley." *Le romantism anglo-americain* (1042), pp. 147-64.

Argues--not always convincingly--that Darwin's ideas influenced W's, and that the style of *The Botanic Garden* is both the model for "Descriptive Sketches" and the butt of W's 1802 Preface.

1045. Kuhn, Daniel K. "The Joy of the Absolute: A Comparative Study of the Romantic Visions of William Wordsworth and C.S. Lewis." _Imagination and the Spirit: Essays in Literature and the Christian Faith Presented to Clyde S. Kilby_, ed. Charles A. Huttar. Grand Rapids, MI: Eerdmans, 1971, pp. 189-214.

Compares and contrasts the writers' religious views in particular, arguing that Lewis's more Christian faith sustained him whereas W's faith, with its intuitive basis, its stress on God's immanence rather than elevation, and an inadequate vision of evil, failed. Attributes W's poetic decline to the "inadequacy" of his faith, but without considering his subsequent movement toward orthodoxy. Considers "Tintern Abbey," the 1850 _Prelude_, and the Ode.

1046. Kuriyama, Minoru. "The Images of Old Age in _The Prelude_." _Studies in English Literature (Tokyo)_ 48,i (1971): 43-56.

Compares the discharged-soldier and the blind-beggar passages (1805 _Prelude_, books 4 and 7), arguing that W progresses in the poem toward a "deepened knowledge of reality."

1047. Mavrocordato, Alexandre. "The Fountain of Youth, or Wordsworth's Ode on Immortality." _Le romantism anglo-americain_ (1042), pp. 103-16.

A rather vague and unfocused reading, which sees the poem as achieving consolation by revising its view of the child.

1048. Rajiva, Stanley F. "Wordsworth and Beethoven as 'Romantic' Artists: Some Parallels." _Literary Criterion_ 10, i(1971): 14-20.

A clichéd description of both artists' Romanticism, chiefly in terms of their reaction to the Eighteenth Century.

1049. Whitaker, Thomas R. "Voices in the Open: Wordsworth, Eliot, and Stevens." _Iowa Review_ 2,iii(1971): 96-112.

On the effort of the poet's "solitary voice to name its calling," the discussion of W (pp. 97-101) suggesting that he achieves "shared solitude" (cf. 127) by finding "reflexive" voices in nature and previous selves. Looks briefly at "To the Cuckoo" ("O blithe newcomer!"), "Tintern Abbey," "Resolution and Independence," and "The Solitary Reaper."

1972

1050 Bluestone, Stephen. "On Wordsworth's Political Sonnets of 1802-1803." Rackham Literary Studies 2(1972): 79-86.

Not a well focused essay, commenting on changes in W's political views.

1051. Breyer, B.R. "Wordsworth's Pleasure: An Approach to his Poetic Theory." Southern Humanities Review 6(1972): 123-31.

Stresses the importance of pleasure in W's poetic, and points out his disagreement with C on the subject.

1052. Chaffee, Alan J. "The Rendezvous of Mind." The Wordsworth Circle 3(1972): 196-203.

Compares Blake's and W's mythical powers, finding that while Blake "exploits symbol, or mythic thought turning to man's inner world," W employs metaphor to transform the outer world of Nature; but both use myth to mediate between tradition and revolution. Focuses chiefly on The Prelude.

1053. Duffy, Edward T. "The Cunning Spontaneities of Romanticism." The Wordsworth Circle 3(1972): 232-40.

Argues that the Romantics parodied traditional forms and styles "in self-defense," and cites W's dedication scene (Prelude 4) and Stanza 7 of the Ode as examples.

1054. Fogle, Richard Harter. "Nathaniel Hawthorne and the Great English Romantic Poets." Keats-Shelley Journal 21-22(1972-73): 219-35.

Pages 219-20, 232-34 describe W's influence as "substantial," though not so great as C's or Shelley's.

1055. Garrison, Joseph M., Jr. "Knowledge and Beauty in Wordsworth's 'Composed Upon Westminster Bridge.'" Research Studies 40(1972): 46-47.

Sees the poem as progressing from a false comparison to a more genuine because absolute appreciation of the city's beauty.

1056. Gomme, A.H. "Wordsworth Remembered." London Times Literary Supplement, 24 Nov. 1972, p. 1429.

Letter to the editor, provoked by comments on W in an article on Ruskin (TLS, 10 Nov. 1972, p. 1353), noting the vividness and permanence of Wordsworthian vision.

1057. Havely, Cicely. Wordsworth. The Age of Revolutions Series, Units 13-14. Bletchley Bucks, England: The Open University, 1972. 70 pp. pbk.

An introduction to W, made to be used in conjunction with broadcasts in England's Open University system.

1058. Huntley, Frank L. "William Wordsworth, 1770-1970." Michigan Quarterly Review 11(1972): 191-96.

A remarkably misinformed bicentenary essay.

1059. Miller, J. Hillis. "The Stone and the Shell: The Problem of Poetic Form in Wordsworth's Dream of the Arab." In Mouvements premiers: etudes critiques offerts à Georges Poulet. Paris: Jose Corti, 1972, pp. 125-47.

Argues that the passage (1850 Prelude, book 5) is structured on a series of displacements or substitutions, such as that of the book for the human body, and that its theme is language, which similarly works by substitution (metaphor).

1060. Morris, David B. The Religious Sublime: Christian Poetry and Critical Tradition in 18th-Century England. Lexington: University of Kentucky, 1972. 260 pp. indexed.

A short section on C and W (pp. 186-96) places them in the tradition, not of Burke's sublime and beautiful (contrast 212), but of the religious sublime.

1061. Owen, W.J.B. "Annotating Wordsworth." In Editing Texts of the Romantic Period: Papers Given at the Conference on Editorial Problems, University of Toronto, November 1971, ed. John D. Baird. Toronto: A.M. Hakkert, 1972, pp. 47-71.

Comments on the relation of annotation to textual and literary criticism, using examples from the Prose Works edited by Owen and Smyser (30) and from The Prelude.

1062. Pleasance, Antony C.E. "William Wordsworth and 'Lucy'--Victor Hugo and 'Leopoldine': A Study." In Pacific Northwest Conference on Foreign Languages. Twenty-Third Annual Meeting, April 28-29, 1972. Corvallis: Oregon State University, 1973, pp. 51-57.

Compares and contrasts W's Lucy Poems with Hugo's poems for his daughter.

1063. Ruotolo, Lucio P. "Wordsworth's Religious Hope: A Study of the Margaret Story." Renascence 24(1972): 96-101.

Argues that Margaret's impossible hope, her "ability to wait" for her husband's return, anticipates the values of modern theology.

1064. Sharrock, Roger. "The Figure in a Landscape: Wordsworth's Early Poetry." Proceedings of the British Academy 58(1972): 313-33.

Pointing out that "An Evening Walk" and "Descriptive Sketches" are not really similar, Sharrock argues that the poems adumbrate much of what is to come, and reveal a progress through the picturesque to the sublime. Sensitive criticism of the former in particular.

1065. Waldoff, Leon. "Wordsworth's Healing Power: Basic Trust in 'Tintern Abbey.'" Hartford Studies in Literature 4 (1972): 147-66.

Finds "Tintern Abbey" a powerful consolation for an age losing its grip on theological affirmations, and explains what Arnold (98) calls W's "healing power" in psychological terms, arguing that it begins in unconscious defensive reactions to the loss (in Erik Erikson's phrase) of "basic trust."

INDEX OF AUTHORS, EDITORS, AND REVIEWERS

Editors or compilers are designated by the letter E, reviewers by the letter R, before the reference number. Asterisks indicate indirect references--e.g., under "Abrams," "*145" refers the reader to a work mentioned in the annotation to item 145. Cross-references have not been indexed.

SELECTIVE TOPIC INDEX

This index contains references not only to works of the poet, but also to people, critical schools, and special topics, though the citations (especially for topics) are of course not exhaustive. Parenthetical notations are intended only to serve as preliminary guides. While we have avoided abbreviations as much as possible in the bibliography, we have had to use a number of them here; where appropriate we adopt Reed's in his _Chronology of the Middle Years_ (82). In addition, within a listing we occasionally use the initial of that topic: for instance, "b" stands for "biography" in notations under that heading.

AM	_The Ancient Mariner_
ap(s).	appendix(es)
BL	_Biographia Literaria_
BW	"Benjamin the Waggoner" and "The Waggoner" (see Cornell Edition, 22)
C	Coleridge
CC	_Concerning the Relations of Great Britain, Spain, and Portugal...as Affected by the Convention of Cintra_
DeQ	Thomas De Quincey
DS	_Descriptive Sketches_
DW	Dorothy Wordsworth
DWJ	_Journals of Dorothy Wordsworth_
ES	_Ecclesiastical Sonnets_
esp.	especially
EW	_An Evening Walk_
Exc.	_The Excursion_
FQ	_The Faerie Queen_
Guide	_W's Guide through the District of the Lakes_
HG	"Home at Grasmere"
infl.	influence
LB	_Lyrical Ballads_
ms(s).	manuscript(s)
n	footnote
OCB	"The Old Cumberland Beggar"
OMT	"Old Man Travelling. Animal Tranquillity and Decay"
_P1815_	_Poems by William Wordsworth_ (London, 1815). 2 vols.
PB	"Peter Bell"

PL	Paradise Lost
PR	Paradise Regained
Prel.	Thirteen-Book and Fourteen-Book Preludes, or The Prelude considered generally. Following numbers refer to books in the 14-book Prelude.
PP	Pilgrim's Progress
P2V	Poems, in Two Volumes (1807)
R&I	"Resolution and Independence"
Rec.	The Recluse
RC	"The Ruined Cottage"
SA	Samson Agonistes
SP	"Salisbury Plain," or related poems (see Cornell Edition, 21)
S&B	"The Sublime and the Beautiful"
TA	"Lines Composed a Few Miles above Tintern Abbey..."
TB	The Borderers
TP	"The Tuft of Primroses"
W	William Wordsworth
WD	The White Doe of Rylstone
2Prel	Two-Part Prelude
5Prel	Five-Book Prelude
17th-c	Seventeenth-century
18th-c	Eighteenth-century
*	indirect reference, to a work not listed separately but mentioned in an annotation--e.g., "*539" refers to Hall's essay, mentioned in the annotation to 539.

SELECTIVE TOPIC INDEX